John Moore

A View of Society and Manners in Italy

With Anecdotes Relating to Some Eminent Characters

John Moore

A View of Society and Manners in Italy
With Anecdotes Relating to Some Eminent Characters

ISBN/EAN: 9783741198908

Manufactured in Europe, USA, Canada, Australia, Japa

Cover: Foto ©Suzi / pixelio.de

Manufactured and distributed by brebook publishing software
(www.brebook.com)

John Moore

A View of Society and Manners in Italy

A

V I E W

O F

SOCIETY AND MANNERS

I N

I T A L Y:

W I T H

ANECDOTES relating to some EMINENT CHARACTERS.

BY JOHN MOORE, M.D.

VOL. II.

Strenua nos exercet inertia: navibus atque
Quadrigis petimus bene vivere. Quod petis, hic est,
Hor.

THE SECOND EDITION.

LONDON:
Printed for W. Strahan; and T. Cadell, in the Strand.
MDCCLXXXI.

CONTENTS

OF THE

SECOND VOLUME.

A 2

CONTENTS. v

5

vi   C O N T E N T S.

CONTENTS. vii

CONTENTS.

LETTER LXXVI. p. 421.

Commerce.—Jews.—Actors.—The Chapel of St. Lorenzo.—The rich not envied by the poor.—The Palazzo Pitti.—Observations on the Madonna della Seggiola.

LETTER LXXVII. p. 431.

A public Discourse by a Professor at the Academy of Arts at Bologna.—Procession of CorpusDomini.—Modena.—Parma.—Different opinions respecting a famous picture of Correggio.

LETTER LXXVIII. p. 441.

Milan.—The Cathedral.—Museum.—Manners.

LETTER LXXIX. p. 451.

Turin.—St. Ambrose.—A Procession.—Mount Cenis.—Modane.—Aiguebelle.—Hannibal's passage into Italy.

A VIEW

A
V I E W

OF

SOCIETY AND MANNERS

IN

I T A L Y.

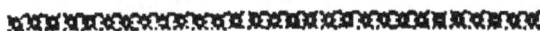

LETTER XLVI.

Rome.

I BEG you may not fufpect me of affectation, or that I wifh to affume the character of a connoiffeur, when I tell you, that I have very great pleafure in contemplating the antique ftatues and bufts, of which there are fuch numbers in this city. It is a natural curiofity, and I have had it all my life in

VOL. II.　　　B　　　a ftrong

a ftrong degree, to fee celebrated men, thofe whofe talents and great qualities can alone render the prefent age an interefling object to pofterity, and prevent its being loft, like the dark ages which fucceeded the deftruction of the Roman empire, in the oblivious vortex of time, leaving fcarcely a wreck behind. The durable monuments raifed to fame by the infpiring genius of *Pitt*, and the invincible fpirit of *Frederick*, will command the admiration of future ages, outlive the power of the empires which *they* aggrandized, and forbid the period in which *they* flourifhed, from ever paffing away like the bafelefs fabric of a vifion. The bufts and ftatues of thofe memorable men will be viewed, by fucceeding generations, with the fame regard and attention which we now beftow on thofe of Cicero and Cæfar. We expect to find fomething peculiarly noble and expreffive in features which were animated, and which, we imagine, muft

have

have been in fome degree modelled, by the
fentiments of thofe to whom they belonged. It is not rank, it is character
alone which interefts pofterity. We know
that men may be feated on thrones, who
would have been placed more fuitably to
their talents on the working-table of a
taylor; we therefore give little attention
to the bufts or coins of the vulgar emperors. In the countenance of Claudius, we
expect nothing more noble than the phlegmatic tranquillity of an acquiefcing
cuckold; in Caligula or Nero, the unrelenting frown of a negro-driver, or the
infolent air of any unprincipled ruffian
in power. Even in the high-praifed Auguftus we look for nothing effentially great,
nothing fuperior to what we fee in thofe
minions of fortune, who are exalted, by a
concurrence of incidents, to a fituation in
life to which their talents would never
have raifed them, and which their characters never deferved. In the face of Julius

we

we expect to find the traces of deep re-flection, magnanimity, and the anxiety natural to the man who had overturned the liberties of his native country, and who muſt have ſecretly dreaded the re-ſentment of a ſpirited people; and in the face of Marcus Brutus we look for inde-pendence, conſcious integrity, and a mind capable of the higheſt effort of virtue.

It is natural to regret, that, of the number of antique ſtatues which have come to us tolerably entire, ſo great a pro-portion are repreſentations of gods and goddeſſes. Had they been intended for real perſons, we might have had a perfect knowledge of the face and figure of the greateſt part of the moſt diſtinguiſhed citizens of ancient Greece and Rome. A man of unrelaxing wiſdom would ſmile with contempt, and aſk, if our having perfect repreſentations of all the heroes, poets, and philoſophers recorded

in

in hiftory, would make us either wifer or more learned? to which I anfwer, That there are a great many things, which neither can add to my ,fmall ftock of learning nor wifdom, and yet give me more pleafure and fatisfaction than thofe which do; and, unfortunately for mankind, the greateft part of them refemble me in this particular.

But though I would with pleafure have given up a great number of the Jupiters and Apollos and Venufes, whofe ftatues we have, in exchange for an equal, or even a fmaller, number of mere mortals whom I could name; I by no means confider the ftatues of thofe deities as uninterefting. Though they are imaginary beings, yet each of them has a diftinct character of his own of claffical authority, which has long been impreffed on our memories; and we affume the right of deciding on the artift's fkill, and applaud-

B 3   ing

ing or blaming, as he has fucceeded or
failed in expreffing the eftablifhed character of the god intended.   From the
ancient artifts having exercifed their
genius in forming the images of an order
of beings fuperior to mankind, another
and a greater advantage is fuppofed to
have followed; it prompted the artifts to
attempt the uniting in one form, the
various beauties and excellencies which
nature had difperfed in many. This was
not fo eafy a tafk as may by fome be
imagined; for that which has a fine effect
in one particular face or perfon, may
appear a deformity when combined with
a different complexion, different features,
or a different fhape.   It therefore required
great judgment and tafte to collect thofe
various graces, and combine them with
elegance and truth ; and repeated efforts
of this kind are imagined to have infpired
fome of the ancient fculptors with fublimer
ideas of beauty than nature herfelf ever
exhibited,

exhibited, as appears in fome of their works which have reached our own times.

Though the works of no modern artift can ftand a comparifon with the great mafter-pieces now alluded to, yet nothing can be more abfurd than the idea which fome people entertain, that all antique ftatues are of more excellent workmanfhip than the modern. We fee, every day, numberlefs fpecimens of every fpecies of fculpture, from the largeft ftatues and baffos-relievos, to the fmalleft cameos and intaglios, that are undoubtedly antique, and yet far inferior, not only to the works of the beft artifts of Leo the Tenth's time, but alfo to thofe of many artifts now alive in various parts of Europe. The paffion for fculpture, which the Romans caught from the Greeks, became almoft univerfal. Statues were not only the chief ornaments of their temples and palaces, but alfo of the houfes of the middle, and even the loweft, order of citizens. They were prompted to adorn them with the figures of a few favourite deities, by religion, as well as vanity : no man, but an atheift or a beggar, could be without them. This being the cafe, we may eafily conceive what gracelefs divinities many of them muft have been; for in this, no doubt, as in every other manufactory, there muft occafionally have been bungling workmen employed, even In the moft flourifhing æra of the arts, and goods finifhed in a very carelefs and hurried manner, to anfwer the conftant demand, and fuit the dimenfions of every purfe. We muft have a very high idea of the number of ftatues of one kind, or other, which were in old Rome, when we confider, how many are ftill to be feen; how many have at different periods been carried away, by the curious, to every country in Europe ; how many were mutilated and deftroyed by the gothic brutality

lity of Barbarians, and the ill-directed zeal of the early Chriftians, who thought it a duty to exterminate every image, without diftinction of age or fex, and without confidering whether they were of God or man. This obliged the wretched heathens to hide the ftatues of their gods and of their anceftors in the bowels of the earth, where unqueftionably great numbers of them ftill remain. Had they not been thus barbaroufly hewed to pieces, and buried, I had almoft faid, alive, we might have had feveral equal to the great mafterpieces in the Vatican; for it is natural to imagine, that the rage of the zealots would be chiefly directed againft thofe ftatues which were in the higheft eftimation with the heathens; and we muft likewife imagine, that thefe would be the pieces which they, on their part, would endeavour, by every poffible means, to preferve from their power, and bury in the earth. Of thofe which have been dug

up,

up, I shall mention only a very few, beginning with the Farnesian Hercules, which has been long admired as an exquisite model of masculine strength; yet, admirable as it is, it does not please all the world. I am told that the women in particular find something unsatisfactory, and even odious, in this figure; which, however majestic, is deficient in the charms most agreeable to them, and which might have been expected in the son of Jupiter and the beauteous Alcmena. A lady whom I accompanied to the Farnese palace, turned away from it in disgust. I could not imagine what had shocked her. She told me, *after recollection*, that she could not bear the stern severity of his countenance, his large brawny limbs, and the club with which he was armed; which gave him more the appearance of one of those giants that, according to the old romances, carried away virgins and shut them up in gloomy castles, than the gallant

Hercules,

Hercules, the lover of Omphale. Finally, the lady declared, fhe was convinced this ftatue could not be a juft reprefentation of Hercules; for it was not in the nature of things, that a man fo formed could ever have been a reliever of diftreffed damfels.

Without fuch powerful fupport as that of the fair fex, I fhould not have expofed myfelf to the refentment of connoiffeurs, by any expreffion which they might conftrue an attack upon this favourite ftatue; but, with their fupport, I will venture to affert, that the Farnefe Hercules is faulty both in his form and attitude: the former is too unwieldy for active exertion, and the latter exhibits vigour *exhaufted*. A refting attitude is furely not the moft proper in which the all-conquering god of ftrength could be reprefented. Reft implies fatigue, and fatigue ftrength exhaufted. A repofing Hercules is almoft a

contra-

contradiction. Invincible activity, and in-
exhauftible ftrength, are his characterif-
tics. The ancient artift has erred, not only
in giving him an attitude which fuppofes
his ftrength wants recruiting, but in the
nature of the ftrength itfelf, the character
of which fhould not be paffive, but
active.

Near to Hercules, under the arcades of
the fame Palezzo Farnefe, is a moft beautiful ftatue of Flora. The great advantage
which ancient artifts had in attending the
exercifes of the gymnafia, has been repeatedly urged as the reafon of their fuperiority over the moderns in fculpture.
We are told, that befides the ufual exercifes
of the gymnafia, all thofe who propofed
to contend at the Olympic games, were
obliged, by the regulations, to prepare themfelves, by exercifing publicly for a year
at Elis; and the ftatuaries and painters
conftantly attended on the Arena, where

they

they had opportunities of beholding
the fineft fhaped, the moft graceful,
and moft vigorous of the Grecian youth
employed in thofe manly fports, in which
the power of every mufcle was exerted,
and all their various actions called forth;
and where the human form appeared in an
infinite variety of different attitudes. By
a conftant attendance at fuch a fchool, independent of any other circumftance, the
artifts are fuppofed to have acquired a more
animated, true, and graceful ftyle, than
poffibly can be caught from viewing the
tame, mercenary models, which are exhibited in our academies. On the other
hand, I have heard it afferted, that the
artift, who formed the Farnefian Flora,
could not have improved his work, or derived any of its excellencies, from the circumftances above enumerated; becaufe the
figure is in a ftanding pofture, and clothed.
In the light, eafy flow of the drapery, and
in

in the contour of the body being as diftinct-
ly pronounced through it, as if the figure
were naked, the chief merit of this ftatue
is thought to confift. But this reafoning
does not feem juft; for the daily opportunities the ancient artifts had of feeing
naked figures, in every variety of action
and attitude, muft have given them advantages over the moderns, in forming even
drapery figures. At Sparta, the women,
upon particular occafions, danced naked.
In their own families, they were feen every
day clothed in light draperies; and fo fecondary was every confideration, even that
of decency, to art, that the prettieft virgins of Agrigentum, it is recorded, were
called upon by the legiflature, without diftinction, to fhew themfelves naked to a
painter, to enable him to paint a Venus.
Whilft the moderns, therefore, muft acknowledge their inferiority to the ancients
in the art of fculpture, they may be allowed

ed merit, on account of the caufe, to which it feems, in fome meafure at leaft, to be owing.

The fineft fpecimens of antique fculpture are to be feen in the Vatican. In thefe the Greek artifts difplay an unqueftionable fuperiority over the moft fuccefsful efforts of the moderns. For me to attempt a defcription of thefe mafter-pieces, which have been defcribed a thoufand times, and imitated as often, without once having had juftice done them, would be equally vain and fuperfluous. I confine myfelf to a very few obfervations. The moft infenfible of mankind muft be ftruck with horror at fight of the Laocoon. On one of my vifits to the Vatican, I was accompanied by two perfons, who had never been there before: one of them is accufed of being perfectly callous to every thing which does not immediately touch his own perfon; the other is a worthy, good man: the firft, after ftaring for fome time with

marks .

marks of terror at the groupe, at length recovered himself; exclaiming with a laugh,—" Egad, I was afraid thefe d—d " ferpents would have left the fellows they " are devouring, and made a fnap at me; " but I am happy to recollect they are of " marble."——" I thank you, Sir, moft " heartily," faid the other, " for putting " me in mind of that circumftance; till " you mentioned it, I was in agony for " thofe two youths."

Nothing can be conceived more admirably executed than this affecting groupe; in all probability, it never would have entered into my own head that it could have been in any refpect improved. But when I firft had the happinefs of becoming acquainted with Mr. Lock, a period of my life which I fhall always recollect with peculiar pleafure, I remember my converfing with him upon this fubject; and that Gentleman, after mentioning the execution
cution

cution of this piece, in the higheſt terms
of praiſe, obſerved that, had the figure of
Laocoon been *alone*, it would have been
perfect. As a man ſuffering the moſt ex-
cruciating bodily pain with becoming for-
titude, it admits of no improvement; his
proportions, his form, his action, his expreſſion, are exquiſite. But when his ſons
appear, he is no longer an inſulated, ſuffering individual, who, when he has met
pain and death with dignity, has done all
that could be expected from man; he
commences *father*, and a much wider field
is opened to the artiſt. We expect the
deepeſt pathos in the exhibition of the ſub-
limeſt character that art can offer to the
contemplation of the human mind: A father forgetting pain, and inſtant death, to
ſave his children. This Sublime and Pathetic the artiſt either did not ſee, or de-
ſpaired of attaining. Laocoon's ſufferings
are merely corporal; he is deaf to the cries
of his agonizing children, who are calling

Vol. II.   C   on

on him for affiftance. But had he been throwing a look of anguifh upon his fons, had he feemed to have forgotten his own fufferings in theirs, he would have commanded the fympathy of the fpectator in a much higher degree. On the whole, Mr. Lock was of opinion, that the execution of this groupe is perfect, but that the conception is not equal to the execution. I fhall leave it to others to decide whether Mr. Lock, in thefe obfervations, fpoke like a man of tafte: I am fure he fpoke like a father. I have fenfibility to feel the beauty and juftnefs of the remark, though I had not the ingenuity to make it.

It is difputed whether this groupe was formed from Virgil's defcription of the death of Laocoon and his fons, or the defcription made from the groupe; it is evident, from their minute refemblance, that one or other muft have been the cafe. The Poet mentions a circumftance, which could

not

not be reprefented by the fculptor; he fays that, although every other perfon around fought fafety by flight, the father was attacked by the ferpents, while he was advancing to the affiftance of his fons—

———auxilio fubeuntem ac tela ferentem.

This deficiency in the fculptor's art would have been finely fupplied by the improvement which Mr. Lock propofed.

Refle&ing on the dreadful condition of three perfons entangled in the horrid twinings of ferpents, and after contemplating the varied anguifh fo ftrongly expreffed in their countenances, it is a relief to turn the eye to the heavenly figure of the Apollo. To form an adequate idea of the beauty of this ftatue, it is abfolutely neceffary to fee it. With all the advantages of colour and life, the human form never appeared fo beautiful; and we never can fufficiently admire the artift, who has endowed marble
C 2   with

with a finer expreſſion of grace, dignity,
and underſtanding, than ever were ſeen in
living features. In the forming of this in-
imitable figure, the artiſt ſeems to have
wrought after an ideal form of beauty, ſuperior to any in nature, and which exiſted
only in his own imagination.

The admired ſtatue of Antinous is in the
ſame Court. Nothing can be more light,
elegant, and eaſy; the proportions are exact, and the execution perfect. It is an
exquiſite repreſentation of the moſt beautiful youth that ever lived.

The ſtatue of Apollo repreſents ſomething ſuperior, and the emotions it excites
are all of the ſublime caſt.

LETTER XLVII.

Rome.

THE prefent Pope, who has affumed the name of Pius the Sixth, is a tall, well-made man, about fixty years of age, but retaining in his lock all the frefh-nefs of a much earlier period of life. He lays a greater ftrefs on the ceremonious part of religion than his predeceffor Gan-ganelli, in whofe reign a great relaxation of church-difcipline is thought to have taken place. The late Pope was a man of moderation, good fenfe, and fimplicity of manners; and could not go through all the oftentatious parade which his ftation required, without reluctance, and marks of difguft. He knew that the opinions of mankind had undergone a very great

C 3   change

change fince thofe ceremonies were eſtabliſhed; and that fome of the moſt refpectable of the fpectators confidered as perfectly frivolous many things which formerly
had been held as facred. A man of good
fenfe may feem to lay the greateſt weight
on ceremonies which he himfelf confiders
as ridiculous, provided he thinks the people, in whofe fight he goes through them,
are impreffed with a conviction of their
importance; but if he knows that fome of
the beholders are entirely of a different
way of thinking, he will be ſtrongly
tempted to evince, by fome means or other,
that he defpifes the fooleries he performs,
as much as any of them. This, in all
probability, was the cafe with Ganganelli;
who, befides, was an enemy to fraud and
hypocrify of every kind. But, however
remifs he may have been with regard to the
etiquette of his fpiritual functions, every
body acknowledges his diligence and activity in promoting the temporal good of his
subjects.

subjects. He did all in his power to revive trade, and to encourage manufactures and industry of every kind. He built no churches, but he repaired the roads all over the ecclefiaftical state; he reftrained the malevolence of bigots, removed abfurd prejudices, and promoted fentiments of charity and good-will to mankind in general, without excepting even heretics. His enemies, the Jefuits, with an intention to make him odious in the eyes of his own subjects, gave him the name of the Proteftant Pope. If they fuppofed that this calumny would be credited, on account of the conduct above mentioned, they at once paid the higheft compliment to the Pope and the Proteftant religion. The carelefs manner in which Ganganelli performed certain functions, and the general tenour of his life and fentiments, were lamented by politicians, as well as by bigots. However frivolous the former might think many ceremonies in themfelves, they ftill confidered

them

them as of political importance, in fuch a government as that of Rome; and the Conclave held on the death of the late Pope,
are thought to have been in fome degree
influenced by fuch confiderations in chufing his fucceffor. The prefent Pope, before he was raifed to that dignity, was
confidered as a firm believer in all the te-
nets of the Roman Church, and a ftrict and
fcrupulous obferver of all its injunctions
and ceremonials. As his pretenfions, in
point of family, fortune, and connexions,
were fmaller than thofe of moft of his brother cardinals, it is the more probable that
he owed his elevation to this part of his
character, which rendered him a proper
perfon to check the progrefs of abufes that
had been entirely neglected by the late
Pope; under whofe adminiftration free-
thinking was faid to have been counte-
nanced, Proteftantifm in general regarded
with diminifhed abhorrence, and the Cal-
vinifts in particular treated with a degree
of

of indulgence, to which their inveterate enmity to the church of Rome gave them no title. Several inflances of this are enumerated, and one in particular, which, I dare fay, you will think a flronger proof of the late Pope's good fenfe and good humour, than of that negligence to which his enemies imputed it.

A Scotch prefbyterian having heated his brain, by reading the Book of Martyrs, the cruelties of the Spanifh Inquifition, and the Hiftories of all the perfecutions that ever were raifed by the Roman Catholics againft the Proteftants, was feized with a dread, that the fame horrors were juft about to be renewed. This terrible idea difturbed his imagination day and night; he thought of nothing but racks and fcaffolds; and, on one occafion, he dreamt that there was a continued train of bonfires, with a tar-barrel and a Proteftant in each, all the way from Smithfield to St. Andrews.

He

He communicated the anxiety and dif-
tref of his mind to a worthy fenfible clergyman who lived in the neighbourhood.
This gentleman took great pains to quiet
his fears, proving to him, by ftrong and
obvious arguments, that there was little or
no danger of fuch an event as he dreaded.
Thefe reafonings had a powerful effect
while they were delivering, but the impreffion did not laft, and was always ef-
faced by a few pages of the Book of Martyrs. As foon as the clergyman remarked
this, he advifed the relations to remove
that, and every book which treated of
perfecution or martyrdom, entirely out of
the poor man's reach. This was done accordingly, and books of a lefs gloomy
complexion were fubftituted in their place ;
but as all of them formed a ftrong contraft
with the colour of his mind, he could not
bear their perufal, but betook himfelf to
the ftudy of the Bible, which was the only
book of his ancient library which had

7   been

been left; and fo ftrong a hold had his former ftudies taken of his imagination, that he could relifh no part of the Bible, except the Revelation of St. John, a great part of which, he thought, referred to the whore of Babylon, or in other words, the Pope of Rome. This part of the fcripture he perufed continually with unabating ardor and delight. His friend the clergyman, having obferved this, took occafion to fay, that every part of the Holy Bible was, without doubt, moft fublime, and wonderfully inftructive; yet he was furprifed to fee that he limited his ftudies entirely to the laft book, and neglected all the reft. To which the other replied, That *he* who was a divine, and a man of learning, might, with propriety, read all the facred volume from beginning to end; but, for his own part, he thought proper to confine himfelf to what he could underftand; and *therefore*, though he had a due refpect for all the fcripture, he acknowledged

knowledged he gave a preference to the
Revelation of St. John. This anfwer entirely fatisfied the clergyman; he did not
think it expedient to queftion him any
farther; he took his leave, after having
requefted the people of the family with
whom this perfon lived, to have a watch-
ful eye on their relation. In the mean time,
this poor man's terrors, with regard to the
revival of popery and perfecution, daily
augmented; and nature, in all probability,
would have funk under the weight of
fuch accumulated anxiety, had not a
thought occurred which relieved his mind
in an inftant, by fuggefting an infallible
method of preventing all the evils which
his imagination had been brooding over
for fo long a time. The happy idea
which afforded him fo much comfort, was
no other, than that he fhould immediately
go to Rome, and convert the Pope from
the Roman Catholic to the Prefbyterian
religion. The moment he hit on this
                                    fortunate

fortunate expedient, he felt at once the ſtrongeſt impulſe to undertake the taſk, and the fulleſt conviction that his undertaking would be crowned with ſuccefs; it is no wonder, therefore, that his countenance threw off its former gloom, and that all his features brightened with the heart-felt thrillings of happineſs and ſelf-applauſe. While his relations congratulated each other on this agreeable change, the exulting viſionary, without communicating his deſign to any mortal, ſet out for London, took his paſſage to Leghorn, and, in a ſhort time after, arrived in perfect health of body, and in exalted ſpirits, at Rome.

He directly applied to an ecclefiaſtic of his own country, of whoſe obliging temper he had previouſly heard, and whom he confidered as a proper perſon to procure him an interview neceſſary for the accompliſhment of his project. He informed
that

that gentleman, that he earneflly wifhed to have a conference with the Pope, on a bufinefs of infinite importance, and which admitted of no delay. It was not difficult to perceive the flate of this poor man's mind; the good-natured ecclefiaftic endeavoured to footh and amufe him, putting off the conference till a diftant day; in hopes that means might be fallen on, during the interval, to prevail on him to return to his own country. A few days after this, however, he happened to go to St. Peter's church, at the very time when his Holinefs was performing fome religious ceremony. At this fight our impatient miffionary felt all his paffions inflamed with irrefiftible ardour; he could no longer wait for the expected conference, but burfling out with zealous indignation, he exclaimed, " O thou beaft of nature, with feven " heads and ten horns! thou mother of " harlots, arrayed in purple and fcarlet, " and decked with gold and precious " ftones

" ftones and pearls! throw away the golden
" cup of abominations, and the filthinefs
" of thy fornication !"

You may eafily imagine the aftonifhment and hubbub that fuch an apoftrophe,
from fuch a perfon, in fuch a place, would
occafion; he was immediately carried to
prifon by the Swifs halberdiers.

When it was known that he was a Britifh fubject, fome who underftood Englifh
were ordered to attend his examination.
The firft queftion afked of him was, " What
" had brought him to Rome?" He anfwered,
" To anoint the eyes of the fcarlet whore
" with eye-falve, that fhe might fee her
" wickednefs." They afked, " Who he
" meant by the fcarlet whore?" He anfwered,
" Who elfe could he mean, but her who
" fitteth upon feven mountains, who hath
" feduced the kings of the earth to com-
" mit fornication, and who hath gotten
" drunk

" drunk with the blood of the faints, and
", the blood of the martyrs ?" Many other
queftions were afked, and fuch provoking
anfwers returned, that fome fufpected the
man affected madnefs, that he might give
vent to his rancour and petulance with
impunity; and they were for condemning
him to the gallies, that he might be taught
more fenfe, and better manners. But
when they communicated their fentiments to
Clement the Fourteenth, he faid, with great
good humour, " That he never had heard
" of any body whofe underftanding, or
" politenefs, had been much improved at
" that fchool; that although the poor
" man's firft addrefs had been a little rough
" and abrupt, yet he could not help con-
" fidering himfelf as obliged to him for
" his good intentions, and for his under-
" taking fuch a long journey with a view
" to do good." He afterwards gave orders to treat the man with gentlenefs
while he remained in confinement, and

to put him on board the firſt ſhip bound
from Civita Vecchia to England, defraying
the expence of his paſſage. However
humane and reaſonable this conduct may
be thought by many, there were people
who condemned it as an injudicious piece
of lenity, which might have a tendency
to ſink the dignity of the ſacred office, and
expoſe it to future inſults. If ſuch behaviour as this did not paſs without blame,
it may be eaſily ſuppoſed, that few of the
late Pope's actions eſcaped uncenſured;
and many who loved the eaſy amiable
diſpoſitions of the man, were of opinion,
that the ſpirit of the times required a different character on the Papal throne.
This idea prevailed among the Cardinals
at the late election, and the Conclave is
ſuppoſed to have fixed on Cardinal Braſchi
to be Pope, from the ſame motive that
the Roman ſenate ſometimes choſe a Dic-
tator to reſtore and enforce the ancient diſ-
cipline.

VOL. II.   D

LETTER XLVIII.

Rome.

PIUS the Sixth performs all the religious functions of his office in the most solemn manner; not only on public and extraordinary occasions, but also in the most common acts of devotion. I happened lately to be at St. Peter's church, when there was scarcely any other body there; while I lounged from chapel to chapel, looking at the sculpture and paintings, the Pope entered with a very few attendants; when he came to the statue of St. Peter, he was not satisfied with bowing, which is the usual mark of respect shewn to that image; or with kneeling, which is performed by more zealous persons; or with kissing the foot, which I formerly imagined concluded the climax of devotion;

votion; he bowed, he knelt, he kiffed the foot, and then he rubbed his brow and his whole head with every mark of humility, fervour, and adoration, upon the facred ftump.—It is no more, one half of the foot having been long fince worn away by the lips of the pious; and if the example of his Holinefs is univerfally imitated, nothing but a miracle can prevent the leg, thigh, and other parts from meeting with the fame fate. This uncommon appearance of zeal in the Pope, is not imputed to hypocrify or to policy, but is fuppofed to proceed entirely from a conviction of the efficacy of thofe holy frictions; an opinion which has given people a much higher idea of the ftrength of his faith, than of his underftanding. This being jubilee year, he may poffibly think a greater appearance of devotion neceffary now, than at any other time. The firft jubilee was inftituted by Boniface the Eighth, in the year 1300. Many cere-

monies

---

monies and inſtitutions of the Roman Catholic church are founded on thoſe of the old Heathens. This is evidently an imitation of the Roman ſecular games, which were exhibited every hundredth year in honour of the gods*; they laſted three days and three nights; they were attended with great pomp, and drew vaſt numbers of people to Rome, from all parts of Italy, and the moſt diſtant provinces. Boniface, recollecting this, determined to inſtitute ſomething analagous, which would immortalize his own name, and promote the intereſt of the Roman Catholic religion in general, and that of the city of Rome in particular. He embraced the favourable opportunity which the beginning of a century preſented; he invented a few extraordinary ceremonies, and declared the year 1300 the firſt jubilee

* The Carmen Seculare of Horace was compoſed on occaſion of thoſe celebrated by Auguſtus in the year of Rome 736.

year,

year, during which he affured mankind, that heaven would be in a particular manner propitious, in granting indulgences, and remiffion of fins, to all who fhould come to Rome, and attend the functions there to be performed, at this fortunate period, which was not to occur again for a hundred years. This drew a great concourfe of wealthy finners to Rome; and the extraordinary circulation of money it occafioned, was ftrongly felt all over the Pope's dominions. Clement the Sixth, regretting that thefe advantages fhould occur fo feldom, abridged the period, and declared there would be a jubilee every fifty years; the fecond was accordingly celebrated in the year 1350. Sixtus the Fifth, imagining that the interval was ftill too long, once more retrenched the half; and ever fince there has been a jubilee every twenty-fifth year *. It is not likely that any fu-

* To this laft abridgement I am Indebted for having feen the ceremonies and proceffions on the termination of this facred year.

D 3   ture

ture Pope will think of shortening this period; if any alteration were again to take place, it most probably would be, to restore the ancient period of fifty or a hundred years; for, instead of the wealthy pilgrims who flocked to Rome from every quarter of Christendom, ninety-nine in a hundred of those who come now, are supported by alms during their journey, or are barely able to defray their own expences by the strictest œconomy; and his Holiness is supposed at present to derive no other advantage from the uncommon fatigue he is obliged to go through on the jubilee year, except the satisfaction he feels, in reflecting on the benefit his labours confer on the souls of the beggars, and other travellers, who resort from all corners of Italy to Rome, on this blessed occasion.   The States which border on the Pope's dominions, suffer many temporal inconveniencies from the zeal of the

peasants

peafants and manufacturers, the greater
part of whom ftill make a point of vifiting St. Peter's on the jubilee year; the
lofs fuftained by the countries which fuch
emigrants abandon, is not balanced by
any advantage transferred to that to which
they refort; the good arifing on the whole,
being entirely of a fpiritual nature. By
far the greater number of pilgrims come
from the kingdom of Naples, whofe inhabitants are faid to be of a very devout
and very amorous difpofition. The firft
prompts them to go to Rome in fearch of
that abfolution which the fecond renders
neceffary; and on the year of jubilee,
when indulgences are to be had at an
eafier rate than at any other time, thofe
who can afford it generally carry away
fuch a ftock, as not only is fufficient to
clear old fcores, but will alfo ferve as an
indemnifying fund for future tranf-
greffions.

There

There is one door into the church of St, Peter's, which is called the Holy Door. This is always walled up, except on this diftinguifhed year; and even then no perfon is permitted to enter by it, but in the humbleft pofture. The pilgrims, and many others, prefer crawling into the church upon their knees, by this door; to walking in, the ufual way, by any other. I was prefent at the fhutting up of this Holy Door. The Pope being feated on a raifed feat, or kind of throne, furrounded by Cardinals and other ecclefiaftics, an anthem, was fung, accompanied by all forts of mufical inftruments. During the performance, his Holinefs defcended from the throne, with a golden trowel in his hand, placed the firft brick, and applied fome mortar; he then returned to his feat, and the door was inftantly built up by more expert, though lefs hallowed, workmen; and will remain as it is now, till the beginning

ginning of the nineteenth century, when
it will be again opened, by the Pope then
in being, with the same solemnity that it
has been now shut. Though his Holiness
places but a single brick, yet it is very remarkable that this never fails to communicate its influence, in such a rapid and
powerful manner, that, within about an
hour, or at most an hour and a half, all
the other bricks, which form the wall of
the Holy Door, acquire an equal degree of
sanctity with that placed by the Pope's own
hands. The common people and pilgrims
are well acquainted with this wonderful
effect. At the beginning of this Jubilee-
year, when the late wall was thrown down,
men, women, and children scrambled and
fought for the fragments of the bricks and
mortar, with the same eagerness which less
enlightened mobs display, on days of public rejoicing, when handfuls of money are
thrown among them. I have been often
assured that those pieces of brick, besides
their

their fanctity, have alfo the virtue of curing
many of the moft obftinate difeafes: and, if
newfpapers were permitted at Rome, there is
not the leaft reafon to doubt, that thofe
cures would be attefted publicly by the patients, in a manner as fatisfactory and
convincing as are the cures performed
daily by the pills, powders, drops, and
balfams advertifed in the London newfpapers. After the fhutting of the Holy
Door, mafs was celebrated at midnight;
and the ceremony was attended by vaft
multitudes of people. For my own part,
I fufpended my curiofity till next day,
which was Chriftmas-day, when I returned
again to St. Peter's church, and faw the
Pope perform mafs on that folemn occafion.
His Holinefs went through all the evolutions of the ceremony with an addrefs and
flexibility of body, which are rarely to be
found in thofe who wear the tiara; who
are, generally fpeaking, men bowing under
the load of years and infirmities. His
                                        prefent

prefent Holinefs has hitherto fuffered from
neither. His features are regular, and he
has a fine countenance; his perfon is
ftraight, and his movements graceful.
His leg and foot are remarkably well made,
and always ornamented with filk ftockings,
and red flippers, of the moft delicate conftruction. Notwithftanding that the papal
uniforms are by no means calculated to fet
off the perfon to the greateft advantage,
yet the peculiar neatnefs with which they
are put on, and the nice adjuftment of their
moft minute parts, fufficiently prove that
his prefent Holinefs is not infenfible of the
charms of his perfon, or unfolicitous about
his external ornaments. Though verging
towards the winter of life, his cheeks ftill
glow with autumnal rofes, which, at a little
diftance, appear as blooming as thofe of the
fpring. If he himfelf were lefs clear-
fighted than he feems to be, to the beauties
of his face and perfon, he could not alfo
be deaf to the voices of the women, who

break

break out into exclamations, in praife of
both, as often as he appears in public. On
a public occafion, lately, as he was carried
through a particular ftreet, a young woman
at a window exclaimed, " Quanto e bello!
" O quanto e bello!" and was immediately
anfwered by a zealous old lady at the window oppofite, who, folding her hands in
each other, and raifing her eyes to heaven,
cried out, with a mixture of love for his
perfon, and veneration for his facred office,
" Tanto e bello, quanto e fanto!" When
we know that fuch a quantity of incenfe is
daily burnt under his facred noftrils, we
ought not to be aftonifhed, though we
fhould find his brain, on fome occafions, a
little intoxicated.

Vanity is a very comfortable failing;
and has fuch an univerfal power over
mankind, that not only the gay bloffoms
of youth, but even the fhrivelled bofom of
age, and the contracted heart of bigotry,
open,

open, expand, and difplay ftrong marks of
fenfibility under its influence.

After mafs, the Pope gave the benediction to the ~eople affembled in
the Grand Court, before the church of
St. Peter's. It was a remarkably fine
day; an immenfe multitude filled that fpacious and magnificent area; the horfe and
foot guards were drawn up in their moft
fhowy uniform. The Pope, feated in an
open, portable chair, in all the fplendour
which his wardrobe could give, with the
tiara on his head, was carried out of a large
window, which opens on a balcony in the
front of St. Peter's. The filk hangings and
gold trappings with which the chair was em-
bellifhed, concealed the men who carried it;
fo that to thofe who viewed him from the area
below, his Holinefs feemed to fail forward,
from the window felf-balanced in the air,
like a celeftial being. The inftant he appeared, the mufic ftruck up, the bells rung from
every

I

every church, and the cannon thundered
from the caflle of St. Angelo in repeated
peals. During the intervals, the church of
St. Peter's, the palace of the Vatican, and
the banks of the Tiber, re-echoed the ac-
clamations of the populace. At length his
Holinefs arofe from his feat, and an immediate and awful filence enfued. The multitude fell upon their knees, with their
hands and eyes raifed towards his Holinefs,
as to a benign Deity. After a folemn
paufe, he pronounced the benediction,
with great fervour; elevating his outftretch-
ed arms as high as he could; then clofing
them together, and bringing them back to
his breaft with a flow motion, as if he had
got hold of the blefling, and was drawing
it gently from heaven. Finally, he threw
his arms open, waving them for fome time,
as if his intention had been to fcatter the
benediction with impartiality among the
people.

No

No ceremony can be better calculated for ſtriking the ſenſes, and impoſing on the underſtanding, than this of the Supreme Pontiff giving the bleſſing from the balcony of St. Peter's. For my own part, if I had not, in my early youth, received impreſſions highly unfavourable to the chief actor in this magnificent interlude, I ſhould have been in danger of paying him a degree of reſpect, very inconſiſtent with the religion in which I was educated.

LETTER XLIX.

Rome.

IN my laſt, I informed you of my having been ſeduced almoſt into idolatry, by the influence of example, and the pomp which ſurrounded the idol. I muſt now confeſs that I have aɗually bowed the knee to Baal, from mere wantonneſs. We are told that, to draw near to that Being, who ought to be the only objeɗ of worſhip, with our lips, while our hearts are far from him, is a mockery. Such daring and abſurd hypocriſy I ſhall always avoid: but to have drawn near to *him*, who ought not to be an objeɗ of worſhip, with the lips only, while the heart continued at a diſtance, I hope will be conſidered as no more than a venial tranſgreſſion. In ſhort, I truſt,

I truft, that it will not be looked on as a mortal fin in Proteftants to have kiffed the Pope's toe. If it fhould, fome of your friends are in a deplorable way, as you fhall hear.—It is ufual for ftrangers to be prefented to his Holinefs, before they leave Rome. The D— of H——, Mr. K——, and myfelf, have all been at the Vatican together, upon that important bufinefs. Your young acquaintance Jack, who, having now got a commiffion in the army, confiders himfelf no longer as a boy, defired to accompany us. We went under the aufpices of a certain ecclefiaftic, who ufually attends the Englifh on fuch occafions.

He very naturally concluded, that it would be moft agreeable to us to have the circumftance of kiffing the flipper difpenfed with. Having had fome converfation, therefore, with his Holinefs, in his own apartment, while we remained in another room, previous to our introduction; he afterwards returned, and informed us, that the Pontiff, indulgent to the prejudices of the British nation, did not infift on that part of the ceremonial; and therefore a very low bow, on our being prefented, was all that would be required of us.

A bow! cried the D— of H—; I fhould not have given myfelf any trouble about the matter, had I fufpected that all was to end in a bow.   I look on kiffing the toe as the only amufing circumftance of the whole; if that is to be omitted, I will not be introduced at all.   For if the moft ludicrous part is left out, who would wait for the reft of a farce?

This was a thunderftroke to our negociator, who expected thanks, at leaft, for the honourable terms he had obtained; but who, on the contrary, found himfelf in the fame difagreeable predicament with other negociators, who have met with abufe and
reproach

reproach from their countrymen, on account of treaties for which they expected univerfal applaufe.

The D— of H—— knew nothing of the treaty which our introducer had juft concluded; otherwife he would certainly have prevented the negociation. As I perceived, however, that our ambaffador was mortified with the thoughts that all his labour fhould prove abortive, I faid, that, although he had prevailed with his Holinefs to wave that part of the ceremonial, which his Grace thought fo entertaining, yet it would unqueftionably be ftill more agreeable to him that the whole fhould be performed to its utmoft extent: this new arrangement, therefore, needed not be an obftruction to our being prefented.

The countenance of our Conductor brightened up at this propofal. He im-

mediately

mediately ushered us into the presence of
the Supreme Pontiff. We all bowed to the
ground; the suppleft of the company had
the happiness to touch the sacred slipper
with their lips, and the least agile were
within a few inches of that honour. As
this was more than had been bargained
for, his Holiness seemed agreeably sur-
prised; raised the D— with a smiling
countenance, and conversed with him in
an obliging manner, asking the common
queslions, How long he had been in Italy?
Whether he found Rome agreeable? When
he intended to set out for Naples?—He
said something of the same kind to each of
the company; and, after about a quarter
of an hour or twenty minutes, we took
our leave.

Next day, his Holiness sent his compliments to the D—, with a present of two
medals, one of gold, and the other
of silver; on both of which the head
                                     of

of the Pontiff is very accurately en-
graved.

The manner in which the generality of
sovereign princes pass their time, is as far
from being amusing or agreeable, as one
can possibly imagine. Slaves to the tire-
some routine of etiquette; martyrs to the
oppressive fatigue of pomp; constrained to
walk every levee-day around the same dull
circle, to gratify the vanity of fifty or a
hundred people, by whispering a something
or a nothing into the ears of each; obliged to wear a smiling countenance, even
when the heart is oppressed with sadness;
besieged by the craving faces of those,
who are more displeased at what is withheld, than grateful for the favours they
have received; surrounded, as he con-
stantly is, by adepts in the art of simula-
tion, all professing the highest possible regard; how shall the puzzled monarch dis-
tinguish real from assumed attachment?

and

and what a rifk does he run, of placing his confidence where he ought to have directed his indignation! And, to all thefe inconveniencies, when we add this, that he is precluded from thofe delightful fenfations which fpring from difinterefled friendſhip, fweet equality, and the gay, carelefs enjoyments of focial life, we mufl acknowledge, that all that is brilliant in the condition of a fovereign, is not fufficient to compenfate for fuch reflraints, fuch dangers, and fuch deprivations.

So far indeed are we from confidering that envied condition as enviable, that great part of mankind are more apt to think it infupportable; and are furprifed to find, that thofe unhappy men, whom fate has condemned to fuffer the pains of royalty for life, are able to wait with patience for the natural period of their days. For, flrange as it may appear, hiftory does not furnifh us with an inflance, not even

in

in Great Britain itfelf, of a king, who
hanged, or drowned, or put himfelf to
death in any other violent manner, from
mere tædium, as other mortals, difgufted
with life, are apt to do. I was at a lofs to
account for fuch an extraordinary fact, till
I recollected that, however void of refources and activity the minds of mo-
narchs may be, they are feldom allowed to reft in repofe. The ftorms to
which people in their lofty fituation are
expofed, occafion fuch agitations as prevent
the ftagnating flime of tædium from gathering on their minds. That kings do
not commit fuicide, therefore, affords only
a very flender prefumption of the happinefs of their condition: although it is a
ftrong proof, that all the hurricanes of life
are not fo infupportable to the human
mind, as that infipid, fearlefs, hopelefs
calm, which envelopes men who are devoid
of mental enjoyments, and whofe fenfes
are palled with fatiety. If there is any
truth in the above reprefentation of the re-

E 4   gal

gal condition, would not you imagine that
of all others it would be the moſt ſhunned?
Would not you imagine that every human
being would ſhrink from it, as from certain miſery; and that at leaſt every wiſe
man would ſay, with the Poet,

I envy none their pageantry and ſhow,
I envy none the gilding of their woe?

Not only every wiſe man, but every fooliſh
man, will adopt the ſentiment, and act
accordingly; provided his rank in life re-
moves him from the poſſibility of ever attaining the objects in queſtion.   For what
is ſituated beyond the ſphere of our hopes,
very ſeldom excites our deſires; but bring
the powerful magnets a little nearer, and
they attract the human paſſions with a
force which reaſon and philoſophy cannot
controul.   Placed within their reach, the
wiſe and the fooliſh graſp with equal eager-
neſs at crowns and ſceptres, in ſpite of all
the thorns with which they are ſurrounded.
Their alluring magic ſeems to have the
power

power of changing the very characters and
natures of men. In purfuit of them, the
indolent have been excited to the moft
active exertions, the voluptuous have re-
nounced their darling pleafures; and even
thofe who have long walked in the direct
road of integrity, have deviated into all
the crooked paths of villany and fraud.

There are paffions, whofe indulgence is
fo exceedingly flattering to the natural
vanity of men, that they will gratify them,
though perfuaded that the gratification
will be attended by difappointment and
mifery. The love of power and fove-
reignty is of this clafs. It has been a general belief, ever fince the kingly office
was eftablifhed among men, that cares and
anxiety were the conftant attendants of
royalty. Yet this general conviction
never made a fingle perfon decline an opportunity of embarking on this fea of
troubles. Every new adventurer flatters
himfelf

himfelf that he fhall be guided by fome
happy ftar undifcovered by former navi-
gators; and thofe who, after trial, have re-
linquifhed the voyage—Charles, Chriftina,
Amadeus, and others--when they had quitted
the helm, and were fafely arrived in port,
are faid to have languifhed, all the reft
of their lives, for that fituation which
their own experience taught them was
fraught with mifery.

Henry the Fourth of England did not
arrive at the throne by the natural and direct road. Shakefpear puts the following
Addrefs to Sleep, into the mouth of this
monarch:

———O Sleep! O gentle Sleep!
Nature's foft nurfe, how have I frighted thee,
That thou no more wilt weigh my eyelids
    down,
And fteep my fenfes in forgetfulnefs?
Why rather, Sleep, lieft thou in fmoky cribs,
Upon uneafy pallets ftretching thee,

And

And hufh'd with bufy night-flies to thy
    flumber;
Than in the perfum'd chambers of the Great,
Under the canopies of coftly ftate,
And lull'd with founds of fweeteft melody?
O thou dull God! why ly'ft thou with the
    vile
In loathfome beds; and leav'ft the kingly
    couch?
A watch-cafe, or a common 'larum bell?
Wilt thou, upon the high and giddy maft,
Seal up the fhip-boy's eyes, and rock his
    brains
In cradle of the rude imperious furge;
And in the vifitation of the winds,——
Who take the ruffian billows by the top,
Curling their monftrous heads, and hanging
    them
With deaf'ning clamours in the flipp'ry
    fhrouds,——
Canft thou, O partial Sleep! give thy repofe
To the wet fea-boy in an hour fo rude;
And, in the calmeft and moft ftilleft night,
With all appliances and means to boot,
Deny it to a King?——

However eager and impatient this Prince
may have formerly been to obtain the
8   crown,

crown, you would conclude that he was
quite cloyed by poſſeſſion at the time he
made this ſpeech; and therefore, at firſt ſight,
you would not expect that he ſhould afterwards diſplay any exceſſive attachment to
what gives him ſo much uneaſineſs. But
Shakeſpear, who knew the ſecret wiſhes,
perverſe deſires, and ſtrange inconſiſt-
encies of the human heart, better than
man ever knew them, makes this very
Henry ſo tenaciouſly fond of that which
he himſelf conſidered as the cauſe of all
his inquietude, that he cannot bear to have
the crown one moment out of his ſight,
but orders it to be placed on his pillow
when he lies on his death-bed.

Of all diadems, the Tiara, in my opinion, has the feweſt charms; and nothing
can afford a ſtronger proof of the ſtrength
and perſeverance of man's paſſion for ſovereign power, than our knowledge, that
even this eccleſiaſtical crown is ſought after

ter with as much eagernefs, perhaps with more, than any other crown in the world, although the candidates are generally in the decline of life, and all of a profeffion which avows the moft perfect contempt of worldly grandeur. This appears the more wonderful when we reflect, that, over and above thofe fources of wearinefs and vexation, which the Pope has in common with other fovereigns, he has fome which are peculiar to himfelf.—The tirefome religious functions which he muft perform, the ungenial folitude of his meals, the exclufion of the company and converfation of women, reftriction from the tendereft and moft delightful connexions in life, from the endearments of a parent, and the *open acknowledgment* of his own children; his mind oppreffed with the gloomy reflection, that the man for whom he has the leaft regard, perhaps his greateft enemy, may be his immediate fucceffor; to which is added, the pain of feeing his

influence,

influence, both fpiritual and temporal, declining every day; and the mortification of knowing, that all his ancient lofty pretenfions are laughed at by one half of the Roman Catholics, all the Proteftants, and totally difregarded by the reft of mankind. I know of nothing which can be put in the other fcale to balance all thofe peculiar difadvantages which his Holinefs labours under, unlefs it is the fingular felicity which he lawfully may, and no doubt does enjoy, in the contemplation of his own infallibility.

LETTER L.

Rome.

IN their external deportment, the Italians
have a grave folemnity of manner,
which is fometimes thought to arife from
a natural gloominefs of difpofition. The
French, above all other nations, are apt
to impute to melancholy, the fedate ferious
air which accompanies reflection.

Though in the pulpit, on the theatre,
and even in common converfation, the
Italians make ufe of a great deal of
action; yet Italian vivacity is different
from French; the former proceeds from
fenfibility, the latter from animal fpirits.

The inhabitants of this country have
not the brifk look, and elaftic trip, which

is

is univerfal in France; they move rather
with a flow compofed pace: their fpines
never having been forced into a ftraight
line, retain the natural bend; and the people of the moft finifhed fafhion, as well
as the neglected vulgar, feem to prefer the
unconftrained attitude of the Antinous,
and other antique ftatues, to the artificial
graces of a French dancing-mafter, or the
erect ftrut of a German foldier. I imagine I perceive a great refemblance between
many of the living countenances I fee
daily, and the features of the ancient
bufts and ftatues ; which leads me to believe, that there are a greater number of
the genuine defcendants of the old Romans in Italy, than is generally imagined.

I am often ftruck with the fine character
of countenance to be feen in the ftreets of
Rome. I never faw features more expreffive
of reflection, fenfe, and genius; in the
very loweft ranks there are countenances

which

which announce minds fit for the higheſt
and moſt important ſituations; and we cannot help regretting, that thoſe to whom
they belong, .have not received an education adequate to the natural abilities
we are convinced they poſſeſs, and placed
where theſe abilities could be brought into
action.

Of all the countries in Europe, Switzerland is that in which the beauties of
nature appear in the greateſt variety of
forms, and on the moſt magnificent ſcale;
in that country, therefore, the young
landſcape painter has the beſt chance of
ſeizing the moſt ſublime ideas : but Italy
is the beſt ſchool for the hiſtory painter,
not only on account of its being enriched
with the works of the greateſt maſters,
and the nobleſt models of antique ſculpture ; but alſo on account of the fine expreſſive ſtyle of the Italian countenance.
Here you have few or none of thoſe fair,

fat, gliftening, unmeaning faces, fo common in the more northern parts of Europe. I happened once to fit by a foreigner of my acquaintance at the Opera in the Hay-market, when a certain Nobleman, who at that time was a good deal talked of, entered. I whifpered him— " That is Lord ——." " Not furely the " famous Lord ——," faid he. " Yes," faid I, " the very fame." " It muft be " acknowledged then," continued he, " that " the noble Earl does infinite honour to " thofe who have had the care of his " education." " How fo?" rejoined I. " Becaufe," replied the foreigner, " a " countenance fo completely vacant, " ftrongly indicates a deficiency of natural " abilities; the refpectable figure he makes " in the fenate, I therefore prefume muft " be entirely owing to inftruction."

Strangers, on their arrival at Rome, form no high idea of the beauty of the
Roman

Roman women, from the fpecimens they fce in the fafhionable circles to which they are firft introduced. There are fome exceptions; but in general it muft be acknowledged, that the prefent race of women of high rank, are more diftinguifhed by their other ornaments, than by their beauty. Among the citizens, however, and in the lower claffes, you frequently meet with the moft beautiful countenances. For a brilliant red and white, and all the charms of complexion, no women are equal to the Englifh. If a hundred, or any greater number, of Englifh women were taken at random, and compared with the fame number of the wives and daughters of the citizens of Rome, I am convinced, that ninety of the Englifh would be found handfomer than ninety of the Romans; but the probability is, that two or three in the hundred Italians, would have finer countenances than any of the Englifh. Englifh beauty is more

remarkable

remarkable in the country, than in towns;
the peafantry of no country in Europe can
ftand a comparifon, in point of looks, with
thofe of England. That race of people
have the conveniencies of life in no other
country in fuch perfection; they are no
where fo well fed, fo well defended from
the injuries of the feafons; and no where
elfe do they keep themfelves fo perfectly
clean, and free from all the vilifying effects of dirt. The Englifh country girls,
taken collectively, are, unqueftionably, the
handfomeft in the world. The female
peafants of moft other countries, indeed,
are fo hard worked, fo ill fed, fo much
tanned by the fun, and fo dirty, that it is
difficult to know whether they have any
beauty or not. Yet I have been informed,
by fome Amateurs, fince I came here, that,
in fpite of all thefe difadvantages, they
fometimes find, among the Italian peafantry, countenances highly interefting, and
.   which

which they prefer to all the cherry checks of Lancashire.

Beauty, doubtlefs, is infinitely varied; and happily for mankind, their taftes and opinions, on the fubject, are equally vari-ous. Notwithftanding this variety, how-ever, a ftyle of face, in fome meafure pe-culiar to its own inhabitants, has been found to prevail in each different nation of Europe. This peculiar countenance is again greatly varied, and marked with every de-gree of difcrimination between the ex-tremes of beauty and uglinefs. I will give you a fketch of the general ftyle of the moft beautiful female heads in this country, from which you may judge whether they are to your tafte or not.

A great profufion of dark hair, which feems to encroach upon the forehead, rendering it fhort and narrow; the nofe

generally

generally either aquiline, or continued in a
ſtraight line from the lower part of tho
brow; a full and ſhort upper lip; by the
way, nothing has a worſe effect on a countenance, than a large interval between the
noſe and mouth; the eyes are large, and
of a ſparkling black. The black eye certainly labours under one diſadvantage,
which is, that, from the iris and pupil
being of the ſame colour, the contraction
and dilatation of the latter is not ſeen, by
which the eye is abridged of half its
powers. Yet the Italian eye is wonderfully expreſſive; ſome people think it ſays
too much. The complexion, for the moſt
part, is of a clear brown, ſometimes fair,
but very ſeldom florid, or of that bright
fairneſs which is common in England and
Saxony. It muſt be owned, that thoſe
features which have a fine expreſſion of
ſentiment and meaning in youth, are more
apt, than leſs expreſſive faces, to become
ſoon ſtrong and maſculine. In England
and

and Germany, the women, a little advanced in life, retain the appearance of youth longer than in Italy.

With countenances so favourable for the pencil, you will naturally imagine, that portrait painting is in the higheſt perfection here. The reverſe, however, of this is true; that branch of the art is in the loweſt eſtimation all over Italy. In palaces, the beſt furniſhed with piⁿures, you ſeldom ſee a portrait of the proprietor, or any of his family. A quarter length of the reigning Pope is ſometimes the only portrait, of a living perſon, to be ſeen in the whole palace. Several of the Roman Princes affect to have a room of ſtate, or audience chamber, in which is a raiſed ſeat like a throne, with a canopy over it. In thoſe rooms the effigies of the Pontiffs are hung; they are the work of very inferior artiſts, and ſeldom coſt above three or four ſequins. As ſoon as his Holineſs

F 4   departs

departs this life, the portrait difappears, and the face of his fucceffor is in due time hung up in its ftead. This, you will fay, is treating their old fovereign a little un-kindly, and paying no very expenfive compliment to the new; it is not fo œconomical, however, as what was practifed by a certain perfon. I fhall not inform you whether he was a Frenchman or an Englifhman, but he certainly was a courtier, and profeffed the higheft poffible regard for all living mo-narchs; but confidered them as no better than any other piece of clay when dead. He had a full length picture of his own Sovereign in the principal room of his houfe; on his majefty's death, to fave himfelf the expence of a frefh body, and a new fuit of ermine, he employed a painter to brufh out the face and periwig, and clap the new King's head on his grand-father's fhoulders; which, he declared, were in the moft perfect prefervation, and

fully

fully able to wear out three or four fuch heads as painters ufually give in thefe degenerate days.

The Italians, in general, very feldom take the trouble of fitting for their pictures. They confider a portrait as a piece of painting, which engages the admiration of nobody but the perfon it reprefents, or the painter who drew it. Thofe who are in circumftances to pay the beft artifts, generally employ them in fome fubject more univerfally interefting, than the reprefentation of human countenances ftaring out of a piece of canvas.

Pompeio Battoni is the beft Italian painter now at Rome. His tafte and genius led him to hiftory painting, and his reputation was originally acquired in that line; but by far the greater part of his fortune, whatever that may be, has flowed through a different channel. His

chief

chief employment, for many years paſt, has been painting the portraits of the young Engliſh, and other ſtrangers of fortune, who viſit Rome. There are artiſts in England, ſuperior in this, and every other branch of painting, to Battoni. They, like him, are ſeduced from the free walks of genius, and chained, by intereſt, to the ſervile drudgery of copying faces. Beauty is worthy of the moſt delicate pencil; but, gracious heaven! why ſhould every periwig-pated fellow, without countenance or character, inſiſt on ſeeing his chubby cheeks on canvas?

" Could you not give a little expreſſion " to that countenance?" ſaid a gentleman to an eminent Engliſh painter, who ſhowed him a portrait which he had juſt finiſhed. "I made that attempt already," replied the painter; " but what the picture gained " in expreſſion, it loſt in likeneſs; and by " the time there was a little common ſenſe
" in

" in the countenance, nobody knew for
" whom it was intended. I was obliged,
" therefore, to make an entire new pic-
" ture, with the face perfectly like, and
" perfectly meaningless, as you see it."

Let the colours for ever remain, which
record the last fainting efforts of Chatham;
the expiring triumph of Wolf; or the in-
decision of Garrick, equally allured by the
two contending Mufes! But let them pe-
rish and fly from the canvas, which blind
felf-love fpreads for infipidity and uglinefs! Why should pofterity know, that the
firft genius of the age, and thofe whofe
pencils were formed to fpeak to the heart,
and delineate beauteous Nature, were chiefly employed in copying faces? and many
of them, faces that imitate humanity fo
abominably, that, to ufe Hamlet's expreffion, they feem not the genuine work of
Nature, but of Nature's journeymen.

To this ridiculous felf-love, equally pre-
valent among the great vulgar and fmall,
                                        fome

fome of the beft painters in France, Germany, and Great Britain, are obliged for
their fubfiftence. This creates a fufpicion,
that a tafte for the real beauties of painting,
is not quite fo univerfal, as a fenfibility to
their own perfonal beauties, among the
individuals of thefe countries. And nothing can be a ftronger proof of the important light in which men appear in their
own eyes, and their fmall importance in
thofe of others, than the different treatment which the generality of portraits receive, during the life, and after the death,
of their conftituents. During the firft of
thefe periods, they inhabit the fineft apartments of the houfes to which they belong;
they are flattered by the guefts, and always
viewed with an eye of complacency by the
landlord. But, after the commencement
of the fecond, they begin to be neglected;
in a fhort time are ignominioufly thruft up
to the garret; and, to fill up the meafure
of their affliction, they finally are thrown
out of doors, in the moft barbarous man-

ner,

ner, without diftinction of rank, age, or fex. Thofe of former times are fcattered, like Jews, with their long beards and brown complexions, all over the face of the earth; and, even of the prefent century, Barons of the moft ancient families, armed cap-a-pee, are to be purchafed for two or three ducats, in moft of the towns of Germany. French Marquifes, in full fuits of embroidered velvet, may be had at Paris ftill cheaper; and many worfhipful citizens of London are to be feen dangling on the walls of an auction-room, when they are fcarce cold in their graves.

LETTER LI.

Rome.

THERE are no theatrical entertainments permitted in this city, except
during the Carnival; but they are then
attended with a degree of ardour unknown
in capitals whofe inhabitants are under no
fuch reftraint. Every kind of amufement,
indeed, in this gay feafon, is followed
with the greateft eagernefs. The natural gravity of the Roman citizens is
changed into a mirthful vivacity; and
the ferious, fombre city of Rome exceeds Paris itfelf in fprightlinefs and gaiety. This fpirit feems gradually to augment, from its commencement; and is at
its height in the laft week of the fix which
comprehend the Carnival. The citizens
then appear in the ftreets, mafked, in
the

the characters of Harlequins, Pantaloons, Punchinellos, and all the fantaftic variety of a mafquerade. This humour fpreads to men, women, and children; defcends to the loweft ranks, and becomes univerfal. Even thofe who put on no mafk, and have no defire to remain unknown, reject their ufual clothes, and affume fome whimfical drefs. The coachmen, who are placed in a more confpicuous point of view than others of the fame rank in life, and who are perfectly known by the carriages they drive, generally affect fome ridiculous difguife : Many of them chufe a woman's drefs, and have their faces painted, and adorned with patches. However dull thefe fellows may be, when in breeches, they are, in petticoats, confidered as the pleafanteft men in the world; and excite much laughter in every ftreet in which they appear. I obferved to an Italian of my acquaintance, that, confidering the ftalenefs of the joke, I was furprifed at the mirth it .

2   feemed

feemed to raife. " When a whole city," anfwered he, " are refolved to be merry " for a week together, it is exceedingly " convenient to have a few eftablifhed " jokes ready made; the young laugh at " the novelty, and the old from prefcrip- " tion. This metamorphofis of the coach- " men is certainly not the moft refined " kind of wit; however, it is more harm- " lefs than the burning of heretics, which " formerly was a great fource of amufe- " ment to our populace."

The ftreet, called the Corfo, is the great fcene of thefe mafquerades. It is crowded every night with people of all conditions : Thofe of rank come in coaches, or in open carriages, made on purpofe. A kind of civil war is carried on by the company, as they pafs each other. The greateft mark of attention you can fhew your friends and acquaintance, is, to throw a handful of little white balls, refembling fugar-plums,

full

full in their faces; and, if they are not deficient in politenefs, they will inftantly return you the compliment. All who wifh to make a figure in the Corfo, come well fupplied in this kind of ammunition..

Sometimes two or three open carriages, on a fide, with five or fix perfons of both fexes in each, draw up oppofite to each other, and fight a pitched battle. On thefe occafions, the combatants are provided with whole bags full of the fmall fhot above mentioned, which they throw at each other, with much apparent fury, till their ammunition is exhaufted, and the field of battle is as white as fnow.

The peculiar dreffes of every nation of the globe, and of every profeffion, befides all the fantaftic characters ufual at mafque-rades, are to be feen on the Corfo. Thofe of Harlequin and Pantaloon are in great vogue among the men. The citizens wives and daughters generally affect the

VOL. II.　　G　　pomp

pomp of women of quality; while their
brothers, or other relations, appear as
train-bearers and attendants. In general,
they seem to delight in characters the moſt
remote from their own. Young people
aſſume the long beard, tottering ſtep,
and other concomitants of old age; the
aged chuſe the bib and rattle of childhood;
and the women of quality, and women
of the town, appear in the characters of
country maidens, nuns, and veſtal virgins.
All endeavour to ſupport the aſſumed characters, to the beſt of their ability; but
none, in my opinion, ſucceed ſo well as
thoſe who repreſent children.

Towards the duſk of the evening, the
horſe-race takes place. As ſoon as this is
announced, the coaches, cabriolets, tri-
umphal cars, and carriages of every kind,
are drawn up, and line the ſtreet; leaving
a ſpace in the middle for the racers to paſs.
Theſe are five or ſix horſes, trained on
purpoſe

purpofe for this diverfion; they are drawn
up a-breaft in the Piazza del Popolo, exactly where the Corfo begins. Certain
balls, with little fharp fpikes, are hung
along their fides, which ferve to fpur them
on. As foon as they begin to run, thofe
animals, by their impatience to be gone,
fhew that they underftand what is required
of them, and that they take as much pleafure as the fpectators in the fport. A
broad piece of canvas, fpread acrofs the
entrance of the ftreet, prevents them from
ftarting too foon: the dropping that canvas
is the fignal for the race to begin. The
horfes fly off together, and, without riders,
exert themfelves to the utmoft; impelled
by emulation, the fhouts of the populace,
and the fpurs above mentioned. They run
the whole length of the Corfo; and the
proprietor of the victor is rewarded by a
certain quantity of fine fcarlet or purple
cloth, which is always furnifhed by the
Jews.

This

This diverfion, fuch as it is, feems highly entertaining to the Roman populace; though it appears a mighty foolifh bufinefs in the eyes of Englifhmen. An acquaintance of mine, who had entirely ruined a fine fortune at Newmarket, told me, that Italian horfe-races were the moft abfurd things in the world; that there were not a hundred guineas loft or won during a whole Carnival; and nothing could be a greater proof of the folly of the people, than their fpending their time in fuch a filly manner.

Mafking and horfe-races are confined to the laft eight days; but there are theatrical entertainments, of various kinds, during the whole fix weeks of the Carnival. The Serious Opera is moft frequented by people of fafhion, who generally take boxes for the whole feafon. The opera, with which this theatre opened, was received with the higheft applaufe, though the-

the mufic only was new. The Italians do not think it always neceffary to compofe. new words for what is called a new opera; they often fatisfy themfelves with new mufic to the affecting dramas of Metafta- fio. The audience here feem to lend a more profound and continued attention to the mufic, than at Venice. This is probably owing to the entertainment being a greater rarity in the one city than in the other; for I could perceive that the people of fafhion, who came every night, began, after the opera had been repeated feveral nights, to abate in their attention, to re- ceive vifitors in their boxes, and to liften only when fome favourite airs were fing- ing: whereas the audience in the pit uni- formly preferve the moft perfect filence, which is only interrupted by gentle mur- murs of pleafure from a few individuals, or an univerfal burft of applaufe from the whole affembly. I never faw fuch genuine marks of fatisfaction difplayed by any af-

G 3   fembly,

fembly, on any occafion whatever. The
fenfibility of fome of the audience gave me
an idea of the power of founds, which the
dulnefs of my own auditory nerves could
never have conveyed to my mind. At certain airs, filent enjoyment was exprefled in
every countenance; at others, the hands
were clafped together, the eyes half fhut,
and the breath drawn in, with a prolonged
figh, as if the foul was expiring in a torrent of delight. One young woman, in
the pit, called out, " O Dio, dove fono!
" che piacer via caccia l'alma ?"

On the firft night of the opera, after
one of thefe favourite airs, an univerfal
fhout of applaufe took place, intermingled
with demands that the compofer of the
mufic fhould appear. Il Maeftro! il Maeftro! refounded from every corner of the
houfe. He was prefent, and led the band
of mufic; he was obliged to ftand upon
the bench, where he continued, bowing to
the

the fpectators, till they were tired of ap-
plauding him. One perfon, in the middle
of the pit, whom I had remarked difplaying great figns of fatisfaction from the beginning of the performance, cried out,
" He deferves to be made chief mufician
" to the Virgin, and to lead a choir of
" angels!" This expreffion would be
thought ftrong, in any country ; but it has
peculiar energy here, where it is a popular
opinion, that the Virgin Mary is very fond,
and an excellent judge, of mufic. I received this information on Chriftmas morning, when I was looking at two poor Ca-
labrian pipers doing their utmoft to pleafe
her, and the Infant in her arms. They
played for a full hour to one of her images
which ftands at the corner of a ftreet. All
the other ftatues of the Virgin, which are
placed in the ftreets, are ferenaded in the
fame manner every Chriftmas morning.
On my enquiring into the meaning of that
ceremony, I was told the above-mentioned
G 4 circumftance

circumstance of her character, which,
though you may have always thought
highly probable, perhaps you never before knew for certain. My informer was
a pilgrim, who stood listening with great
devotion to the pipers. He told me, at
the same time, that the Virgin's taste was
too refined to have much satisfaction in
the performance of those poor Calabrians,
which was chiefly intended for the Infant;
and he desired me to remark, that the
tunes were plain, simple, and such as
might naturally be supposed agreeable to
the ear of a child of his time of life.

Though the serious opera is in highest
estimation, and more regularly attended
by people of the first fashion; yet the
opera buffas, or burlettas, are not entirely neglected, even by them, and are
crowded, every night, by the middle and
lower classes. Some admired singers have
performed there during the Carnival, and
the

the mufical compofers have rendered them
highly pleafing to the general tafte.

The ferious and burlefque operas prevail infinitely over the other theatrical entertainments at Rome, in fpite of the
united efforts of Harlequin, Pantaloon, and
Punchinello.

The prohibition of female performers
renders the amufement of the Roman
theatre very infipid, in the opinion of
fome unrefined Englifhmen of your acquaintance who are here. In my own
poor opinion, the natural fweetnefs of the
female voice is ill fupplied by the artificial trills of wretched caftratos ; and the
aukward agility of robuft finewy fellows
dreffed in women's clothes, is a moft deplorable fubftitution for the graceful movements
of elegant female dancers. Is not the horrid
practice which is encouraged by this manner of fupplying the place of female
fingers,

fingers, a greater outrage on religion and morality, than can be produced by the evils which their prohibition is intended to prevent? Is it poffible to believe, that purity of fentiment will be preferved by producing eunuchs on the ftage? I fhould fear it would have a different effect. At the funeral of Junia, the wife of Caffius, and fifter of Brutus, the ftatues of all the great perfons connected with her family by blood or alliance, were carried in proceffion, except thofe of her brother and hufband. This *deficiency* ftruck the people more than any part of the proceffion, and brought the two illuftrious Romans into their minds with more force than if their ftatues had been carried with the others.— Præfulgebant Caffius atque Brutus, fays Tacitus, eo ipfo, quod effigies eorum non vifebantur.

LETTER LII.

Naples.

I TAKE the firſt opportunity of in-
forming you of our arrival in this
city. Some of the principal objects which
occurred on the road, with the ſentiments
they ſuggeſted to my mind, ſhall form the
ſubject of this letter.

It is almoſt impoſſible to go out of the
walls of Rome, without being impreſſed
with melancholic ideas. Having left that
city by St. John de Lateran's gate, we ſoon
entered a ſpacious plain, and drove for
ſeveral miles in ſight of ſepulchral monuments and the ruins of ancient aqueducts.
Sixtus the Fifth repaired one of them, to
bring water into that part of Rome where
Diocleſian's

Dioclefian's baths formerly flood : this
water is now called *aqua felice*, from Felix,
the name of that pontiff, while he was
only a Cordelier. Having changed horfes
at the Torre de Mezzo Via, fo called from
an old tower near the poft-houfe, we proceeded through a filent, deferted, unwhole-
fome country. We fcarce met a paffenger
between Rome and Marino, a little town
about twelve miles from the former, which
has its name from Caius Marius, who had
a villa there; it now belongs to the Co-
lonna family. While frefh horfes were
harneffing, we vifited two churches, to fee
two pictures which we had heard com-
mended; the fubject of one is as difagreeable, as that of the other is difficult to
execute. The connoiffeur who directed us
to thefe pieces, told me, that the firft, the
flaying of St. Bartholomew, by Guercino,
is in a great ftyle, finely coloured, and the
mufcles convulfed with pain in the fweeteft
manner imaginable; he could have gazed

at

at it for ever. " As for the other," added
he " which reprefents the Trinity, it is na-
" tural, well grouped, and eafily under-
" ftood; and that is all that can be faid
". for it."

From Marino, the road runs for feveral
miles over craggy mountains. In afcending
Mons Albanus, we were charmed with a
fine view of the country towards the fea;
Oftia, Antium, the lake Albano, and the
fields adjacent. The form and component
parts of this mountain plainly fhew, that
it has formerly been a volcano. The lake
of Nemi, which we left to the right, feems,
like that of Albano, to have been formed
in the cavity of a crater.

We came next to Veletri, an inconfiderable town, fituated on a hill. There is
one palace here, with fpacious gardens,
which, when kept in repair, may have
been magnificent. The ftair-cafe, they af-

I   fured

fured us, is ftill worthy of admiration.
The inhabitants of Valetri affert, that
Auguftus was born there. Suetonius fays,
he was born at Rome. It is certainly of
no importance where he was born. Perhaps it would have been better for Rome,
and for the world in general, that he
never had been born at all. The Vale-
trians are fo fond of emperors, that they
claim a connection even with Tiberius and
Caligula, who had villas in their neighbourhood. The ruins of Otho's palace are
ftill to be feen about a mile from this
city, at a place called Colle Ottone. Of
thofe four emperors, the laft-mentioned
was by much the beft worth the claiming
as a countryman. As for Caligula, he was
a mifchievous madman. Tiberius feems
to have been born with wicked difpofitions,
which he improved by art. Auguftus was
naturally wicked, and artificially virtuous;
and Otho feems to have been exactly the
reverfe. Though educated in the moft vi-

5   cious

cious of courts, and the favourite and companion of Nero, he still preserved, in some degree, the original excellence of his character; and, at his death, displayed a magnanimity of sentiment, and noble-nefs of conduct, of which the highly flattered Augustus was never capable. " Alii diutius imperium tenuerint," says Tacitus ; " nemo tam fortiter reliquerit." Convinced that, if he continued the contest with Vitellius, all the horrors of a civil war would be prolonged, he determined to sacrifice his life to the quiet of his country, and to the safety of his friends *. " To in- " volve you in fresh calamities," said this generous prince to the officers who offered still to support his cause, " is purchasing

---

* Hunc animum, hanc virtutem vestram, ultra peri-culis objicere, nimis grande vitæ meæ pretium puto. An ego tantum Romanæ pubis, tot egregios exercitus, sternl rurfus et republicâ eripi patiar? Esse superstites, nec diu moremur; ego incolumitatem vestram, vos constantiam meam. De nemine queror, nam incufare deos vel homi-nas, ejus est, qui vivere velit.   TACIT. Hist. lib. ii.

" life

" life at a price beyond what, in my opi-
" nion, is its value. Shall Roman armies
" be led againſt each other, and the Roman
" youth be excited to mutual ſlaughter, on
" my account ? No ! for your ſafety, and
" to prevent ſuch evils, I die contented;
" Let me be no impediment to your treat-
" ing with the enemy; nor do you any
" longer oppoſe my fixed reſolution. I
" complain not of my fate, nor do I ac-
" cuſe any body. To arraign the conduct
" of gods or men, is natural to thoſe only
" who wiſh to live."

Though they are not to be compared in
other reſpects, yet the *death* of Otho may
vie with that of Cato ; and is one of the
ſtrongeſt inſtances to be found in hiſtory,
that a life of effeminacy and voluptuouſ-
neſs does not always eradicate the ſeeds
of virtue and benevolence.

In the middle of the ſquare of Viletri,
is a bronze ſtatue of Urban the Eighth.
I think

I think they told us it is the workmanfhip
of Bernini.

Defcending from that town by a rough
road, bordered by vineyards and fruit-
trees, we traverfed an unfalubrious plain
to Sermonetta; between which, and the
poft-houfe, called Cafa Nuova, a little to
the left of the highway, are fome vaults
and ruins, not greatly worthy of the
notice of the mere antiquarian. Yet
paffengers of a fingular caft of mind,
who feel themfelves as much interefted in
the tranfactions recorded in the New Tefta-
ment, as men of tafte are in paintings or
heathen antiquities, ftop a little here to
contemplate the *Tres Tabernæ*, which are
faid to be the three Taverns mentioned in the
Acts of the Apoftles, where the Chriftian
brethren from Rome came to meet St.
Paul, when he was on his journey to that
city. I have feen, however, fome Chriftian travellers, who, without being connoiffeurs, were of opinion, that old ruined
houfes derived little value from the cir-

cumflance above mentioned, and who preferred a good modern inn to all the
antiquities, facred or profane, that they
met with on their grand tours. Without
prefuming to blame any fet of men for
their particular tafte, I may venture to fay,
that a traveller, who loves always to fee a
well-peopled and well-cultivated country,
who infifts on good eating every day, and
a neat comfortable bed every night, would
judge very wifely in never travelling out
of England.—I am certain he ought not to
travel between Rome and Naples; for on
this road, efpecially the part which runs
through the Ecclefiaflical State, the traveller's
chief entertainment muft arife from a lefs
fubflantial foundation; from the ideas
formed in the mind, at fight of places
celebrated by favourite authors; from a
recollection of the important fcenes which
have been acted there; and even from the
thought of treading the fame ground, and
viewing the fame objects, with certain
perfons who lived there fifteen hundred or

two

two thoufand years ago. Strangers, therefore, who come under the firft defcription,
whofe fenfes are far more powerful than
their fancy, when they are fo ill advifed as
to come fo far from home, generally make
this journey in very ill humour, fretting at
Italian beds, fuming againft Italian cooks,
and execrating every poor little Italian flea
that they meet with on the road. But he
who can put up with indifferent fare cheerfully, whofe ferenity of temper remains
unfhaken by the affaults of a flea, and who
can draw amufement from the ftores of
memory and imagination, will find the
powers of both wonderfully excited during
this journey. Sacred hiftory unites with
profane, truth confpires with fable, to afford
him entertainment, and render every object
interefting.

Proxima Circeæ raduntur littora terræ.

Driving along this road, you have a
fine view of Monte Circello, and

———— the Ææan bay,
Where Circe dwelt, the daughter of the Day;

Goddefs

Goddefs and queen, to whom the powers belong
Of dreadful magic and commanding fong.

This abode of the enchantrefs Circe has
been generally defcribed as an ifland;
whereas it is, in reality, a promontory,
united to the continent by a neck of land.
The adventures of Ulyffes and his companions at this place, with all the extraordinary things which Homer has recorded
of Circe, muft ferve to amufe you between Cafa Nuova and Piperno; the road
affords no other.

At Piperno, anciently Privernum, you
quit Circe, for Virgil's Camilla, a lady of
a very different character, whofe native
city this is *.

Near to Piperno, an abbey, called Foffa
Nuova, is fituated on the ruins of the
little town of Forum Appii, the fame of

* Hos fuper advenit Volfcâ de gente Camilla,
Agmen agens equitum et florentes ære catervæ,
Bellatrix: Non illa colo calathifve Minervæ
Fœmineas affueta manus; fed prœlia virgo
Dera pati, curfuque pedum prævertere ventos.
                                       Æneid. lib. vii.

which

which mention is made in the Acts of the Apostles, and by Horace, in his account of his journey to Brundusium.

———— Inde Forum Appi
Differtum nautis, cauponibus atque malignis.

The abbey of Foffa Nuova is faid to have made a very valuable acquifition of late, no lefs than the head of St. Thomas Aquinas. We are told, in the memoirs of that Saint, that he was taken ill as he pafled this way, and was carried to this convent, where he died. His body was afterward required by the king of France, and ordered to be carried to Thouloufe; but before the remains of this holy perfon were removed from the convent, one of the monks, unwilling to allow the whole of fuch a precious depofite to be carried away, determined to retain the moft valuable part, and actually cut off the faint's head, fubftituting another in its ftead, which was carried to Thouloufe, very nicely ftitched to the body of the faint. The monk, who was guilty of this pious fraud, hid the true head in the wall of the convent, and died without revealing the fecret to any mortal. From that time the fuppofititious head remained unfufpected at Thouloufe; but as impostures are generally detected fooner or later, the venerable brethren of Fossa Nuova (this happened much about the time that the Cock-lane ghost made fuch a noife in London) were difturbed with ftrange knockings and fcratchings at a particular part of the wall.—On this noife being frequently repeated, without any visible agent, and the people of the neighbourhood having been often affembled to hear it, the monks at length agreed to pull down part of the wall at the place where the fcratching and knocking were always heard. This was no fooner done, than the true head of St. Thomas Aquinas was found as frefh as the day it was cut off;—on the veffel in which it was contained was the following infcription:

Caput divi Thomæ Aquinatis.

And

And near it a paper, containing a faithful narrative of the whole tranfaction, figned by the monk who did the deed.

Some people, not making a proper allowance for the difference between a faint's head and their own, fay, this cannot poffibly be the head of Thomas Aquinas, which muft have putrified fome centuries ago; they fay, the paper is written in a character by much too modern; they fay, the monks contrived the whole affair, to give an importance to their convent; they fay—but what fignifies what they fay? In this age of incredulity, fome people will fay any thing. We next came to Terracina, and here I muft finifh my letter; in my next I fhall carry you to Naples.

H 4

LETTER LIII.

Naples.

TErracina, formerly called Anxur, was the capital of the warlike Volfci*. The principal church was originally a temple of Jupiter, who was fuppofed to have a partiality for this town, and the country around it. Virgil calls him Jupiter Anxurus. Enumerating the troops who came to fupport the caufe of Turnus, he mentions thofe who plough the Rutulian hills:

Circeumque jugum; queis Jupiter Anxurus
    arvis
Præfidet, et viridi gaudens Feronia luco:
Qua faturæ jacet atra palus, &c.

Near this place we fell in again with the Appian Way, and beheld, with aftonifh-

* Anxur fuit quæ nunc Terracinæ funt; urbs prona in paludes.   TIT. LIV. lib. iv.

ment,

ment, the depth of rock that has here
been cut, to render it more convenient for
paſſengers. This famous road is a paved
cauſeway, begun in the year of Rome 441,
by Appius Claudius Cæcus the Cenſor, and
carried all the way from Rome to Capua. It
would be ſuperfluous to inſiſt on the ſubſtan-
tial manner in which it has been originally
made, ſince it ſtill remains in many places.
Though travellers are now obliged to make
a circuit by Caſa Nuova and Piperno, the
Via Appia was originally made in a ſtraight
line through the Palude Pontine, or Palus
Pomptina, as that vaſt marſh was anciently
called : it is the Ater Palus above mentioned, in the lines quoted from Virgil.
That part of the Appian road is now quite
impaſſable, from the augmentation of this
noxious marſh, whoſe exhalations are diſ-
agreeable to paſſengers, and near which it
is dangerous to ſleep a ſingle night.

Keyſler and ſome others ſay, that Appius
made this road at his own expence. I
do not know on what authority they make

I   this

this aſſertion; but, whatever their authority may be, the thing is incredible.
Could a Roman citizen, at a period when
the inhabitants of Rome were not rich,
bear an expence which we are ſurpriſed
that even the State itſelf could ſupport?
Though this famous road has received its
name from Appius, I can hardly imagine
it was completed by him. The diſtance
from Rome to Capua is above one hundred
and thirty miles; a prodigious length for
ſuch a road as this to have been made,
during the ſhort courſe of one Cenſorſhip;
for a man could be Cenſor only once in his
life. This was an office of very great dignity; no perſon could enjoy it till he had
previouſly been Conſul. It was originally
held for five years; but, a hundred years
before the time of Appius, the term was
abridged to eighteen months. He, however, who, as Livy tells us, poſſeſſed all
the pride and obſtinacy of his family,
refuſed to quit the Cenſorſhip at the end
of that period; and, in ſpite of all the ef-

forts

forts of the Tribunes, continued three
years and a half beyond the term to which
the office had been reftricted by the Æmi-
lian Law. But even five years is a very
fhort time for fo great a work; yet this
was not the only work he carried on during his Cenforfhip. " Viam munivit,"
fays the Hiftorian, " et aquam in urbem
" duxit." The Appian road was carried
on, afterwards, from Capua to Brundufium, and was probably completed fo far,
in the time of Horace; as appears by this
verfe, in one of his Epiftles addrcffed to
Lollius:

> Brundufium Numici melius via ducat, an
> Appi.

Terracina is the laft town of the Ecclefiaftical, and Fundi the firft of the Neapolitan, dominions. This laft town ftands
on a plain, fheltered by hills, which is
feldom the cafe with Italian towns : it probably derives its name from its fituation.
There is nothing very attractive in this

3   place,

place, now, more than in Horace's time; so we left it as willingly as he did:

Fundos Aufidio Lusco Prætore *libenter* Linquimus.

Continuing our route, partly on the Appian way, we came to Mola di Gaeta, a town built on the ruins of the ancient Formiæ. Horace compliments Ælius Lamia, on his being descended from the first founder of this city:

Auctore ab illo ducis originem,
Qui Formiarum mœnia dicitur,
Princeps.

The same Poet puts the wine, made from the grapes of the Formian hills, on a footing with the Falernian:

————mea nec Falernæ
Temperant vites, neque Formiani
Pocula colles.

Cicero had a villa near this place; and it was on this coast where that great orator was murdered in his litter, as he was endea-

vouring

vouring to make his escape to Greece.
The fortress of Gaeta is built on a promontory, about three miles from Mola;
but travellers, who have the curiosity to
go to the former, generally cross the
gulph between the two; and immediately, as the most remarkable thing in the
place, they are shewn a great cleft in
a rock, and informed that it was mira-
culously split in this manner at the death
of our Saviour. To put this beyond doubt,
they shew, at the same time, something
like the impression of a man's hand on the
rock, of which the following account is
given.—A certain person having been told
on what occasion the rent took place,
struck the palm of his hand on the marble,
declaring he could no more believe their
story, than that his hand would leave its
stamp on the rock; on which, to the terror and confusion of this infidel, the stone
yielded like wax, and the impression remains till this day.

Nothing

Nothing is fo injurious to the caufe of truth, as attempts to fupport it by fiction. Many evidences of the juftnefs of this ob-'fervation occur in the courfe of a tour through Italy. That mountains were rent at the death of our Saviour, we know from the New Teflament; but, as none of them are there particularized, it is prefumptuous in others to imagine they can point out what the Evangelifts have thought proper to conceal.

This rock, however, is much reforted to by pilgrims; and the Tartanes, and other veffels, often touch there, that the feamen may be provided with little pieces of marble, which they earneftly requeft may be taken as near the fiffure as poffible. Thefe they wear conftantly in their pockets, in cafe of fhipwreck, from a perfuafion, that they are a more certain prefervative from drowning, than a cork jacket. Some of thefe poor people have the misfortune to be drowned, notwithftanding; but

the

the facred marble lofes none of its reputation on that account. Such accidents are
always imputed to the weight of the unfortunate perfon's fins, which have funk him
to the bottom, in fpite of all the efforts of
the marble to keep him above water; and
it is allowed on all hands, that a man fo
oppreffed with iniquity, as to be drowned
with a piece of this marble in his pocket,
would have funk much fooner, if, inftead
of that, he had had nothing to keep him
up but a cork jacket.

Strangers are next led to the Caftle,
and are fhewn, with fome other curiofities,
the fkeleton of the famous Bourbon, Con-
ftable of France, who was killed in the
fervice of the emperor Charles the Fifth,
as he fcaled the walls of Rome.

It is remarkable that France, a nation
which values itfelf fo much on an affect011on-
ate attachment to its princes, and places
loyalty at the head of the virtues, fhould
have produced, in the courfe of the two

laſt centuries, ſo many illuſtrious rebels: Bourbon, Coligni, Guiſe, Turenne, and the Condés; all of them were, at ſome period of their lives, in arms againſt their ſovereign.

That it is the duty of ſubjects to preſerve their allegiance, however unjuſtly and tyrannically their prince may conduct himſelf, is one of the moſt debaſing and abſurd doctrines that ever was obtruded on the underſtanding of mankind. When Francis forgot the ſervices which the gallant Bourbon had rendered him at Mirignan; when, by repeated acts of oppreſſion, he forgot the duty of a king; Bourbon ſpurned at his allegiance, as a ſubject. The Spaniſh nobleman, who declared that he would pull down his houſe, if Bourbon ſhould be allowed to lodge in it, either never had heard of the injurious treatment which that gallant ſoldier had received, or he betrayed the ſentiments of a ſlave, and meant to inſinuate his own implicit loyalty

to

to the Emperor. Mankind in general have
a partiality for princes. The fenfes are
impofed on by the fplendour which fur-
rounds them; and the refpect due to the
office of a king, is naturally converted into
an affection for his perfon: there muft
therefore be fomething highly unpopular
in the character of the monarch, and highly oppreffive in the meafures of government, before people can be excited to re-
bellion. Subjects feldom rife through a defire of attacking, but rather from an impatience of fuffering. Where men are
under the yoke of feudal lords, who can
force them to fight in any caufe, it may be
otherwife; but when general difcontent
pervades a free people, and when, in confequence of this, they take arms againft
their prince, they muft have juftice on
their fide. The higheft compliment which
fubjects can pay, and the beft fervice they
can render, to a good prince, is, to behave
in fuch a manner, as to convince him that
they would rebel againft a bad one.

From Mola we were conducted by the Appian way, over the fertile fields washed by the silent Liris:

——Rura quæ Liris quieta
Mordet aqua, taciturnus amnis.

This river bounded Latium. On its banks are still seen some ruins of the ancient Minturnæ. After Manlius Torquatus, in what some will call a phrenzy of virtue, had offered up his son as a sacrifice to military discipline; and his colleague Decius, immediately after, devoted himself in a battle against the Latins; the broken army of that people assembled at Minturnæ, and were a second time defeated by Manlius, and their lands divided by the senate among the citizens of Rome. The first battle was fought near Mount Vesuvius, and the second between Sinuessa and Minturnæ. In the morasses of Minturnæ, Caius Marius, in the seventieth year of his age, was taken, and brought a prisoner to that city, whose magistrates ordered an as-

8   saffin

faffin to put him to death, whom the fierce
veteran difarmed with a look. What
mortal, fays. Juvenal, would have been
thought more fortunate than Marius, had
he breathed out his afpiring foul, furrounded by the captives he had made, his
victorious troops, and all the pomp of
war, as he defeended from his Teutonic
chariot, after his triumph over the
Cimbri.

> ——Quid illo cive tuliffet
> Natura in terris, quid Roma beatius un-
>   quam?
> Si circumducto captivorum agmine, et
>   omni
> Bellorum pompâ, animam exhalaffet opi-
>   mam,
> Cum de Teutonico vellet defcendere curru.

Several writers, in their remarks on
Italy, obferve, that it was on the banks of
the Liris that Pyrrhus gained his dear-
bought victory over the Romans. They
have fallen into this miftake, by confound-
ing the Liris with the Siris, a river in
Magna Græcia, near Heraclea; in the

I 2   neighbour-

neighbourhood of which Pyrrhus defeated
the Romans by the means of his elephants.

Leaving Garilagno, which is the modern
name of the Liris, we pass the rising
ground where the ancient Sinuessa was
situated; the city where Horace met his
friends Plotius, Varius, and Virgil. The
friendly glow with which this admirable
painter has adorned their characters, conveys an amiable idea of his own.

——Animæ, quales neque candidiores
Terra tulit; neque queis me sit devinctior
alter.
O, qui complexus et gaudia quanta fuerunt !
Nil ego contulerim jucundo sanus amico.

Do you not share in the happiness of such
a company? And are you not rejoiced that
they happened to meet near the Ager Fa-
lernus, where they could have the best Maf-
fic and Falernian wines ?

New Capua, through which the road
from Rome to Naples lies, is a small town
of no importance. The ancient city of that
name

name was fituated two miles diflant from
the new. The ruins of the amphitheatre,
which are ftill to be feen, give fome idea
of the ancient grandeur of that city. Before the amphitheatre of Vefpafian was
built, there was none in Rome of equal
fize with this. Old Capua is faid, at one
period, to have vied in magnificence with
Rome and Carthage:

> Altera dicta olim Carthago, atque altera
> Roma,
> Nunc proftrata jacet, proprioque fepulta
> fepulchro.

The army of Hannibal is faid to have
been conquered by the luxuries of this
place; but the judicious Montefquieu obferves, that the Carthaginian army, enriched by fo many victories, would have found
a Capua wherever they had gone. Whether Capua brought on the ruin of
Hannibal or not, there can be no doubt
that Hannibal occafioned the ruin of
Capua.

I 3   Having

Having broken their connection with Rome, and formed an alliance with her enemy, the Capuans were, in the course of the war, befieged by the Confuls Fulvius and Appius. Hannibal exerted all his vaft abilities for the relief of his new friends; but was not able to bring the Roman army to a battle, or to raife the fiege. When every other expedient had failed, he marched directly to Rome, in the hopes of drawing the Roman army after him to defend the capital. A number of alarming events confpired, at this time, to deprefs the fpirit of the Roman Senate. The Proconful Sempronius Gracchus, who commanded an army in Lucania, had fallen into an ambufcade, and was maffacred. The two gallant brothers, the Scipios, who were their generals in Spain, had been defeated and killed; and Hannibal was at their gates. How did the Senate behave at this crifis? Did they fpend their time in idle harangues and mutual accufations? Did they

they throw out reflections againſt thoſe
ſenators who were againſt entering into a
treaty with the Carthaginians till their
army ſhould be withdrawn from Italy?
Did they recall their army from Capua?
Did they ſhew any mark of deſpondence?
In this ſtate of affairs, the Roman Senate
ſent orders to Appius to continue the ſiege
of Capua; they ordered a reinforcement to
their army in Spain; the troops for that
ſervice marching out at one gate of Rome,
while Hannibal threatened to enter by
ſtorm at another. How could ſuch a people fail to become the maſters of the world!

The country between Capua and Naples
diſplays a varied ſcene of laviſh fertility,
and with great propriety might be named
Campania Felix, if the richeſt and moſt generous ſoil, with the mildeſt and moſt
agreeable climate, were ſufficient to render
the inhabitants of a country happy.

I 4

LETTER LIV.

Naples,

THE day after our arrival at this place, we waited on Sir W—— H——, his Majesty's minister at this court. He had gone early that morning on a hunting party with the King; but the Portuguese ambassador, at L—y H——'s desire, undertook to accompany the D— on the usual round of visits; Sir W—— was not expected to return for several days, and the laws of etiquette do not allow that important tour to be delayed so long. As we have been continually driving about ever since our arrival, I am already pretty well acquainted with this town, and the environs.

Naples was founded by the Greeks. The charming situation they have chosen, is

one

one proof among thoufands, of the fine tafte of that ingenious people.

The bay is about thirty miles in circumference, and twelve in diameter; it has been named Crater, from its fuppofed refemblance to a bowl. This bowl is ornamented with the moft beautiful foliage, with vines; with olive, mulberry, and orange trees; with hills, dales, towns, villas, and villages.

At the bottom of the bay of Naples, the town is built in the form of a vaft amphitheatre, floping from the hills towards the fea.

If, from the town, you turn your eyes to the eaft, you fee the rich plains leading to mount Vefuvius, and Portici. If you look to the weft, you have the Grotto of Paufilippo, the mountain on which Virgil's tomb is placed, and the fields leading to Puzzoli and the coaft of Baia. On the north, are the fertile hills, gradually rifing from the fhore to the Campagna Felice.

lice. On the South, is the bay, confined by the two promontories of Mifenum and Minerva, the view being terminated by the iflands Procida, Ifchia, and Caprea; and as you afcend to the caftle of St. Elmo, you have all thefe objects under your eye at once, with the addition of a great part of the Campagna.

Independent of its happy fituation, Naples is a very beautiful city. The ftyle of architecture, it muft be confeffed, is inferior to what prevails at Rome; but though Naples cannot vie with that city in the number of palaces, or in the grandeur and magnificence of the churches, the private houfes in general are better built, and are more uniformly convenient; the ftreets are broader and better paved. No ftreet in Rome equals in beauty the Strada di Toledo at Naples; and ftill lefs can any of them be compared with thofe beautiful ftreets which are open to the bay. This is the native country of the Zephyrs; here

the

the exceffive heat of the Sun is often tempered with fea breezes, and with gales, wafting the perfumes of the Campagna Felice.

The houfes, in general, are five or fix flories in height, and flat at the top; on which are placed, numbers of flower vafes or fruit trees, in boxes of earth, producing a very gay and agreeable effect.

The fortrefs of St. Elmo is built on a mountain of the fame name. The garrifon flationed here, have the entire command of the town, and could lay it in afhes at pleafure. A little lower, on the fame mountain, is a convent of Carthufians. The fituation of this convent is as advantageous and beautiful as can be imagined; and much expence has been lavifhed to render the building, the apartments, and the gardens, equal to the fituation.

To beflow great fums of money in adorning the retreat of men who have abandoned the world for the exprefs purpofe

pofe of paffing the remainder of their lives in felf-denial and mortification, feems to be very ill judged ; and might, on fome occafions, counteract the defign of. their retreat. I expreffed this fentiment to a Neapolitan lady at Sir W—— H——'s affembly, the evening after I had vifited this convent. She faid, " that the elegant " apartments, the gardens, and all the ex- " penfive ornaments I had particularifed, " could not much impede a fyftem of felf- " denial; for they foon became infipid to " thofe who had them conftantly before their " eyes, and proved no compenfation for the " want of other comforts." " In that cafe," `faid I, " the whole expence might have " been faved, or beftowed in procuring " comforts to others who have made no " vows of mortification." " Tolga iddio !" cried the lady, forgetting her former argument, " for none have fo good a title " to every comfortable and pleafant thing " in this world, as thofe who have re- " nounced it, and placed their affections en- " tirely

" tirely on the next; inſtead of depriving
" theſe ſanctified Carthuſians of what they
" already poſſeſs, it would be more meri-
" torious to give them what they have
" not."

" Give them then, ſaid I, what will afford
" ſome ſatisfaction, inſtead of the luxuries
" of ſculpture, and painting, and architec-
" ture, which, as you ſay, become ſo
" ſoon inſipid; let them have enjoyments
" of a different kind. Why ſhould their
" diet be confined to fiſh and vegetables?
" Let them enjoy the pleaſures of the table
" without any limitation. And ſince they
" are ſo very meritorious, why is your ſex
" deprived of the happineſs of their con-
" verſation, and why are they denied the
" pleaſure which the ſociety of women
" might afford them ?"

" Criſto benedetto!" cried the lady,
" You do not underſtand this matter.——
" Though none deſerve the pleaſures of
" this world, but thoſe who think only

"" on

" on the next; yet none can obtain the
" joys of the next, who indulge in the
" pleafures of this."

" That is unlucky," faid I.

" Unlucky! to be fure it is the moft
" unlucky thing that could have happen-
" ed, *ecco dove mi doleva*," added the
lady.

Though Naples is admirably fituated
for commerce, and no kingdom produces
the neceffaries and luxuries of life in
greater profufion, yet trade is but in a
languifhing condition; the beft filks
come from Lyons, and the beft woollen
goods from England.

The chief articles manufactured here, at
prefent, are, filk ftockings, foap, fnuff-
boxes, or tortoife fhells; and the lava of
Mount Vefuvius, tables, and ornamental
furniture, of marble.

They are thought to embroider here
better than even in France; and their ma-.
caroni

caroni is preferred to that made in any
other part of Italy. The Neapolitans excel alſo in liqueurs and confections; particularly in one kind of confection, which
is ſold at a very high price, called Diabo-
lonis. This drug, as you will gueſs from
its name, is of a very hot and ſtimulat-
ing nature, and what I ſhould think by
no means requiſite to Neapolitan con-
ſtitutions.

The inhabitants of this town are computed at three hundred and fifty thouſand.
I make no doubt of their amounting to
that number; for though Naples is not
one third of the ſize of London, yet many
of the ſtreets here are more crowded than
the Strand. In London and Paris, the
people who fill the ſtreets are mere paſſengers, hurrying from place to place on
buſineſs; and when they chooſe to converſe, or to amuſe themſelves, they reſort
to the public walks or gardens: at Naples,
the citizens have fewer avocations of buſineſs to excite their activity; no public
walks,

walks, or gardens, to which they can refort;
and are, therefore, more frequently feed
fauntering and converfing in the ftreets;
where a great proportion of the pooreft
fort, for want of habitations, are obliged
to fpend the night as well as the day;
While you fit in your chamber at London,
or at Paris, the ufual noife you hear from
the ftreets, is that of carriages; but at
Naples, where they talk with uncommon
vivacity, and where whole ftreets full of
talkers are in continual employment, the
noife of carriages is completely drowned
in the aggregated clack of human voices:
In the midft of all this idlenefs, fewer
riots or outrages of any kind happen,
than might be expected in a town where
the police is far from being ftrict, and
where fuch multitudes of poor unemployed people meet together every day;
This partly proceeds from the national
character of the Italians; which, in my
opinion, is quiet, fubmiffive, and averfe
to riot or fedition; and partly to the

common

common people being univerſally ſober, and never inflamed with ſtrong and ſpirituous liquors, as they are in the northern countries. Iced water and lemonade are among the luxuries of the loweſt vulgar; they are carried about in little barrels, and ſold in half-penny's worth. The half naked lazzarone is often tempted to ſpend the ſmall pittance deſtined for the maintenance of his family, on this bewitching beverage, as the moſt diſſolute of the low people in London ſpend their wages on gin and brandy; ſo that the ſame extravagance which cools the mob of the one city, tends to inflame that of the other to acts of exceſs and brutality.

There is not, perhaps, a city in the world, with the ſame number of inhabitants, in which ſo few contribute to the wealth of the community by uſeful, or by productive labour, as Naples; but the numbers of prieſts, monks, fiddlers, lawyers, nobility, footmen, and lazzaronis, furpaſs all reaſonable proportion; the laſt alone are computed at thirty or forty thouſand. If theſe poor fellows are idle, it is not their own fault; they are continually running about the ſtreets, as we are told of the artificers of China; offering their ſervice, and begging for employment; and are conſidered, by many, as of more real utility than any of the claſſes above mentioned.

LETTER LV.

Naples.

THERE is an affembly once a week
at the houfe of the Britifh minifter;
no affembly in Naples is more numerous,
or more brilliant, than this. Exclufive
of that gentleman's good qualities, and
thofe accomplifhments which procure
efteem in any fituation, he would meet
with every mark of regard from the Neapolitan nobles, on account of the high
favour in which he ftands with their Sovereign. Sir W——'s houfe is open to
ftrangers of every country who come to
Naples properly recommended, as well as
to the Englifh; he has a private concert
almoft every evening. L—y H—— un-
derftands mufic perfectly, and performs in
fuch a manner, as to command the admiration even of the Neapolitans. Sir W——,

'   K 2   who

who is the happiest tempered man in the world, and the easiest amused, performs alfo, and succeeds perfectly in amusing himfelf, which is a more valuable attainment than the other.

The Neapolitan nobility are exceffively fond of fplendour and fhow. This appears in the brilliancy of their equipages, the number of their attendants, the richnefs of their drefs, and the grandeur of their titles.

I am affured, that the King of Naples counts a hundred perfons with the title of Prince, and ftill a greater number with that of Duke, among his fubjects. Six or feven of thefe have eftates, which produce from ten to twelve or thirteen thoufand pounds a year; a confiderable number have fortunes of about half that value; and the annual revenue of many is not above one or two thoufand pounds. With refpect to the inferior orders of nobility, they are much poorer; many

Counts

Counts and Marquiffes have not above
three or four hundred pounds a year of
paternal eflate, many flill lefs, and not a
few enjoy the title without any eflate
whatever.

When we confider the magnificence of
their entertainments, the fplendour of
their equipages, and the number of their
fervants, we are furprifed that the richeft
of them can fupport fuch expenfive efta-
blifhmerits. I dined, foon after our arrival,
at the Prince of Franca Villa's; there were
about forty people at table; it was meagre
day; the dinner confifled entirely of fifh
and vegetables, and was the moft magnificent entertainment I ever faw, comprehending an infinite variety of difhes, a
vaft profufion of fruit, and the wines of
every country in Europe. I dined fince
at the Prince Iacci's. I fhall mention two
circumftances, from which you may form
an idea of the grandeur of an Italian
palace, and the number of domeftics
K 3 which

which some of the nobility retain. We passed through twelve or thirteen large rooms before we arrived at the dining room; there were thirty-six persons at table, none served but the Prince's domestics, and each guest had a footman behind his chair; other domestics belonging to the Prince remained in the adjacent rooms, and in the hall. We afterwards passed through a considerable number of other rooms in our way to one from which there is a very commanding view.

No estate in England could support such a number of servants, paid and fed as English servants are; but here the wages are very moderate indeed, and the greater number of men servants, belonging to the first families, give their attendance through the day only, and find beds and provisions for themselves. It must be remembered, also, that few of the nobles give entertainments, and those who do not,

not, are faid to live very fparingly; fo
that the whole of their revenue, whatever
that may be, is exhaufted on articles of
fhow.

As there is no Opera at prefent, the
people of fafhion generally pafs part of
the evening at the Corfo, on the fea-fhore.
This is the great fcene of Neapolitan fplendour and parade; and, on grand occafions,
the magnificence difplayed here will ftrike
a ftranger very much. The fineft carriages
are painted, gilt, varnifhed, and lined, in
a richer and more beautiful manner, than
has as yet become fafhionable either in
England or France; they are often drawn
by fix, and fometimes by eight horfes. As
the laft is the number allotted to his Bri-
tannic Majefty when he goes to parliament, fome of our countrymen are offended that any individuals whatfoever
fhould prefume to drive with the fame
number.

K 4

It

It is the mode here, to have two running footmen, very gaily dreſſed, before
the carriage, and three or four ſervants in
rich liveries behind; theſe attendants are
generally the handſomeſt young men that
can be procured. The ladies or gentlemen
within the coaches, glitter in all the brilliancy of lace, embroidery, and jewels.
The Neapolitan carriages, for gala days,
are made on purpoſe, with very large
windows, that the ſpectators may enjoy a
full view of the parties within. Nothing
can be more ſhowy than the harneſs of the
horſes; their heads and manes are ornamented with the rareſt plumage, and their
tails ſet off with riband and artificial
flowers, in ſuch a graceful manner that
you are apt to think they have been
adorned by the ſame hands that dreſſed the
heads of the ladies, and not by common
grooms.

After all, you will perhaps imagine the
amuſement cannot be very great.   The
.6   carriages

carriages follow each other in two lines, moving in oppofite directions. The company within fmile, and bow, and wave the hand, as they pafs and repafs their acquaintance; and doubtlefs imagine, that they are the moft important figures in the proceffion. The horfes, however, feem to be quite of a different way of thinking, and to confider themfelves as the chief objects of admiration, looking on the livery fervants, the volantis, the lords, and the ladies, as their natural fuit on all fuch folemn occafions.

LETTER LVI.

Naples.

THE greatest part of kings, whatever may be thought of them after their death, have the good fortune to be reprefented, at fome period of their lives, generally at the beginning of their reigns, as the greateft and moft virtuous of mankind. They are never compared to characters of lefs dignity than Solomon, Alexander, Cæfar, or Titus; and the comparifon ufually concludes to the advantage of the living monarch. They differ in this, as in many other particulars, from thofe of the moft diftinguifhed genius and exalted merit among their fubjects, That the fame of the latter, if any awaits them, feldom arrives at its meridian till many years after their death; whereas the glory of the former is at its fulleft fplendour during their lives;

lives; and moft of them have the fatisfaction of hearing all their praifes with their
own ears. Each particular monarch, taken
feparately, is, or has been, confidered as a
ftar of great luftre; yet any number of
them, taken without felection, and placed
in the hiftorical galaxy, add little to its
brightnefs, and are often contemplated
with difguft. When we have occafion to
mention kings in general, the expreffion
certainly does not awaken a recollection of
the moft amiable or moft deferving part of
the human fpecies; and tyranny in no country
is pufhed fo far, as to conftrain men to fpeak
of them, when we fpeak in general terms, as
if they were. It would revolt the feelings,
and roufe the indignation, even of flaves.
Full freedom is allowed therefore on this
topic; and, under the moft arbitrary government, if you chufe to declaim on the
imbecility, profligacy, or corruption of
human nature, you may draw your illuf-
trations from the kings of any country,
provided you take them in groupes, and

hint

hint nothing to the detriment of the reigning monarch. But, when we talk of any
one living fovereign, we fhould never allow it to efcape from our memory, that he
is wife, valiant, generous, and good; and
we ought always to have Solomon, Alexander, Cæfar, and Titus, at our elbow, to
introduce them apropos when occafion of-
fers. We may have what opinion we
pleafe of the whole race of Bourbon; but
it would be highly indecent to deny, that
the reigning kings of Spain and Naples
are very great princes. As I never had
the happinefs of feeing the father, I can
only fpeak of the fon. His Neapolitan
Majefty feems to be about the age of fix or
feven-and-twenty. He is a prince of great
activity of body, and a good conflitution;
he indulges in frequent relaxations from
the cares of government and the fatigue of
thinking, by hunting and other exercifes;
and (which ought to give a high idea of
his natural talents) he never fails to acquire
a very confiderable degree of perfection in
thofe

thofe things to which he applies. He is very fond, like the King of Pruffia, of reviewing his troops, and is perfectly mafter of the whole myftery of the manual exercife. I have had the honour, oftener than once, of feeing him exercife the different regiments which form the garrifon here: he always gave the word of command with his own royal mouth, and with a precifion which feemed to aftonifh the whole Court. This monarch is alfo a very excellent fhot; his uncommon fuccefs at this diverfion is thought to have roufed the jealoufy of his Moft Catholic Majefty, who alfo values himfelf on his fkill as a markfman. The correfpondence between thofe two great perfonages often relates to their favourite amufement.—A gentleman, who came lately from Madrid, told me, that the King, on fome occafion, had read a letter which he had juft received from his fon at Naples, wherein he complained of his bad fuccefs on a fhooting party, having killed no more than eighty birds in a day: and the Spa-

nifh

niſh monarch, turning to his courtiers, said, in a plaintive tone of voice, " Mio " filio piange di non aver' fatto piu di ot- " tante beccacie in uno giorno, quando mi " crederei l'uomo il piu felice del mondo " ſe poteſſe fare quaranta." All who take a becoming ſhare in the afflictions of a royal boſom, will no doubt join with me, in wiſhing better ſucceſs to this good monarch, for the future. Fortunate would it be for mankind, if the happineſs of their princes could be purchaſed at ſo eaſy a rate! and thrice fortunate for the generous people of Spain, if the family connexions of their monarch, often at variance with the real intereſt of that country, ſhould never ſeduce him into a more ruinous war, than that which he now wages againſt the beaſts of the field and the birds of the air. His Neapolitan Majeſty, as I am informed, poſſeſſes many other accompliſhments; I particulariſe thoſe only to which I have myſelf been a witneſs. No king in Europe is ſuppoſed to underſtand the game of

3   billiards

billiards better. I had the pleasure of seeing him strike the most brilliant stroke that
perhaps ever was struck by a crowned
head. The ball of his antagonist was near
one of the middle pockets, and his own in
such a situation, that it was absolutely ne-
cessary to make it rebound from two different parts of the cushion, before it could
pocket the other. A person of less enter-
prise would have been contented with
placing himself in a safe situation, at a
small loss, and never have risqued any of-
fensive attempt against the enemy; but
the difficulty and danger, instead of inti-
midating, seemed rather to animate the
ambition of this Prince. He summoned all
his address; he estimated, with a mathe-
matical eye, the angles at which the ball
must fly off; and he struck it with an un-
daunted mind and a steady hand. It re-
bounded obliquely, from the opposite side-
cushion, to that at the end; from which it
moved in a direct line towards the middle
pocket, which seemed to stand in gaping
expectation

expectation to receive it.—The hearts of
the spectators beat thick as it rolled along;
and they shewed, by the contortions of
their faces and perfons, how much they
feared that it should move one hair-breadth
in a wrong direction.—I must here interrupt this important narrative, to obferve,
that, when I talk of contortions, if you
form your idea from any thing of that kind
which you may have feen around an English billiard-table or bowling-green, you
can have no juft notion of thofe which
were exhibited on this occafion: your imagination must triple the force and energy
of every English grimace, before it can do
juflice to the nervous twift of an Italian
countenance.—At length the royal ball
reached that of the enemy, and with a
fingle blow drove it off the plain. An
univerfal shout of joy, triumph, and applaufe burft from the beholders; but,

> O thoughtlefs mortals, ever blind to fate,
> Too foon dejected, and too foon elate!

the victorious ball, purfuing the enemy too far, fhared the fame fate, and was buried in the fame grave, with the vanquifhed. This fatal and unforefeen event feemed to make a deep impreffion on the minds of all who were witneffes to it; and will no doubt be recorded in the annals of the prefent reign, and quoted by future poets and hiftorians, as a ftriking inftance of the inftability of fublunary felicity.

It is imagined that the cabinet of this Court is entirely guided by that of Spain; which, on its part, is thought to be greatly under the influence of French counfels. The manners, as well as the politics, of France, are faid to prevail at prefent at the Court of Madrid. I do not prefume to fay of what nature the politics of his Neapolitan Majefty are, or whether he is fond of French counfels or not; but no true-born Englifhman exifting can fhew a more perfect contempt of their manners

VOL. II. L than

than he does. In domeftic life, this Prince
is generally allowed to be an eafy mafter,
a good-natured hufband, a dutiful fon, and
an indulgent father.

The Queen of Naples is a beautiful woman, and feems to poffefs the affability,
good-humour, and benevolence, which
diftinguifh, in fuch an amiable manner,
the Auftrian family.

LETTER LVII.

Naples.

THE hereditary jurisdiction of the nobles over their vassals subsists, both in the kingdom of Naples and Sicily, in the full rigour of the feudal government. The peasants therefore are poor; and it depends entirely on the personal character of the masters, whether their poverty is not the least of their grievances. If the land was leased out to free farmers, whose property was perfectly secure, and the leases of a sufficient length to allow the tenant to reap the fruits of his own improvements, there is no manner of doubt that the estates of the nobility would produce much more. The landlord might have a higher rent paid in money, instead of being collected in kind, which subjects him to the salaries and impositions of a nume-

rous train of ftewards; and the tenants,
on their parts, would be enabled to live
much more comfortably, and to lay up,
every year, a fmall pittance for their families. But the love of domineering is fo
predominant in the breafts of men who
have been accuftomed to it from their infancy, that, if the alternative were in their
choice, many of them would rather fubmit
to be themfelves flaves to the caprices of
an abfolute prince, than become perfectly
independent, on the condition of giving
independence to their vaffals. There is
reafon to believe that this ungenerous fpirit prevails pretty univerfally among the
nobility all over Enrope. The German
Barons are more fhocked at the idea of
their peafants becoming perfectly free, like
the farmers of Great Britain, than they
are folicitous to limit the power of their
princes: And, from the fentiments I have
heard expreffed by the French, I very
much doubt, whether their high nobility
would

would accept of the privileges of Englifh peers, at the expence of that infolent fuperiority, and thofe licentious freedoms, with which *they* may, though no Englifh peer can, treat with impunity the citizens and people of inferior rank. We need be the lefs furprifed at this, when we confider that, in fome parts of the Britifh empire, where the equable and generous laws of England prevail, thofe who fet the higheft value on freedom, who fubmit to every hardfhip, and encounter every danger, to fecure it to themfelves, never have fhewn a difpofition of extending its bleffings, or even alleviating the bondage of that part of the human fpecies, which a fordid and unjuftifiable barter has brought into their power.

The Court of Naples has not yet ventured, by one open act of authority, to abolifh the immoderate power of the lords over their tenants. But it is believed that the Minifter fecretly wifhes for its deftruc-

L 3   tion;

tion ; and in cafes of flagrant oppreffion,
when complaints are brought before the le-
gal courts, or directly to the King himfelf, by
the peafants againft their lord, it is generally remarked that the Minifter favours
the complainant.   Notwithftanding this,
the mafters have fo many opportunities of
oppreffing, and fuch various methods of
teafing, their vaffals, that they generally
chufe to bear their wrongs in filence ; and
perceiving that thofe who hold their lands
immediately from the Crown, are in a
much eafier fituation than themfelves,
without raifing their hopes to perfect freedom, the height of their wifhes is to be
fheltered, from the vexations of little ty-
rants, under the unlimited power of one
common mafter.   The objects of royal attention, they fondly imagine, are too fublime, and the minds of kings too generous,
to ftoop to, or even to countenance, in
their fervants, the minute and unreafona-
ble exertions, which are wrung at prefent
from

from the hard hands of the exhaufted labourer.

Though the Neapolitan nobility ftill
retain the ancient feudal authority over the
peafants, yet their perfonal importance depends, in a great meafure, on the favour
of the King; who, under pretext of any
offence, can confine them to their own
eftates, or imprifon them at pleafure; and
who, without any alleged offence, and
without going to fuch extremes, can inflict
a punifhment, highly fenfible to them, by
not inviting them to the amufements of
the Court, or not receiving them with
fmiles when they attend on any ordinary
occafion. Unlefs this Prince were fo very
impolitic as to difguft all the nobility at
once, and fo unite the whole body againft
him, he has little to fear from their refentment. Even in cafe of fuch an union,
as the nobles have loft the affection and attachment of their peafants, what could they
do in oppofition to a ftanding army of

L 4   thirty

thirty thoufand men, entirely devoted to
the Crown ? The eftablifhment of ftanding
armies has univerfally given ftability to
the power of the prince, and ruined that
of the great lords. No nobility in Europe
can now be faid to inherit political importance, or to act independent of, or in oppofition to, the influence of the crown ;
except the *temporal peers of that part of
Great Britain called England.*

As men of high birth are feldom, in
this country, called to the management of
public affairs, or placed in thofe fituations
where great political knowledge is required ; and as his Majefty relies on his
own talents and experience in war for the
direction of the army ; neither the civil
nor military eftablifhments open any very
tempting field for the ambition of the nobles, whofe education is ufually adapted to
the parts in life which they have a probability of acting. Their fortunes and titles
defcend to them, independent of any effort

7   of

of their own. All the literary diftinctions are beneath their regard; it is therefore not thought expedient to cloud the playful innocence of their childhood, or the amiable gaiety of their youth, with fevere ftudy. In fome other countries, where a very fmall portion of literary education is thought becoming for young men of rank, and where even this fmall portion has been neglected, they fometimes catch a little knowledge of hiftory and mythology, and fome ufeful moral fentiments, from the excellent dramatic pieces that are reprefented on their theatres. They alfo fometimes pick up fome notion of the different governments in Europe, and a few political ideas, in the courfe of their travels. But the nobility of this country very feldom travel; and the only dramatic pieces, reprefented here, are operas; in which mufic, not fentiment, is the principal thing attended to. In the other theatrical entertainments, Punchinello is the fhining character. To this difregard of literature among the nobles, it is owing, that in their body are to be found few tirefome, fcholaftic pedants, and none of thofe perturbed fpirits, who ruffle the ferenity of nations by political alarms, who clog the wheels of government by oppofition, who pry into the conduct of minifters, or in any way difturb that total indifference with regard to the public, which prevails all over this kingdom. We are told by a great modern Hiftorian *, that " force of mind, a fenfe " of perfonal dignity, gallantry in enter- " prife, invincible perfeverance in execu- " tion, contempt of danger and of death, " are the characteriftic virtues of uncivil- " ifed nations." But as the nobles of this country have long been fufficiently ci- vilifed, thefe qualities may in them be fup- pofed to have given place to the arts which embellifh a polifhed age ; to gaming, gal- lantry, mufic, the parade of equipage, the refinements of drefs, and other namelefs refinements.

* Vide Dr. Robertfon's Hiftory of the Emperor Charles V. Sect. I.

LETTER LVIII.

Naples.

THE citizens of Naples form a fociety of their own, perfectly diftinct from the nobility; and although they are not the moft induftrious people in the world, yet, having fome degree of occupation, and their time being divided between bufinefs and pleafure, they probably have more enjoyment than thofe, who, without internal refources, or opportunities of active exertion, pafs their lives in fenfual gratifications, and in waiting the returns of appetite around a gaming table. In the moft refpectable clafs of citizens, are comprehended the lawyers, of whom there are an incredible number in this town. The moft eminent of this profeffion hold, indeed, a kind of intermediate rank between the nobility and citizens;

8   the

the reft are on a level with the phyficians; the principal merchants, and the artifts; none of whom can make great fortunes, however induftrious they may be; but a moderate income enables them to fupport their rank in fuciety, and to enjoy all the conveniences, and many of the luxuries, of life.

England is perhaps the only nation in Europe where fome individuals, of every profeffion, even of the loweft, find it poffible to accumulate great fortunes; the effect of this very frequently is, that the fon defpifes the profeffion of the father, commences gentleman, and diffipates, in a few years, what coft a life to gather. In the principal cities of Germany and Italy, we find, that the anceflors of many of thofe citizens who are the moft eminent in their particular bufineffes, have tranfmitted the art to them through feveral generations. It is natural to imagine, that this will tend to the improvement of

the

the art, or science, or profeſſion, as well
as the family fortune; and that the third
generation will acquire knowledge from
the experience, as well as wealth from
the induſtry, of the former two; whereas,
in the caſes alluded to above, the wheel of
fortune moves differently. A man, by
aſſiduity in a particular buſineſs, and by
genius, acquires a great fortune and a high
reputation; the ſon throws away the fortune, and ruins his own character by extravagance; and the grandſon is obliged
to recommence the buſineſs, unaided by
the wealth or experience of his anceſtors.
This, however, is pointing out an evil
which I ſhould be ſorry to ſee remedied;
becauſe it certainly originates in the riches
and proſperity of the country in which it
exiſts.

The number of prieſts, monks, and ec-
cleſiaſtics of all the various orders that
ſwarm in this city, is prodigious; and the
proviſion appropriated for their uſe, is as
ample.

ample. I am affured, that the clergy are in poffeffion of confiderably above one-third of the revenue of the whole kingdom, over and above what fome particular orders among them acquire by begging for the ufe of their convents, and what is gotten in legacies by the addrefs and affiduity of the whole. The unproductive wealth, which is lodged in the churches and convents of this city, amounts alfo to an amazing value. Not to be compared in point of architecture to the churches and convents of Rome, thofe of Naples furpafs them in riches, in the value of their jewels, and in the quantity of filver and golden crucifixes, veffels, and implements of various kinds. I have often heard thefe eftimated at a fum fo enormous as to furpafs all credibility; and which, as I have no opportunity of afcertaining with any degree of precifion, I fhall not mention. This wealth, whatever it amounts to, is of as little ufe to the kingdom, as if it ftill remained in the mines of Peru;

and

and the greater part of it, furely, affords
as little comfort to the clergy and monks
as to any other part of the community; '
for though it belongs to their church, or
their convent, yet it can no more be converted to the ufe of the prieſts and monks
of fuch churches and convents, than to the
tradefmen who inhabit the adjacent ſtreets.
For this reafon I am a good deal furprifed,
that no pretext, or fubterfuge, has been
found, no expedient fallen on, no treaty or
convention made, for appropriating part of
this at leaſt, to the ufe of fome fet of
people or other. If the clergy were to
lay their hands on it, this might be found
fault with by the King; if his Majeſty
dreamt of taking any part of it for the
exigencies of the ſtate, the clergy would
undoubtedly raife a clamour; and if both
united, the Pope would think he had a
right to pronounce his vote: but if all
thefe three powers could come to an underſtanding, and fettle their proportions, I

am

am apt to think a partition might be made
as quietly as that of Poland.

Whatever fcruples the Neapolitan clergy
may have to fuch a project, they certainly have none to the full enjoyment of
their revenues. No clafs of men can be
lefs difpofed to offend Providence by a
peevifh neglect of the good things which
the bounty of heaven has beftowed. Self-
denial is a virtue, which I will not fay
they poffefs in a fmaller degree, but which,
I am fure, they affect lefs than any other
ecclefiaftics I know; they live very much
in fociety, both with the nobles and citizens. All of them, the monks not excepted, attend the theatre, and feem to
join moft cordially in other diverfions
and amufements; the common people are
no ways offended at this, or imagine that
they ought to live in a more reclufe manner. Some of the orders have had the
addrefs to make a concern for their temporal intereft, and a defire of feeing them
live

live full, and in fomething of a jolly manner, be regarded by the common people
as a proof of zeal for religion. I am informed, that a very confiderable diminution in the number of monks has taken
place in the kingdom of Naples fince the
fuppreffion of the Jefuits, and fince a
liberty of quitting the cowl was granted
by the late Pope; but ftill there is no
reafon to complain of a deficiency in this
order of men. The richeft and moft
commodious convents in Europe, both for
male and female votaries, are in this city;
the moft fertile and beautiful hills of the
environs are covered with them; a fmall
part of their revenue is fpent in feeding
the poor, the monks diftributing bread and
foup to a certain number every day before
the doors of the convents. Some of the
friars ftudy phyfic and furgery, and
practife thefe arts with great applaufe.
Each convent has an apothecary's fhop belonging to it, where medicines are delivered gratis to the poor, and fold to thofe

who can afford to pay. On all thefe accounts the monks in general are greater
favourites with the common people than
even the fecular clergy; all the charity of
the friars, however, would not be able to
cover their fins, if the ftories circulated
by their enemies were true,—by which
they are reprefented as the greateft profli-
gates and debauchees in the world. Without giving credit to all that is reported on
this fubject, as the Neapolitan monks are
very well fed, as this climate is not the
moft favourable to contipency (a virtue
which in this place is by no means eftimated in proportion to its rarity), it is
moft likely that the inhabitants of the
convents, like the inhabitants in general,
indulge in certain pleafures with lefs
fcruple or reftraint than is ufual in fome
other places. Be that as it may, it is certain that they are the moft fuperftitious of
mankind; a turn of mind which they
communicate with equal zeal and fuccefs
to a people remarkably ignorant, and re-
8   markably

markably amorous. The feeds of fuperftition thus zealoufly fown on fuch a warm
and fertile, though uncultivated, foil,
fometimes produce the moft extraordinary
crops of fenfuality and devotion that ever
were feen in any country.

The lazzaroni, or black-guards, as has
been already obferved, form a confiderable part of the inhabitants of Naples; and have, on fome well-known occafions, had the government for a fhort
time in their own hands. They are computed at above thirty thoufand; the
greater part of them have no dwelling-
houfes, but fleep every night under por-
ticos, piazzas, or any kind of fhelter they
can find. Thofe of them who have wives
and children, live in the fuburbs of Naples near Paufilippo, in huts, or in ca-
verns or chambers dug out of that
mountain. Some gain a livelihood by
fifhing, others by carrying burdens to and
from the fhipping; many walk about the

M 2   ftreets

ftreets ready to run on errands, or to perform any labour in their power for a very
fmall recompence. As they do not meet
with conftant employment, their wages
are not fufficient for their maintenance ; the
foup and bread diftributed at the door of the
convents fupply the deficiency. The lazzaroni are generally reprefented as a lazy, licentious, and turbulent fet of people;
what I have obferved gives me a very different idea of their character. Their idlenefs is evidently the effect of neceffity,
not of choice; they are always ready to
perform any work, however laborious, for
a very reafonable gratification. It muft
proceed from the fault of Government,
when fuch a number of ftout active citizens remain unemployed; and fo far are
they from being licentious and turbulent,
that I cannot help thinking they are by
much too tame and fubmiffive. Though
the inhabitants of the Italian cities were
the firft who fhook off the feudal yoke,
and

and though in Naples they have long enjoyed the privilege of municipal jurifdic-
tion, yet the external fplendour of the
nobles, and the authority they ftill exercife over the peafants, impofe upon the
minds of the lazzaroni; and however
bold and refentful they may be of injuries
offered by others, they bear the infolence
of the nobility as paffively as peafants
fixed to the foil. A coxcomb of a volanti
tricked out in his fantaftical drefs, or any
of the liveried flaves of the great, make
no ceremony of treating thefe poor fellows
with all the infolence and infenfibility natural to their mafters; and for no vifible
reafon, but becaufe he is dreffed in lace,
and the others in rags. Inftead of calling
to them to make way, when the noife in
the ftreets prevents the common people
from hearing the approach of the carriage, a ftroke acrofs the fhoulders with
the cane of the running footman, is the
ufual warning they receive. Nothing
animates this people to infurrection, but

M 3   fome

fome very prefling and very univerfal caufe;
fuch as a fcarcity of bread: every other griev-
ance they bear as if it were their charter.
When we confider thirty thoufand human
creatures without beds or habitations,
wandering almoft naked in fearch of food
through the ftreets of a well built city;
when we think of the opportunities they
have of being together, of comparing
their own deftitute fituation with the afflu-
ence of others, one cannot help being
aftonifhed at their patience.

Let the prince be diftinguifhed by fplendour and magnificence; let the great and
the rich have their luxuries; but, in the
name of humanity, let the poor, who
are willing to labour, have food in abundance to fatisfy the cravings of nature,
and raiment to defend them from the in-
clemencies of the weather!

If their governors, whether from weaknefs or neglect, do not fupply them with
thefe,

thefe, they certainly have a right to help themfelves.—Every law of equity and common fenfe will juftify them, in revolting againft fuch governors, and in fatisfying their own wants from the fuperfluities of lazy luxury.

M 4

L E T T E R LIX.

Naples.

I HAVE made several visits to the museum at Portici, principally, as you
may believe, to view the antiquities dug
out of Herculaneum and Pompeia. The
work publishing by Government, ornamented with engravings of the chief articles of this curious collection, will, in
all probability, be continued for many
years, as new articles worthy of the
sculptor's art are daily discovered, and as
a vast mine of curiosities is supposed to
be concealed in the unopened streets
of Pompeia. Among the ancient paintings, those which ornamented the theatre
of Herculaneum are more elegant
than any that have hitherto been found
at Pompeia. .All those paintings were
executed upon the stucco which lined the
walls;

walls; they have been fawed off with great labour and addrefs, and are now preferved in glafs cafes; the colours, we are told, were much brighter before they were drawn out of their fubterraneous abode, and expofed to the open air; they are, however, ftill wonderfully lively: the fubjects are underftood at the firft glance by thofe who are acquainted with the Grecian hiftory and mythology. There is a Chiron teaching Achilles to play on the lyre, Ariadne deferted, the Judgment of Paris, fome Bacchantes and Fauns; the largeft piece reprefents Thefeus's victory over the Minotaur. It confifts of feven or eight figures very well grouped, but a Frieze, with a dancing woman, on a black ground, not above ten inches long, is thought the beft.

We ought not, however, to judge of the progrefs which the ancients had made in the art of painting, by the degree of perfection which appears in thofe pictures.

3　　　　　　　　　　It

It is not probable that the beft paintings of ancient Greece or Italy were at Hercula- neum; and, if it could be afcertained that fome of the produdions of the beft mafters were there, it would not follow that thofe which have been difcovered are of that clafs. If a ftranger were to enter at ran- dom a few houfes in London, and fee fome tolerably good pictures there, he could not with propriety conclude that the beft of them were the very beft in London. The paintings brought from Herculaneum are perfect proofs that the ancients had made that progrefs in the art, which thofe pic- tures indicate; but do not form even a prefumption, that they had not made a much greater. It is almoft demonftrable that thefe paintings are not of their beft. The fame fchool which formed the fculp- tor to correctnefs, would form the painter to equal correctnefs in his drawings, how- ever deficient he might be in all the other parts of his art. Their beft ftatues are correct in their proportions, and elegant

in

in their forms: Thefe paintings are not
correct in their proportions, and are comparatively inelegant in their forms.

Among the flatues, the drunken Faun
and the Mercury are the beft. There are
fome fine bronze bufts; the intaglios and
cameos, which hitherto have been found
either in Herculaneum or Pompeia, are
reckoned but indifferent.

The elegance of form, with the admirable workmanfhip, of the ornamental furniture and domeftic utenfils, in filver and
other metals; the variety and beauty of
the lamps, tripods, and vafes; fufficiently
teftify, if there were no other proofs, the
fertile imagination and exquifite execution
of the ancient artifts. And, had their
own poets and hiftorians been quite filent
concerning the Roman refinements in the
art of cookery, and the luxury of their
tables; the prodigious variety of culinary
inftruments, the moulds for jellies, for
confections, and paftry, which are collected

ed in this mufeum, would afford a ftrong prefumption that the great men of our own days have a nearer refemblance to thofe ancient conquerors of the world, than is generally imagined.

Many of the ancient manufcripts found at Herculaneum have been carried to Madrid; but a great number ftill remain at Portici. Great pains have been beftowed, and much ingenuity difplayed, in feparating and unrolling the fheets, without deftroying the writing. This has fucceeded in a certain degree; though, in fpite of all the fkill and attention of thofe who are employed in this very delicate work, the copiers are obliged to leave many blanks where the letters are obliterated. The manufcripts hitherto unrolled and copied, are in the Greek language, and not of a very important nature. As the unrolling thofe papers muft take up a great deal of time, and requires infinite addrefs, it is to be wifhed that his Neapolitan Majefty would

would fend one at leaft to every univerfity in Europe, that the abilities of the moft ingenious men of every country might be exercifed on a fubject fo univerfally interefting. The method which fhould be found to fucceed beft, might be immediately made known, and applied to the unfolding of the remaining manufcripts. The probability of recovering thofe works, whofe lofs the learned have fo long lamented, would by this means be greatly increafed.

Herculaneum and Pompeia were deftroyed by the fame eruption of Mount Vefuvius, about feventeen hundred years ago. The former was a town of much more magnificence than the other ; but it is infinitely more difficult to be cleared of the matter which covers it. Sir William Hamilton, in his accurate and judicious obfervations on Mount Vefuvius, afferts, that there are evident marks that the matter of fix eruptions has taken its courfe
over

over this devoted town, since the great explosion which involved it in the same fate
with Pompeia. These different eruptions
have all happened at considerable distances
of time from each other. This appears by
the layers of good soil which are found
between them. But the matter which immediately covers the town, and with
which the theatre, and all the houses hitherto examined, were found filled, is not
lava, but a sort of soft stone, composed of
pumice and ashes, intermixed with earth.
This has saved the pictures, manu-
scripts, busts, utensils, and other antiquities, which have been recovered out
of Herculaneum, from utter destruc-
tion. For if any of the six succeeding
eruptions had happened previous to this,
and the red-hot liquid lava, of which they
consisted, had flowed into the open city, it
would have filled every street, scorched up
every combustible substance with intense
heat, involving the houses, and all they
contained, in one solid rock of lava, un-
distinguishable,

diftinguifhable, and for ever infeparable, from it. The eruption, which buried the city in cinders, earth, and afhes, has in fome meafure preferved it from the more deftructive effects of the fiery torrents which have overwhelmed it fince.

· When we confider that the intervals be-tween thofe eruptions were fufficiently long to allow a foil to be formed upon the hardened lava of each; that a new city has been actually built on the lava of the laft eruption; and that the ancient city is . from feventy to one hundred feet below the prefent furface of the earth; we muft acknowledge it more furprifing that any, than that fo few, of its ornaments have been recovered. At the beginning of the prefent century, any body would have ima-gined that the bufts, ftatues and pictures of Herculaneum had not a much better chance, than the perfons they reprefent, of appearing again, within a few years, upon the furface of this globe.

The

The cafe is different with regard to Pompeia. Though it was not difcovered till about twenty-five years ago, which is forty years almoft after the difcovery of Herculaneum, yet the probability was greatly in favour of its being difcovered fooner, for Pompeia has felt the effects of a fingle eruption only; it is not buried above twelve feet below the furface of the ground, and the earth, afhes, cinders, and pumice-ftones, with which it is covered, are fo light, and fo little tenacious, that they might be removed with no great difficulty. If the attention of his Neapolitan Majefty were not engroffed with more important concerns, he might have the whole town uncovered in a very fhort fpace of time; half the lazzaroni of Naples could complete the bufinefs in one year. Hitherto only one ftreet and a few detached buildings are cleared; the ftreet is well paved with the fame kind of ftone of which the ancient roads are

are made, narrow caufeways are raifed a
foot and an half on each fide for the conveniency of foot paffengers. The ftreet
itfelf, to my recollection, is not fo broad
as the narroweft part of the Strand, and
is fuppofed to have been inhabited by
tradefpeople. The traces of wheels of
carriages are to be feen on the pavement;
the diftance betwen the traces is lefs than
that between the wheels of a modern poft-
chaife. I remarked this the more as, on
my firft viewing the ftreet, I doubted whether there was room for two modern
coaches to pafs each other. I plainly faw
there was fufficient room for two of the
ancient chariots, whofe wheels were of no
greater diftance than between the traces on
the pavement. The houfes are fmall, and
in a very different ftyle from the modern Italian houfes; for the former give an
idea of neatnefs and conveniency. The
ftucco on the walls is hard as marble,
fmooth and beautiful. Some of the rooms
are ornamented with paintings, moftly

single figures, reprefenting fome animal;
they are tolerably well executed, and on
a little water being thrown on them, the
colours appear furprifingly frefh.

Moft of the houfes are built on the
fame plan, and have one fmall room from
the paffage, which is conjectured to have
been the fhop, with a window to the
ftreet, and a place which feems to have
been contrived for fhewing the goods to
the greateft advantage. The nature of
the traffic carried on at one particular
houfe, is indicated by a figure in alto
relievo of a very expreffive kind, immediately above the door.

It is to be wifhed they would cover one
of the beft houfes with a roof, as nearly
refembling that which originally belonged
to it as they could imagine, with a complete affortment of the antique furniture
of the kitchen and each particular room.
Such a houfe fitted up with accuracy and
judgment, with all its utenfils and ornaments

ments properly arranged, would be an object of univerfal curiofity, and would fwell the heart of the antiquarian with veneration and delight. Only imagine, my dear Sir, what thofe gentlemen muft feel, when they fee the venerable habitations of the ancients in their prefent mournful condition, neglected, defpifed, abandoned to the peltings of rain, and all the injuries of the weather! thofe precious walls, which, were it poffible to tranfport them to the various countries of the world, would be bought with avidity, and placed in the gardens of Princes! How muft the bofoms of all true virtuofos glow with indignation, when they behold the manfions of the ancient Romans ftripped of their ornaments, difhonoured, and expofed, like a parcel of ragged galley flaves, in the moft indecent manner, with hardly any covering to their nakednefs; while a little paltry brick houfe, coming the Lord knows how, from a country which men of tafte have always defpifed, has

been

been received with hofpitality, dreffed in
a fine coat of the richeft marble, adorned with jewels and precious ftones,
and treated with every mark of honourable diftinction !

In another part of the town of Pompeia, there is a rectangular building, with a
colonade, towards the court, fomething in
the ftyle of the Royal Exchange at London,
but fmaller. This has every appearance of a
barrack and guard room; the pillars are
of brick, covered with fhining ftucco, ele-
gantly fluted; the fcrawlings and drawings
ftill vifible on the walls, are fuch as we
might naturally expect on the walls of a
guard room, where foldiers are the de-
figners, and fwords the engraving tools.
They confift of gladiators fighting, fome
with each other, fome with wild beafts;
the games of the circus, as chariot races,
wreftling, and the like; a few figures in
caricatura, defigned probably by fome of
the foldiers, in ridicule of their companions,

4   or

or perhaps of their officers; and there
are abundance of names infcribed on various parts of the wall, according to the
univerfal cuftom of the humbleft candidates for fame in all ages and countries.
It may be fafely afferted, that none of
thofe who have endeavoured to tranfmit
their names to pofterity in this manner,
have fucceeded fo well as the foldiers of
the garrifon of Pompeia.

At a confiderable diftance from the barrack, is a building, known by the infcription upon it, for a temple of the goddefs
Ifis; there is nothing very magnificent in
its appearance; the pillars are of brick ftuc-
coed like thofe of the guard room. The
beft paintings, hitherto found at Pompeia,
are thofe of this temple; they have been
cut out of the walls and removed to
Portici. It was abfolutely neceffary to do
this with the pictures at Herculaneum, becaufe *there* they could not be feen without
the help of torches; but *here*, where they

N 3   could

could be feen by the light of the Sun, they
would, in my humble opinion, have appeared to more advantage, and have had
a better effect in the identical fituation in
which they were placed by the ancient
artift. A few ftill remain, particularly
one, which is confidered by travellers as a
great curiofity; it is a fmall view of a
villa, with the gardens belonging to it.

There is one houfe or villa without the
walls, on a much larger fcale than any of
the others. In a large cellar, or vaulted
gallery, belonging to this houfe, there are
a number of amphoræ, or earthen veffels,
arranged along the walls; moft of them
filled with a kind of red fubftance,
fuppofed to have been wine. This cellar
is funk about two-thirds below the furface of the ground, and is lighted by
fmall narrow windows. I have called it
gallery, becaufe it is about twelve feet in
width, and is the whole length of two
adjoining fides of the fquare which the

villa

villa forms. It was ufed not only as a repofitory for wine, but alfo as a cool retreat for the family during exceffive hot weather. Some of this unfortunate family fought fhelter in this place from the deftructive fhower which overwhelmed the town. Eight fkelctons, four being thofe of children, were found here; where they muft have met a more cruel and lingering death, than that which they fhunned. In one room, the body of a man was found, with an ax in the hand; it is probable he had been endeavouring to cut a paffage into the open air; he had broken and pierced the wall, but had expired before he could clear away the furrounding rubbifh. Few fkeletons were found in the ftreets, but a confiderable number in the houfes. Before the decifive fhower fell, which fmothered the inhabitants of this ill-fated city, perhaps fuch quantities of afhes and cinders were occafionally falling, as frightened, and obliged them to keep within doors.

It

It is impoſſible to view thoſe ſkeletons, and reflect on this dreadful cataſtrophe, without horror and compaſſion. We cannot think of the inhabitants of a whole town being deſtroyed at once, without imagining that their fate has been uncommonly ſevere. But are not the inhabitants of all the towns then exiſting, of whom we think without any emotion of pity, as completely dead as thoſe of Pompeia? And could we take them one by one, and conſider the nature of their deaths, and the circumſtances attending that of each individual; ſome deſtroyed by painful bodily diſeaſes, ſome by the torture of the executioner, ſome bowed to the grave by the weight of accumulated ſorrow, and the ſlow anguiſh of a broken heart, after having ſuffered the pangs of diſſolution, over and over again, in the death of thoſe they loved, after having beheld the dying agonies of their children; could all this, I ſay, be appraiſed, calculated, and compared, the balance of

ſuffering

ſuffering might not be found with the inhabitants of Pompeia, but rather with
thoſe of the contemporary cities, who,
perhaps at that time, as we do now, lamented its ſevere fate.

LETTER LX.

AS I fauntered along the Strada Nuova lately, I perceived a groupe of people liftening, with much attention, to a perfon who harangued them in a raifed; folemn voice, and with great gefticulation. I immediately made one of the auditory, which increafed every moment; men, women, and children bringing feats from the neighbouring houfes, on which they placed themfelves around the orator. He repeated ftanzas from Ariofto, in a pompous, recitativo cadence, peculiar to the natives of Italy; and he had a book in his hand, to affift his memory when it failed. He made occafional commentaries in profe, by way of bringing the Poet's expreffion nearer to the level of his hearers' capacities. His cloak hung loofe from one fhoulder;

his

his right arm was difengaged, for the purpofes of oratory. Sometimes he waved it
with a flow, fmooth motion, which ac-
corded with the cadence of the verfes;
fometimes he prefled it to his breaft, to
give energy to the pathetic fentiments of
the Poet. Now he gathered the hanging
folds of the right fide of his cloak, and
held them gracefully up, in imitation of a
Roman fenator ; and anon he fwung them
acrofs his left fhoulder, like a citizen of
Naples. He humoured the ftanza by his
voice, which he could modulate to the key
of any paffion, from the boifterous burfts
of rage, to the foft notes of pity or love.
But, when he came to defcribe the exploits
of Orlando, he trufted neither to the powers of his own voice, nor the Poet's genius; but, throwing off his cloak, and
grafping his cane, he affumed the warlike
attitude and ftern countenance of that hero; reprefenting, by the moft animated
action, how he drove his fpear through the
bodies of fix of his enemies at once; the

point

point at the fame time killing a feventh,
who would alfo have remained transfixed
with his companions, if the fpear could
have held more than fix men of an ordinary fize upon it at a time.

Il Cavalier d' Anglante ove pui fpeffe
Vide le genti e l'arme, abbaffo l'afta,
Ed uno in quella, e pofcia un altro meffe
E un altro, e un altro, che fembrar di pafta,
E fino a fei ve n'infilzò, e li reffe
Tutti una lancia; e perche' ella non bafta
A piu Capir, lafciò il fettimo fuore
Ferito fi che di quel colpo muore.

This ftanza our declaimer had no occafion
to comment upon, as Ariofto has thought
fit to illuftrate it in a manner which feemed
highly to the tafte of this audience. For,
in the verfe immediately following, Orlando is compared to a man killing frogs
in marfhy ground, with a bow and arrow
made for that purpofe; an amufement very
common in Italy, and ftill more fo in France.

Non altrimente nell' eftrema arena
Veggiam le rane de' canali e foffe

Dal

Dal cauto arcier ne i fianchi, e nella fchiena
L'una vicina all' altera effer percoffe,
Ne dalla freccia, fin che tutta piena
Non fia da un capo all' altero effer rimoffe.

I muft however do this audience the juftice
to acknowledge, that they feemed to feel
the pathetic and fublime, as well as the
ludicrous, parts of the ancient Bard.

This practice of rehearfing the verfes of
Ariofto, Taffo, and other poets, in the
ftreet, I have not obferved in any other
town of Italy; and I am told it is lefs
common here than it was formerly. I remember indeed, at Venice, to have frequently feen mountebanks, who gained
their livelihood by amufing the populace
at St. Mark's Place, with wonderful and
romantic ftories in profe.—" Liften, Gen-
" tlemen," faid one of them; " let
" me crave your attention, ye beauti-
" ful and virtuous ladies; I have fome-
" thing equally affecting and wonderful
" to tell you; a ftrange and ftupendous
" adventure, which happened to a gallant
" knight."

" knight."—Perceiving that this did not
fufficiently intereft the hearers, he exalted
his voice, calling out that his Knight was
uno Cavalliero Crifliano. The audience
feemed ftill a little fluctuating. He raifed
his voice a note higher, telling them that
this Chriftian Knight was one of their own
victorious countrymen, " un' Eroe Vene-
" ziano." This fixed them ; and he proceeded to relate how the Knight, going to
join the Chriftian army, which was on its
march to recover the Sepulchre of Chrift
from the hands of the Infidels, loft his
way in a vaft wood, and wandered at
length to a caftle, in which a lady of tran-
fcendent beauty was kept prifoner by a gi-
gantic Saracen, who, having failed in all
his endeavours to gain the heart of this
peerlefs damfel, refolved to gratify his paffion by force; and had actually begun the
horrid attempt, when the fhrieks of this
chafte maiden reached the ears of the Venetian hero; who, ever ready to relieve
virgins in diftrefs, rufhed into the apartment

ment from whence the cries iſſued. The brutal raviſher, alarmed at the noiſe, quits the ſtruggling lady, at the very inſtant when her ſtrength began to fail; draws his flaming ſword; and a dreadful combat begins between him and the Chriſtian Knight, who performs miracles of courage and addreſs in refiſting the blows of this mighty giant; till, his foot unfortunately ſlipping in the blood which flowed on the pavement, he fell at the feet of the Saracen; who, immediately ſeizing the advantage which chance gave him, raiſed his ſword with all his might, and—— Here the orator's hat flew to the ground, open to receive the contributions of the liſteners; and he continued repeating, " raiſed " his ſword over the head of the Chriſtian " Knight"—" raiſed his bloody, murder- " ous brand, to deſtroy your noble, va- " liant countryman."—But he proceeded no farther in his narrative, till all who ſeemed intereſted in it had thrown ſomething into the hat. He then pocketed the

money

money with great gravity, and went on to inform them, that, at this critical moment, the Lady, feeing the danger which threatened her deliverer, redoubled her prayers to the Bleſſed Mary, who, a virgin herſelf, is peculiarly attentive and propitious to the prayers of virgins. Juſt as the Saracen's fword was defcending on the head of the Venetian, a large bee flew, quick as thought, in at the window, ſtung the former very fmartly on the left temple, diverted the blow, and gave the Chriſtian Knight time to recover himſelf. The fight then recommenced with freſh fury; but, after the Virgin Mary had taken ſuch a decided part, you may believe it was no match. The Infidel foon fell dead at the feet of the Believer. But who do you think this beauteous maiden was, on whoſe account the combat had begun ? Why no other than the fiſter of the Venetian Hero. —This young lady had been ſtolen from her father's houfe, while ſhe was yet a child, by an Armenian merchant, who

dealt

dealt in no other goods than women. He concealed the child till he found means to carry her to Egypt; where he kept her in bondage, with other young girls, till the age of fifteen, and then fold her to the Saracen. I do not exactly remember whether the recognition between the brother and fifter was made out by means of a mole on the young lady's neck, or by a bracelet on her arm, which, with fome other of her mother's jewels, happened to be in her pocket when fhe was ftolen; but, in whatever manner this came about, there was the greateft joy on the happy occafion; and the lady joined the army with her brother, and one of the Chriftian commanders fell in love with her, and their nuptials were folemnized at Jerufalem; and they returned to Venice, and had a very numerous family of the fineft children you ever beheld.

At Rome, thofe ftreet-orators fometimes entertain their audience with interefting paffages of real hiftory. I remember having heard one, in particular, give a full and true account how the bloody heathen emperor Nero fet fire to the city of Rome, and fat at a window of his golden palace, playing on a harp, while the town was in flames. After which the Hiftorian proceeded to relate, how this unnatural emperor murdered his own mother; and he concluded by giving the audience the fatisfaction of hearing a particular detail of all the ignominious circumftances attending the murderer's own death.

This bufinefs of ftreet-oratory, while it amufes the populace, and keeps them from lefs innocent and more expenfive paftimes, gives them at the fame time fome general ideas of hiftory. Street-orators, therefore, are a more ufeful fet of men than another clafs, of which there are numbers at Rome, who entertain companies with extemporaneous verfes on any given fubject. The laft are called Improuvifatoris; and fome

people

people admire thefe performances greatly.
For my own part, I am too poor a judge
of the Italian language either to admire or
condemn them; but, from the nature of
the thing, I fhould imagine they are but
indifferent. It is faid, that the Italian
is peculiarly calculated for poetry, and
that verfes may be made with more facility in this than in any other language. It
may be more eafy to find fmooth lines,
and make them terminate in rhime in
Italian, than in any language; but to
compofe verfes with all the qualities effential to good poetry, I imagine leifure
and long reflection are requifite. Indeed
I underftand, from thofe who are judges,
that thofe extempore compofitions of the
Improuvifatori are in general but mean
productions, confifting of a few fulfome
compliments to the company, and fome
common-place obfervations, put into rhime,
on the fubject propofed. There is, however, a lady of an amiable character, Sig-
nora Corilla, whofe extempore produc-

tions, which fhe repeats in the moft graceful manner, are admired by people of real
tafte. While we were at Rome, this lady
made an appearance one evening, at the
affembly of the Arcadi, which charmed a
very numerous company; and of which our
friend Mr. R—y has given me fuch an account, as makes me regret that I was not prefent. After much entreaty, a fubject being
given, fhe began, accompanied by two vio-
lins, and fung her unpremeditated ftrains with
great variety of thought and elegance of
language. The whole of her performance
lafted above an hour, with three or four
paufes, of about five minutes each, which
feemed neceffary, more that fhe might recover her ftrength and voice, than for recollection; for that gentleman faid, that
nothing could have more the air of
infpiration, or what we are told of the
Pythian Prophetefs. At her firft fetting
out, her manner was fedate, or rather
cold; but gradually becoming animated,
her voice rofe, her eyes fparkled, and the
rapidity

rapidity and beauty of her expreſſions and ideas ſeemed ſupernatural. She at laſt called on another member of the ſociety to ſing alternately with her, which he complied with; but Mr. R——y thought, though they were *Arcades ambo*, they were by no means *cantare pares*.

Naples is celebrated for the fineſt opera in Europe. This however happens not to be the ſeaſon of performing; but the common people enjoy *their* operas at all ſeaſons. Little concerts of vocal and inſtrumental muſic are heard every evening in the Strada Nuova, the Chiaca, the Strada di Toledo, and other ſtreets; and young men and women are ſeen dancing to the muſic of ambulatory performers all along this delightful bay. To a mere ſpectator, the amuſements of the common people afford more delight, than thoſe of the great; becauſe they ſeem to be more enjoyed by the one claſs, than by the other. This is the caſe every where, except in

France;

France; where the high appear as happy as
thofe of middle rank, and the rich are very
near as merry as the poor. But, in moft
other countries, the people of great rank and
fortune, though they flock to every kind
of entertainment, from not knowing what
to do with themfelves, yet feem to enjoy
them lefs than thofe of inferior rank and
fortune.

The Englifh particularly are faid to be
in this predicament. This may be true in
fome degree; though I imagine there is
more appearance than reality in it; owing
to an abfurd affectation of indifference, or
what the French call *nonchalance*, which has
prevailed of late years. A few infipid
characters in high life, whofe internal
vacancy leads them to feek amufement in
public places, and whofe infenfibility prevents them from finding it, have probably
brought this appearance of a want of all
enjoyment into fafhion. Thofe who wifh
to be thought of what is called the *ton*,
imitate

imitate the mawkifh infipidity of their fu-
periors in rank, and imagine it diftin-
guifhes them from the vulgar, to fupprefs
all the natural expreffions of pity, joy, or
admiration, and to feem, upon all occafions, in a ftate of complete apathy.
Thofe amiable creatures frequent public
places, that it may be faid of them, *They
are not as other men are.* You will feé
them occafionally at the playhoufe, placed
in the boxes, like fo many bufts, with un-
changing features; and, while the reft of
the audience yield to the emotions excited
by the poet and the actors, thofe men of
the *ton* preferve the moft dignified ferenity
of countenance; and, except that they
from time to time pronounce the words
Pfhaw! and *Stuff!*—one would think them
the exprefs reprefentatives of the Pagan
gods, who *have eyes but do not fee, and
ears but do not hear.*

I know not what may be the cafe at the
opera; but I can affure you there are none
of

of thofe bufts among the auditories which the
ftreet-performers at Naples gather around
them. I faw very lately a large clufter of
men, women, and children, entertained to
the higheft degree, and to all appearance
made exceedingly happy, by a poor fellow with a mafk on his face, and a guitar
in his hands. He affembled his audience
by the fongs he fung to the mufic of his
inftrument, and by a thoufand merry ftories he told them with infinite drollery.
This affembly was in an open place, facing
the bay, and near the palace. The old
women fat liftening, with their diftaffs,
fpinning a kind of coarfe flax, and wetting
the thread with their fpittle ; their grand-
children fprawled at their feet, amufed
with the twirling of the fpindle. The
men and their wives, the youths and their
miftreffes, fat in a circle, with their eyes
fixed on the mufician, who kept them
laughing for a great part of the evening
with his ftories, which he enlivened occafionally

fionally with tunes upon the guitar. At
length, when the company was moft numerous, and at the higheft pitch of good
humour, he fuddenly pulled off his mafk,
laid down his guitar, and opened a little
box which ftood before him, and addreffed
the audience in the following words, as
literally as I can tranflate them:——
" Ladies and gentlemen, there is a time
" for all things; we have had enough
" of jefting; innocent mirth is excellent
" for the health of the body, but other
" things are requifite for the health of
" the foul. I will now, with your per-
" miffion, my honourable mafters and mif-
" treffes, entertain you with fomething
" ferious, and of infinitely greater import-
" ance; fomething for which all of you
" will have reafon to blefs me as long as you
" live." Here he fhook out of a bag a
great number of little leaden crucifixes.—
" I am juft come from the Holy Houfe of
" Loretto, my fellow chriftians," continued
he, " on purpofe to furnifh you with
" thofe

" those jewels, more precious than all the
" gold of Peru, and all the pearls of the
" ocean. Now, my beloved brethren and
" sisters, you are afraid that I shall de-
" mand a price for those sacred crosses,
" far above your abilities, and something
" correspondent with their value, by way
" of indemnification for the fatigue and
" expence of the long journey which I
" have made on your account, all the way
" from the habitation of the Blessed Vir-
" gin to this thrice renowned city of Na-
" ples, the riches and liberality of whose
" inhabitants are celebrated all over the
" globe. No, my generous Neapolitans;
" I do not wish to take the advantage of
" your pious and liberal dispositions. I
" will not ask for those invaluable cruci-
" fixes (all of which, let me inform you,
" have touched the foot of the holy
" image of the Blessed Virgin, which was
" formed by the hands of St. Luke; and,
" moreover, each of them has been shaken
" in

" in the Santiſſima Scodella, the ſacred
" porringer in which the Virgin made the
" pap for the infant Jeſus); I will not,
" I ſay, aſk an ounce of gold, no not
" even a crown of ſilver; my regard for
" you is ſuch, that I ſhall let you have
" them for a penny a piece."

You muſt acknowledge, my friend, that
this morſel of eloquence was a very great
pennyworth; and when we recollect the
ſums that ſome of our acquaintance receive for their oratory, though they never
could produce ſo pathetic a ſpecimen,
you will naturally conclude that eloquence
is a much rarer commodity in England
than in Italy.

LETTER LXI.

Naples.

I HAVE made two vifits to Mount
Vefuvius, the firft in company with
your acquaintance Mr. N———t. Leaving
the carriage at Herculaneum, we mounted
mules, and were attended by three men,
whofe bufinefs it is to accompany ftrangers
up the mountain. Being arrived at a
hermitage, called Il Salvatore, we found
the road fo broken and rough, that we
thought proper to leave the mules at that
place, which is inhabited by a French her-
mit. The poor man mufl have a very bad
opinion of mankind, to choofe the mouth
of Mount Vefuvius for his neareft neigh-
bour, in preference to their fociety. From
the hermitage we walked over various
fields of lava, which have burft out at
different periods. Thefe feemed to be
perfectly

perfectly well known to our guides, who
mentioned their different dates as we paffed. The latest appeared, before we left
Rome, about two months ago; it was, however, but inconfiderable in comparifon of
other eruptions, there having been no
burfting of the crater, or of the fide of
the mountain, as in the eruption of 1767,
fo well defcribed by Sir William Hamilton;
but only a boiling over of lava from the
mouth of the volcano, and that not in
exceffive quantity; for it had done no da-
mage to the vineyards or cultivated parts
of the mountain, having reached no farther than the old black lava on which
foil had not as yet been formed. I was
furprifed to fee this lava of the laft eruption ftill fmoking, and in fome places,
where a confiderable quantity was confined in a kind of deep path like a dry
ditch, and fhaded from the light of the
Sun, it appeared of a glowing red colour.
In other places, notwithftanding its being
perfectly black and folid, it ftill retained
fuch

fuch a degree of heat, that we could not
ftand upon it for any confiderable time, but
were obliged very frequently to ftep on the
ground, or on older lava, to cool our feet. We
had advanced a good way on a large piece of
the lateft lava, which was perfectly black
and hard, and feemed cooler than the reft;
while from this we looked at a ftream
of liquid lava, which flowed fluggifhly
along a hollow way at fome diftance. I
accidentally threw my eyes below my feet,
and perceived fomething, which mightily
difcompofed my contemplations. This was
a fmall ftream of the fame matter, gliding
to one fide from beneath the black cruft
on which we ftood. The idea of this cruft
giving way, and our finking into the glowing liquid which it covered, made us fhift
our ground with great precipitation; which
one of our guides obferving, he called out,
" Animo, animo, Signori;" and immediately
jumped on the incruftation which we had
abandoned, and danced above it, to fhew
that

that it was fufficiently ftrong, and that
we had no reafon to be afraid. We afterwards threw large ftones of the heavieft
kind we could find, into this rivulet, on
whofe furface they floated like cork in
water ; and on thrufting a ftick into the
ftream, it required a confiderable exertion
of ftrength to make it enter. About this
time the day began to overcaft; this deftroyed our hopes of enjoying the view
from the top of the mountain, and we
were not tempted to afcend any farther.

Some time after, I went to the fummit
with another party;—but I think it fair
to inform you, that I have nothing new
to fay on the fubject of volcanos, nor any
philofophical remarks to make upon lavas.
I have no guefs of what time may be neceffary for the formation of foil, nor do I
know whether it accumulates in a regular
progreffion, or is accelerated or retarded
by various accidents, which may lead us
into infinite errors, when we calculate

7   time

time by fuch a rule. I have not the fmalleft
wifh to infinuate that the world is an hour
older than Mofes makes it; becaufe I
imagine thofe gentlemen whofe calculations
differ from his, are very nearly as liable
to be miftaken as he was; becaufe an attempt to prove it more ancient, can be
no fervice to mankind; and finally, becaufe,
unlefs it could at the fame time be proved
that the world has acquired wifdom in
proportion to its years, fuch an attempt
conveys an oblique reflection on its character; for many follies may be overlooked
and forgiven to a world of only five or
fix thoufand years of age, which would
be quite unpardonable at a more advanced
period of exiftence. Having forewarned
you that I fhall treat of none of thofe
matters, but fimply defcribe what I faw,
and mention perhaps a few incidents,
none of which, I confefs, are of great
importance, I leave it in your choice to
afcend the mountain with me, or not, as
you pleafe.

Having

Having proceeded on mules as far as on the former occafion, we walked to that part of the mountain which is almoft perpendicular. This appears of no great height, yet thofe who have never before attempted this afcent, fatigue themfelves here much more than during all the reft of the journey, notwithftanding their being affifted by laying hold of the belts which the guides wear about their waifts for that purpofe. This part of the mountain appearing much fhorter than it really is, people are tempted to make a violent effort, in the expectation of furmounting the difficulty at once; but the cinders, afhes, and other droffy materials, giving way, the foot generally finks back twothirds of each ftep; fo that befides the height being greater than it appears, you have all the fatigue of afcending a hill three times as high as this is in reality. Thofe, therefore, who fet out too brifkly at firft, and do not hufband their ftrength at the beginning, have reafon to repent

their

their imprudence, being obliged to throw many a longing look, and make many a fruitless vow, before they, with the wretched guide who lugs them along, can arrive, panting and breathless, at the top; like those young men who, having wasted their vigour in early excesses, and brought on premature old age, link themselves to some ill-fated woman, who drags them, tormenting and tormented, to the grave.

Those who wish to view Mount Vesuvius to the greatest advantage, must begin their expedition in the evening; and the darker the succeeding night happens to be, so much the better. By the time our company had arrived at the top of the mountain, there was hardly any other light than that which issued by interrupted flashes from the volcano.

Exclusive of those periods when there are actual eruptions, the appearance and quantity of what issues from the mountain are very various; sometimes, for a long

3   space

fpace of time together, it feems in a ftate
of almoft perfect tranquillity; nothing but
a fmall quantity of fmoke afcending from
the volcano, as if that vaft magazine of
fuel, which has kept it alive for fo many
ages, was at laft exhaufted, and nothing
remained but the dying embers; then,
perhaps, when leaft expected, the cloud
of fmoke thickens, and is intermixed with
flame; at other times, quantities of pumice ftone and afhes are thrown up with
a kind of hiffing noife. For near a week
the mountain has been more turbulent
than it has been fince the fmall eruption,
or rather boiling over of lava, which
took place about two months ago; and
while we remained at the top, the explofions were of fufficient importance to fatisfy our curiofity to the utmoft. They
appeared much more confiderable there
than we had imagined while at a greater
diftance; each of them was preceded by
a noife like thunder within the mountain;
a column of thick black fmoke then iffued

out with great rapidity, followed by a blaze of flame; and immediately after, a shower of cinders and ashes, or red hot stones, were thrown into the sky. This was succeeded by a calm of a few minutes, during which nothing issued but a moderate quantity of smoke and flame, which gradually increased, and terminated in thunder and explosion as before. These accesses and intervals continued with varied force while we remained.

When we first arrived, our guides placed us at a reasonable distance from the mouth of the volcano, and on the side from which the wind came, so that we were no way incommoded by the smoke. In this situation the wind also bore to the opposite side the cinders, ashes, and other fiery substances, which were thrown up; and we ran no danger of being hurt, except when the explosion was very violent, and when red hot stones, and such heavy substances, were thrown like sky-rockets,

rockets, with a great noife and prodigious force, into the air; and even thefe make fuch a flaming appearance, and take fo much time in defcending, that they are eafily avoided.

Mr. Brydone, in his admirable account of Mount Ætna, tells us, he was informed, that, in an eruption of that mountain, large rocks of fire were difcharged, with a noife much more terrible than that of thunder; that the perfon who informed him, reckoned from the time of their greateft elevation till they reached the ground, and found they took twenty-one feconds to defcend; from whence he concludes their elevation had been feven thoufand feet. This unqueftionably required a power of projeɕtion far fuperior to what Vefuvius has been known to exert. He himfelf meafured the height of the explofions of the latter by the fame rule; and the ftones thrown the higheft, never took above nine feconds to defcend; which,

by

by the fame method of calculating, fhews they had rifen to little more than twelve hundred feet.—A pretty tolerable height, and might have fatisfied the ambition of Vefuvius, if the ftones of Ætna had not been faid to have mounted fo much higher. But before fuch an exceffive fuperiority is granted to the latter, thofe who are acquainted with Mr. Brydone will recollect, that they have his own authority for the one fact, and that of another perfon for the other.

After having remained fome time at the place where they were pofted by the guides, our company grew bolder, as they became more familiarifed to the object. Some made the circuit of the volcano, and by that means increafed the rifque of being wounded by the ftones thrown out. Your young friend Jack was a good deal hurt by a fall, as he ran to avoid a large portion of fome fiery fubftance, which feemed to be falling directly on his head.

Confidering

Confidering the rafh and frolicfome difpofition of fome who vifit this mountain, it is very remarkable that fo few fatal accidents happen. I have heard of young Englifh gentlemen betting, who fhould venture fartheft, or remain longeft, near the mouth of the Volcano. A very dreadful event had nearly taken place while our company remained. The bank, if it may be fo called, on which fome of them had ftood when they looked into the Volcano, actually fell in before we left the fummit of the mountain. This made an impreffion on all prefent, and inclined them to abandon fo treacherous a neighbourhood. The fleep hill of drofs and cinders, which we had found it fo difficult to afcend, we defcended in a twinkling; but, as the night was uncommonly dark, we had much trouble in paffing over the rough valley between that and the Hermitage, near which the mules waited. I ought to be afhamed, however, to mention the fatigue of this expedition ; for two ladies,

dies, natives of Geneva, formed part of
the company. One of them, big with
child, accompanied her hufband as far as
the Hermitage, and was then with difficulty perfuaded to go back; the other actually went to the fummit, and returned
with the reft of the company.

Before we fet out for Naples, we were
refreſhed, at a little inn at the bottom of
the mountain, with fome glaffes of a very
generous and palatable wine, called *La-
chrima Chrifti*; and experienced the truth
of what an Italian Poet obferved, that the
effects of this wine form a ftrong contraft
with its name:

> Chi fu, de Contadini il più indifcreto,
>   Che à ſbigottir la gente,
>   Diede nome dolente,
> Al vin, che fopra ogn' altro il cuor fà lieto?
> Lachrima dunque appellaraſſi un' rifo,
> Parto di nobiliſſima vindemia.

LETTER LXII.

Naples.

YOUR account of our Friend's state of health gives me much concern; the more, as I cannot approve the change he has made of a phyfician. You fay, the doctor, under whofe care he is at prefent, has employed his mind fo entirely in medical refearches, that he fcarcely difplays a grain of common fenfe, when the converfation turns on any other fubject; and that, although he feems opinionative, vain, and oftentatious in his profeffion, and full of falfe and abfurd ideas in the common affairs of life, yet he is a very able phyfician, and has performed many wonderful cures. Be affured, my dear Sir, that this is impoffible; for medical fkill is not like the rod of an inchanter, which may be found accidentally, and which transfers

9   its

its miraculous powers indifcriminately to a blockhead or a man of fenfe. The number of weak, goffipping men, who have made fortunes by this profeffion, do not prove the contrary. I do not fay that men of that kind cannot make fortunes; I only affert they are not the moft likely to cure difeafes. An intereft with apothecaries, nurfes, and a few talkative old ladies, will enable them to do the firft; but a clear underftanding, and a confiderable fhare of natural fagacity, are qualities effentially neceffary for the fecond, and for every bufinefs which requires refleâion. Without thefe, falfe inferences will be drawn from experience itfelf; and learning will tend to confirm a man in his errors, and to render him more completely a coxcomb.

The profeffion of phyfic is that, of all others, in which the generality of mankind have the feweft lights, by which they can difcern the abilities of its profeffors; becaufe the ftudies which lead to it are

more

more out of the road of ufual education,
and the practice more enveloped in technical terms and hieroglyphical figns. But
I imagine the fafeft criterion by which
men, who have not been bred to that profeffion, can form a judgment of thofe
who have, is, the degree of fagacity and
penetration they difcover on fubjects equally open to mankind in general, and which
ought to be underftood by all who live in
fociety. You do not mention particularly
what has been prefcribed by either; only
that the former phyfician feemed to rely
almoft entirely on exercife and regimen,
whereas the prefent flatters our friend
with a fpeedy cure, by the help of the
Pectoral and Balfamic medicines which
he orders in fuch abundance, and which
he declares are fo efficacious in *pulmonary
confumptions.*

Having lamented with you the mournful events which render the name of that
difeafe peculiarly alarming to you, and
knowing

knowing your friendly folicitude about Mr. ———, I do not wonder at your earneft defire to know fomething of the nature of a diftemper with which he is threatened, and which has proved fatal to fo many of our friends. But I am furprifed that you have not chofen a more enlightened inftructor, when you have fo many around you. Though confcious that I have no juft claim to all the obliging expreffions which your partiality to. my opinions has prompted you to make ufe of, yet I am too much flattered by fome of them, to re-fufe complying with your requeft. My fentiments, fuch as they are, will at leaft have the merit of being clearly underftood. I fhall obferve your prohibition, not to re-fer you to any medical book; and fhall carefully avoid all technical terms, which you fo much abominate. With regard to your fhewing my Letter to any of the fa-culty; if you find yourfelf fo inclined, I have not the fmalleft objection; for thofe

who

who have the greatest knowledge in their profeffion, are beft acquainted with its uncertainty, and moft indulgent to the miftakes or errors of others.

Alas, my friend! how is it poffible that phyficians fhould avoid miftakes? If the ableft mechanic were to attempt to remedy the irregular movements of a watch, while he remained ignorant of the ftructure and manner of acting of fome of the principal fprings, would he not be in danger of doing harm inftead of good? Phyficians are in the fituation of fuch a mechanic; for, although it is evident that the nerves are the organs of motion and fenfation, yet their ftructure is not known. Some anatomifts affert they are impervious cords; others, that they are flender tubes, containing a fluid. But what the nature of this fluid is; whether it ferves only to nourifh the nerves themfelves, or is the medium by which they convey feeling and the power of motion to other parts, is not afcer-

afcertained even by thofe who argue for its exiflence; far lefs is it explained in what manner ideas, formed within the brain, can, by the means of folid cords, or by a fluid contained in tubes, communicate motion at pleafure to the legs and arms. We are ignorant why the will, which has no influence over the motion of an animal's heart, fhould find the feet obedient to her dictates; and we can no more explain how a man can move one leg over the other by volition, or the mere act of willing, than how he could, by the fame means, move Offa on the top of Olympus. The one happens every moment, the other would be confidered as a miracle; but they are equally unaccountable. While parts fo infinitely effential to life are not underflood, inflead of being furprifed that fo many difeafes baffle the fkill of the phyfician, we have more reafon to be aftonifhed that any can be alleviated or cured by his art.

The

The pen of the fatirift, no doubt, may be fairly aimed againft the prefumption and ignorance of many individuals of this, as of every other profeffion; but cannot with juftice be directed againft the art it-felf: fince, in fpite of the obfcurity which ftill involves fome parts of the animal eco-nomy, many diforders are relieved, and fome of the fevereft and moft difagreeable to which the human body is liable, are cured with certainty by the art of me-dicine.

Unfortunately for mankind, and in a particular manner for the inhabitants of Great Britain, the pulmonary confumption is not of the number.

This difeafe may originate from various caufes:

1ft. An external bruife or wound.

2d. The difeafe called pleurify, includ-ing in that term an inflammation of the lungs themfelves, as well as the membrane which covers them.

3d.

3d. The burſting of ſome of the blood-veſſels of the lungs, independent of external injury, and owing to a faulty conformation of the cheſt, and the ſlenderneſs of the veſſels.

4th. Certain ſmall tumours, called tubercles, in the lungs.

The firſt cauſe I have mentioned is an external bruiſe or wound.

An accident of that kind happening to the lungs, is more dangerous and difficult to cure, than when the ſame takes place in moſt other parts of the body; becauſe the lungs are vital organs, eſſentially neceſſary to life, and when their motion is impaired, other animal functions are thereby injured; becauſe they are of an uncommonly delicate texture, in which a rupture having once taken place, will be apt to increaſe; becauſe they are in conſtant motion and expoſed to the acceſs of external air, both of which circumſtances are unfavourable to the healing of wounds,

and

and becaufe the mafs of blood diftributed to the whole body palfes previoufly through the lungs, and confequently the blood-veffels of this organ are more numerous than thofe of any other part of the body.

When we confider thefe peculiarities, it is natural to conclude, that every wound of the lungs muft neceffarily prove mortal; but experience has taught the contrary. Many wounds of the lungs heal of themfelves, by what is called, the firft intention. The phyfician may prevent a fever, by ordering the patient to lofe blood in proper quantities, and he may regulate the diet; but the cure muft be left to nature, which fhe will perform with greater certainty, if fhe is not difturbed by any of thofe balfams which the wounded are fometimes directed to fwallow on fuch occafions. But when the wound, either from injudicious treatment, or from its fize, or from the bad habit of the patient, degenerates into an ulcer at-

VoL. II.   Q   tended

tended with hectic symptoms, the difeafe muft be treated as if it had arifen from any of the other caufes.

The pleurify, or inflammation of the lungs, is a difeafe more frequent in cold countries than in mild; in the fpring than in the other feafons; and more apt to feize people of a fanguine conftitution than others.

Plentiful and repeated bleedings, fomentations, blifters near the affected part, and a cooling, diluting regimen, generally remove it, without its leaving any bad confequence. Sometimes, by the omiffion of bleeding in due quantity at the beginning, and fometimes in fpite of all poffible care, it terminates in an abfcefs, which, on burfling, may fuffocate the patient; or, if the matter is coughed up, becomes an open ulcer, and produces the difeafe in queftion.

The third caufe of the pulmonary confumption above mentioned, is, a fpitting

of

of blood, from the burfting of veffels of the lungs, independent of external wound or bruife. People of a fair complexion, delicate fkin, flender make, long neck, and narrow cheft, are more fubject to this than others. Thofe who have a predifpofition to this complaint, by their form, are moft apt to be attacked after their full growth : women from fifteen to three-and-thirty ; men two or three years later. In Great Britain, a fpitting of blood generally occurs to thofe predifpofed to it, in the fpring, or beginning of fummer, when the weather fuddenly changes from cold to excellive hot ; and when the heat is fuppofed to rarify the blood, before the folids are proportionably relaxed from the contracted ftate they acquire during the cold of winter. When a fpitting of blood happens to a perfon who has actually loft brothers or fifters, or other near relations, by the pulmonary confumption, as that circumftance gives reafon to fufpect a family

taint

taint or predifpofition, the cafe will, on
that account, be more dangerous.

Violent exercife may occafion the rupture of blood-veffels in the lungs, even in
thofe who have no hereditary difpofition
to fuch an accident; it ought therefore to be carefully avoided by all who
have. Violent exercife, in the fpring, is
more dangerous than in other feafons;
and, when taken at the top of high mountains, by thofe who do not ufually refide
there, it has been confidered as more dangerous than in vallies. The fudden diminution of the weight of the atmofphere,
co-operating with the exercife, renders
the veffels more apt to break. Of all
things the moft pernicious to people predifpofed to a fpitting of blood, is, playing
upon wind-inftruments. Previous to the
fpitting of blood, fome perceive an uneafinefs in the cheft, an oppreffion on the
breath, and a faltifh tafte in the fpittle;
but thefe fymptoms are not conftant.

Nothing

Nothing can be more infidious than the approaches of this difeafe fometimes are. The fubftance of the lungs, which is fo full of blood-veffels, is not fupplied fo liberally with nerves; the lungs, therefore, may be materially affected, before danger is indicated by acute pain. And it fometimes happens, that people of the make above defcribed are, in the bloom of life, and generally in the fpring of the year, feized with a flight cough, which gradually increafes, without pain, forenefs in the breaft, difficulty of refpiration, or fpitting of blood. A flow fever fupervenes every night, which remits every morning, with fweats. Thefe fymptoms augment daily; and, in fpite of early attention, and what is thought the beft advice, the unfufpecting victims gradually fink into their graves.

Thofe who by their make, or by the difeafe having in former inftances appeared in their family, are predifpofed to this complaint, ought to be peculiarly attentive in the

Q 3   article

article of diet. A fpare and cooling regimen
is the beft. They fhould avoid violent exercife, and every other exciting caufe;
and ufe the precaution of lofing blood in
the fpring. If their circumftances permit,
they ought to pafs the cold months in a
mild climate; but, if they are obliged to
remain during the winter in Great Britain,
let them wear flannel next the fkin, and
ufe every other precaution againft catching
colds.

The fourth caufe above enumerated is,
tubercles in the lungs.

The moift, foggy, and changeable weather, which prevails in Great Britain, renders its inhabitants more liable, than thofe
of milder and more uniform climates, to
catarrhs, rheumatifms, pleurifies, and
other difeafes proceeding from obftructed
perfpiration. The fame caufe fubjects the
inhabitants of Great Britain to obftructions
of the glands, fcrophulous complaints, and
tubercles

tubercles in the fubflance of the lungs.
The fcrophulous difeafe is more frequent
than is generally imagined. For one perfon in whom it appears by fwellings in the
glands below the chin, and other external
marks, many have the internal glands affected by it. This is well known to thofe
who are accuflomed to open dead bodies.
On examining the bodies of fuch as have
died of the pulmonary confumption, befides the open ulcers in the lungs, many
little hard tumours or tubercles are generally found; fome, with matter; others,
on being cut open, difcover a little blueifh
fpot, of the fize of a fmall lead fhot.
Here the fuppuration, or formation of
matter, is juft going to begin; and in fome
the tubercle is perfectly hard, and the colour whitifh, throughout its whole fubftance. Tubercles may remain for a confiderable time in the lungs, in this indolent ftate, without much inconveniency;
but, when excited to inflammation by frequent catarrhs, or other irritating caufes,

Q 4　　　matter

matter is formed, they break, and produce an ulcer. Care and attention may prevent tubercles from inflammation, or may prevent *that* from terminating in the formation of matter; but when matter is actually formed, and the tubercle has become an abfcefs, no remedy can ftop its progrefs. It muft go on till it burfts. If this happens near any of the large air-vef-fels, immediate fuffocation may enfue; but, for the moft part, the matter is coughed up.

From the circumftances above enume-rated of the delicate texture, conftant motion, and numerous blood-veffels of the lungs, it is natural to imagine, that a breach of this nature in their fubftance will be ftill more difficult to heal than a wound from an external caufe. So unquef-tionably it is; yet there are many inftances of even this kind of breach being repaired; the matter expectorated diminifhing in quan-tity every day, and the ulcer gradually healing; not, furely, by the power of medicine,

medicine, but by the conftant difpofition and tendency which exifts in nature, by infcrutable means of her own, to reftore health to the human body.

It may be proper to obferve, that thofe perfons whofe formation of body renders them moft liable to a fpitting of blood, have alfo a greater predifpofition than others to tubercles in the lungs. The dif-eafe, called the fpafmodic afthma, has been reckoned among the caufes of the pulmonary confumption. It would re-quire a much greater degree of confidence in a man's own judgment, than I have in mine, to affert, that this complaint has no tendency to produce tubercles in the lungs; but I may fay, with truth, that I have often known the fpafmodic afthma, in the moft violent degree, attended with the moft alarming fymptoms, continue to harafs the patients for a long period of time, and at length fuddenly difappear, without ever returning; the perfons who have

have been thus afflicted, enjoying perfect health for many years after. It is not probable that tubercles were formed in any of thefe cafes; and it is certain they were not in fome, whofe bodies were opened after their deaths, which happened from other diftempers, the afthma having difappeared feveral years before.

Certain eruptions of the fkin, attended with fever, particularly the fmall-pox, and ftill oftener the mealles, leave after them a foundation for the pulmonary confumption. From whichever of the caufes above enumerated this difeafe takes its origin, when once an ulcer, attended with a hectic fever, is formed in the lungs, the cafe is, in the higheft degree, dangerous. When it ends fatally, the fymptoms are, a quick pulfe, and a fenfation of cold, while the patient's fkin, to the feeling of every other perfon, is hot; irregular fhiverings, a fevere cough, expectoration of matter ftreaked with blood, morning fweats,

a cir-

a circumfcribed fpot of a crimfon colour
on the cheeks, heat of the palms of the
hands, exceffive emaciation, crooking of
the nails, fwelling of the legs, giddinefs,
delirium, foon followed by death.

Thefe fymptoms do not appear in every
cafe. Although the emaciation is greater
in this difeafe than in any other, yet the
appetite frequently remains ftrong and unimpaired to the laft; and although delirium fometimes comes before death, yet
in many cafes the fenfes feem perfect and
intire; except in one particular, that in
fpite of all the foregoing fymptoms, the
patient often entertains the fulleft hopes
of recovery to the laft moment.

Would to heaven it were as eafy to
point out the cure, as to defcribe the fymptoms of a difeafe of fuch a formidable
nature, and againft which the powers of
medicine have been directed with fuch
bad fuccefs, that there is reafon to fear,
its fatal termination has been oftener accelerated

cclerated than retarded by the means employed to remove it! To particularife the drugs which have been long in ufe, and have been honoured with the higheft encomiums for their great efficacy in healing inward bruifes, ulcers of the lungs, and confirmed confumptions, would in many inflances be pointing out, what ought to be fhunned as pernicious, and in others what ought to be neglected as futile.

Salt water, and fome of the mineral fprings, which are unqueflionably beneficial in fcrophulous and other diftempers, have been *found* hurtful, or at leaft inefficacious, in the confumption; there is no fufficient reafon to depend on a courfe of thefe, or any medicine at prefent known, for preventing or diffolving tubercles in the lungs. Mercury, which has been found fo powerful in difpofing other ulcers to heal, has no good effect on ulcers of that organ;—though fome phyficians imagine it may be of fervice in the beginning to
diffolve

diffolve tubercles, before they begin to suppurate; but as there is no abfolute evidence, during life, of indolent tubercles being formed, there can be none that mercury cures them.

Various kinds of gums, with the natural and artificial balfams, were long fuppofed to promote the healing of external wounds and ulcers, and on that account were made the bafis of a vaft variety of ointments and plaifters. It was afterwards imagined, that the fame remedies, adminiftered internally, would have the fame effect on internal ulcers; and of courfe many of thofe gums and balfams were prefcribed in various forms for the pulmonary confumption. The reafoning on which this practice was eftablifhed, however, feems a little fhallow, and is far from being conclufive; for although it were granted, that thefe balfams contributed to the cure of wounds, when applied directly to the part, it does

7   not

not follow that they could carry their healing powers, unimpaired, from the ftomach to the lungs, through the whole procefs of digeftion. But more accurate furgery having made it manifeft, that the granulations which fpring up to fupply the lofs of fubftance in external wounds, and the healing or fkinning over of all kinds of fores, proceeds from no active virtue in the plaifters or ointments with which they are dreffed, but is entirely the work of nature, and beft performed when the mildeft fubftances, or even dry lint only is applied; and that heating gums, refins, and balfams, rather retard than promote their cure; the internal ufe of fuch remedies ought to be rejected now, on the fame principles they were adapted formerly.

No kind of reafoning ought to have weight, when oppofed by fair experience. But phyficians have formed contrary and oppofite conclufions, with refpect to the

effect

effect of the natural and artificial balfams,
even when they have laid all theory and
reafoning afide, and decided on their
powers from practice and experiment
only. This is fufficient to prove, at leaft,
that their efficacy is very problematical.
For my own part, after the faireft trials,
and the moft accurate obfervations I have
been able to make, I cannot fay that I
ever knew them of fervice in any hectic
complaint proceeding from an ulcer in the
lungs; and I have generally found thofe
phyficians, on whofe judgment I have more
reliance than on my own, of the fame
opinion.

It is far from being uncommon to fee
a cure retarded, not to fay any thing
ftronger, by the means employed to
haften it; and phyficians who found their
practice on theoretical reafonings, are not
the only perfons to whom this misfortune may happen. Thofe who profefs to
take experience for their fole guide, if

it

it is not directed by candour, and enlightened by natural fagacity, are liable to
the fame. A man may, for twenty years,
order a medicine, which has in every in-
stance done a little harm, though not always fo much as to prevent nature from
removing the complaint at laft; and if the
reputation of this medicine fhould ever be
attacked, he may bring his twenty years
experience in fupport of it. It ought to be
remembered, that as often as the animal
conflitution is put out of order, by accident
or diftemper, nature endeavours to reftore
health. Happily fhe has many refources,
and various methods of accomplifhing her
purpofe; and very often fhe fucceeds beft
without medical affiftance. Put medical
affiftance being given, fhe frequently fucceeds *notwithftanding*; and it fometimes
happens, that both phyfician and patient
are convinced, that the means which did
not prevent have actually performed the
cure.

A peafant

A peasant is seized with a shivering, followed by feverishness, and accompanied with a slight cough—he goes to bed, and excessive heat and thirst prompt him to drink plentifully of plain water; on the second or third day a copious sweat bursts from all his pores, and terminates the disorder. A person of fortune is seized with the same symptoms, arising from the same cause, and which would have been cured by the same means, in the same space of time; but the apothecary is called, who immediately sends pectoral linctuses to remove the cough, and afterwards gives a vomit, to remove the nausea which the linctuses have occasioned: the heat and fever augment; the physician is called; he orders the patient to be blooded, to abate the violence of the fever, and gives a little physic on some other account. All this prevents the natural crisis by sweat; and the patient being farther teased by draughts or powders every two or three hours, nature cannot shake off the fever so

VOL. II. R soon

foon by fix or feven days, as fhe would
have done had fhe been left to herfelf. She
generally' docs her bufinefs at laft, however; and then the phyfician and apothecary glory in the happy effects of their
fkill, and receive the grateful thanks of
their patient for having cured him of a
dangerous fever.

Every body of common penetration, at
all converfant in medical matters, muft
have feen enough to convince them that
the above defcription is not exaggerated;
but it is not to be inferred from this, that
the art of medicine is of no ufe to mankind. There are many difeafes in which
nature finks, without medical affiftance. It
is the part of the penetrating and experienced phyfician to diftinguifh thefe from
others, and leave it to the knavifh and
weak to affume the merit of cures in cafes
where they know, or ought to know, that
medicine can do nothing.

Some

Some phyficians, who have abandoned the other refins and gums, as ufelefs or hurtful in hectic complaints, ftill adhere to myrrh as a beneficial medicine ; but from what I can learn, the cafes in which. this gum has been thought ferviceable, are hectic complaints, from debility, in confequence of exceffive evacuations of various kinds, and not proceeding from ulcerated lungs. After it is fully eftablifhed that myrrh is of ufe in fuch inftances, it will ftill be worthy of inveftigation, whether it is of more or lefs than Jefuits bark. I have repeatedly mentioned blood-letting, and a fparc, diluting regimen, as the moft powerful means of preventing and curing all affections of the lungs that depend on inflammation. In the cafe of external wounds, or bruifes of the lungs, this method facilitates the immediate cure by the firft intention. It is the chief thing to be depended on for the cure of pleurifies ; and it is often owing to a neglect, or too fparing an ufe of this evacuation, that the com-

R 2

plaint terminates in an abfcefs. In people
- predifpofed by the form of their bodies, or
the nature of their conftitutions, to a fpitting
of blood, it may prevent the turgid veffels
from burfting; and in thofe who have tubercles in the lungs, it is of the greateft
utility, by preventing thofe tumours from
inflaming, and becoming ulcers; but after
the ulcers are actually formed, I have great
doubts with regard to the propriety of attempting a cure by repeated bleedings,
even in fmall quantities. This method has
been often tried; but I fear the fuccefs with
which it has been attended, gives no encouragement to continue the practice. That
fymptoms may be fuch, in every period of
this difeafe, as to require this evacuation,
is not to be denied; but there is a great
difference in the application of what is confidered as an occafional palliative, and that
from which we expect a radical cure. In
the one cafe, it will only be ufed when fome
particular fymptom ftrongly urges; in the
other, it will be ufed at ftated intervals,
whether

whether the symptoms press or not; and
may tend to weaken the already debilitated
patient, without our having the consolation
of knowing, with certainty, that it has had
any other effect.

Blisters do not weaken so much; they
are of undoubted use in pleurisies; perhaps,
by exciting external inflammation, they
may contribute to draw off the inflamma-
tory disposition within the breast: perhaps—
But in whatever way they act, I imagine
I have frequently seen blisters and setons,
particularly the latter, of considerable service, even after the symptoms indicated the
existence of an ulcer in the lungs.

As for the numerous forms of electuaries,
lohochs, and linctuses, composed of oils,
gums, and syrups, and by the courtesy of
dispensatory writers called *pectoral*; I am
convinced they are of no manner of service
in this complaint, and seldom have any
other effect than that of loading the sto-

mach,

mach, and impairing the digeftion of falutary food. So far from being of any permanent fervice to the difeafe, they cannot be depended on for giving even a temporary relief to the cough; when that fymptom becomes troublefome, gentle opiates will be found the beft palliatives. Some practitioners object to thefe medicines, on a fuppofition that they check expectoration; but they only feem to have this effect, by lulling the irritation to cough; the fame quantity will be expectorated in the morning, after the influence of the opiate is over. It is furely better that the matter fhould accumulate, and the patient fpit it up at once, than allow him to be kept from reft, and teafed with coughing and fpitting through the whole night. Thefe palliatives, however, are to be managed with great caution; never exhibited while the patient enjoys a tolerable fhare of *natural* reft. Small dofes fhould be given at firft, and not increafed without abfolute neceffity. Exhibited in this manner, they cannot do harm; and thofe who reject the
affiftance

affiftance of a clafs of medicines, which
afford eafe and tranquillity in the moft de-
plorible ftate of this difeafe, ought to give
better proofs than have hitherto appeared,
that they are able to procure their patients
more valuable and lafting comforts than
thofe they deprive them of.

The known efficacy of the Peruvian
bark, in many diftempers, efpecially in intermittent fevers; the remiffion of the fymptoms, which happens regularly every day at a
particular ftage of the pulmonary confumption, and in fome degree gives it the appearance of an intermittent, joined to the
failure of all other remedies, prompted
phyficians to make trial of that noble medicine in this difeafe. In confequence of
thefe trials, the bark is now pretty generally acknowledged to be ferviceable in
hectical complaints, proceeding from debility, and other caufes, exclufive of ulcerated lungs; but when the difeafe proceeds
from this caufe, the bark is fuppofed, by

R 4   fome

some very refpectable phyficians, always to
do harm. I am moft clearly of the firft
opinion, and perhaps it would not become
me to difpute the fecond. It may be permitted, however, to obferve, that the moft
difcerning practitioners may be led into a
notion, that a very fafe medicine does harm,
when it is exhibited at the worft ftage of a
difcafe, in which hardly any medicine
whatever has been found to do good. In
every ftage of this difeafe, elixir of vitriol
may be ufed. It is a pleafant and fafe medicine, but particularly efficacious when
the patient is troubled with wafting fweats.

Having, in obedience to your requeft,
delivered my fentiments freely, you will
perceive, that, befides the objections already mentioned to the perfon under whofe
care our friend is at prefent, I cannot approve of his being directed to take fo many
drugs, or of his being detained in town, at
a feafon when he may enjoy, in the country, what is preferable to all medicine; I
mean

mean air, exercife, and, let me even add, diet.

Had I known of our friend's complaints earlier, I fhould have advifed him to have met the advancing fpring in the South of France; but at the feafon in which you will receive this letter, the moderate warmth, and refrefhing verdure of England, are preferable to the fultry heats and fcorched fields of the South. From the view I have of his complaints, I can have no hefitation in advifing you to endeavour to prevail on him to quit his drugs, and to leave London without delay. Since he bears riding on horfeback fo well, let him enjoy that exercife in an atmofphere freed from the fmoke of the town, and impregnated with the flavour of rifing plants and green herbage; a flavour which may with more truth be called *pectoral*, than any of the heating refins, or loathfome oils, on which that term has been proftituted. Let him pafs the fummer in drinking the waters, and riding around the environs of Briftol. It will be eafy for him to find a houfe in the free air of the country, at fome diftance from that town; and it will be of ufe to have an additional reafon for rifing early, and riding every morning. It is of the greateft importance that he continue that exercife every day that the weather will permit : a little cloudinefs of the fky fhould not fright him from it ; there is no danger of catching cold during the continuation of that movement which affifts digeftion, promotes the determination of blood from the lungs to the furface of the body, and is more falutary in the morning than after dinner.

With refpect to diet, he fhould carefully obferve the important rule of taking food frequently, in fmall quantities, and never making a full meal ; that the digeftive organs may not be overpowered, or the veffels charged with too large a quantity of chyle at a time ; which never fails to bring on on oppreffive breathing, and augments the fever and flufhing, which in fome degree fucceeds every repaft.

Since all kinds of milk are found to difa-gree with his conflitution, that nourifh-ment, which is in general fo well adapted to fimilar complaints, mufl be omitted, and light broths, with vegetable food, particu-larly of the farinaceous kind, fubflituted in its place.

Acids, efpecially the native acid of vege-tables, are remarkably agreeable and re-frefhing to all who labour under the heat, oppreffion, and languor, which accompany hectic complaints. It is furprifing what a quantity of the juice of lemons the confli-tution will bear, without any inconveni-ency, when it is accuftomed to it by de-grees ; and in thofe cafes where it does not occafion pains in the ftomach and bowels, or other immediate inconveniencies, it has been thought to have a good effect in abat-ing the force of the hectic fever.

2 I have

I have met with two cafes, fince I have been laft abroad, in both of which there feemed to be a quicker recovery than I ever faw, from the fame fymptoms. The firft was that of a young lady, of about feventeen years of age, and apparently of a very healthy conftitution. In bad weather, during the fpring, fhe caught cold: this being neglected in the beginning, gradually grew worfe. When phyficians were at length confulted, their prefcriptions feemed to have as bad an effect as her own neglect. By the middle of fummer her cough was inceffant, accompanied with hectic fever and flufhings, irregular fhiverings, morning fweats, emaciation, expectoration of purulent phlegm ftreaked with blood, and every indication of an open ulcer in the lungs. In this defperate ftate fhe was carried from the town to a finely fituated village in Switzerland, where, for feveral months, fhe lived in the middle of a vineyard, on ripe grapes and bread. She had been directed to a milk and vegetable diet

in

in general. Her own tafte inclined her to
the grapes, which fhe continued, on finding, that, with this diet only, fhe was lefs languid, and of a more natural coolnefs, and that
the cough, fever, and all the other symptoms
gradually abated. She feemed to be brought
from the jaws of death by the change of air,
and this regimen only; and fhe returned to
her own home in high fpirits, and with the
look and vigour of health. The enfuing
winter, after being heated with dancing at
the houfe of a friend, fhe walked home in
a cold night; the cough, fpitting of blood,
and other fymptoms immediately returned,
and fhe died three months after.

In the other cafe, there was not fuch a
degree of fever, but there was an expectoration of matter, frequently ftreaked with
blood, and evident figns of an ulcer in the
lungs. The perfon who laboured under
thefe fymptoms, had tried the ufual remedies of pectorals, pills, linctufes, &c. with
the ufual fuccefs. He grew daily worfe.
He

He had formerly found much relief from
bleeding, but had left it off for many
months, on a fuppofition that it had loft all
effect; and he had allowed an iffue to be
healed, on the fame fuppofition; though
he ftill perfevered in a milk regimen. I
mentioned to him the cafe of the young.
lady, as it is above recited. He immediately took the refolution to confine himfelf
to bread and grapes for almoft his only
food. I advifed him at the fame time to
have the iffue opened, and to continue that
drain for fome time; but this he did not
comply with. He forfook, however, the
town for the country, and paffed as much
of the morning on horfeback, as he could
bear without fatigue. He foon was able
to bear more; and after about three weeks
or a month, his cough had greatly abated.
When he had perfifted in this regimen between two and three months, he had very
little cough; and what he fpit up was pure
phlegm, unmixed with blood or matter.
He has now been well above a year; and
                                    although

although I underftand that he occafionally
takes animal food, he has hitherto felt no
inconveniency from it. He paffed the
fecond autumn, as he had done the firft, at
a houfe in the country, furrounded with
vineyards. The greater part of his food
confifted of ripe grapes and bread. With
fuch a diet, he had not occafion for much
drink of any kind; what he ufed was
fimple water, and he made an ample pro-
vifion of grapes for the fucceeding winter.

Though I have no idea that there is any
fpecific virtue in grapes, for the cure of
the pulmonary confumption, or that they
are greatly preferable to fome other cooling,
fub-acid, mild fruit, equally agreeable to the
tafte, provided any fuch can be found ; yet
I thought it right to particularize what was
ufed on thofe two occafions; leaving it to
others to determine, what fhare of the
happy confequences I have enumerated
were owing to the change of air, how much
may have flowed from the exercife, how
much

much from the regimen, and whether there
is reafon to think, that the favourable turn
in both cafes depended on other circumftances, unobferved by me.

I have now, my dear Sir, complied with
your requeft; and although I have endeavoured to avoid technical verbofity, and all
unneceffary detail, yet I find my letter has
fwelled to a greater fize than I expected.
I fhall be exceedingly happy to hear that
any hint I have given has been ferviceable to
our friend. If the cough fhould ftill continue,
after he has paffed two or three months at
Briftol, I imagine the moft effectual thing
he can do will be, to take a voyage to this
place; he will by that means efcape the
feverity of a Britifh winter. The voyage
itfelf will be of fervice, and at the end of it
he will have the benefit of the mild air of
the Campagna Felice, be refrefhed and
nourifhed by the fineft grapes, and, when
tired of riding, he will have continual opportunities of failing in this charming bay.

LETTER LXIII.

AS I was walking a few days since in the street with two of our countrymen, T—— and N——, we met some people carrying the corpse of a man on an open bier, and others following in a kind of procession. The deceased was a tradesman, whose widow had bestowed the utmost attention in dressing him to the greatest advantage on this solemn occasion; he had a perfectly new suit of clothes, a laced hat upon his head, ruffles, his hair finely powdered, and a large blooming nosegay in his left hand, while the right was very gracefully stuck in his side. It is the custom at Naples to carry every body to church in full dress soon after their death, and the nearest relations display the magnitude of their

Vol. II.   S   grief

grief by the magnificent manner in which
they decorate the corpfe. This poor woman, it feems, was quite inconfolable,
and had ornamented the body of her late
hufband with a profufion fhe could ill
afford. When the corpfe arrives in church,
the fervice is read over it. That ceremony
being performed, and the body carried
home, it is confidered as having no farther
occafion for fine clothes, but is generally
ftript to the fhirt, and buried privately.

" Can any thing be more ridiculous,"
fays N——, " than to trick a man out in
" his beft clothes after his death?" " No-
" thing," replied T——; " unlefs it be
" to order a fantaftical drefs at a greater
" expence on purpofe, as if the dead
" would not be fatisfied with the clothes
" they wore when alive, but delighted in
" long flowing robes in a particular ftyle
" of their own."

T—— has long refided abroad, and
now prefers many foreign cuftoms to thofe
of

of his own country, which frequently involves him in difputes with his countrymen.

The Princefs of —— drove paft.
" There fhe goes," fays N——, " with
" her cavalieros, her volantis, and all
" the fplendour of a fovereign; yet the
" wife of a plain Englifh gentleman is in
" a far more enviable fituation. With all
" her titles and her high rank, fhe is a
" meer fervant of the Queen's, a depen-
" dant on the caprice of another; a frown
" from her Majefty would annihilate
" her." " Thofe who are *nothing*, ex-
" clufive of court favour," replied T——,
" ought not be cenfured for devoting their
" time to court attendance. But did you
" never hear of any who are dazzled
" with the glitter of court fhackels in the
" boafted land of liberty; people whom
" riches, rank, and the moft flattering
" favours of fortune cannot make inde-
" pendent; whofe minds feem the more

" abject,

" abject, as their fituation lays them un-
" der the lefs neceffity of remaining in
" fervitude; who, withered with age, and
" repining with envy, facrifice every do-
" meftic duty, and ftalk around the man-
" fions of royalty, as ghofts are faid to
" haunt thofe abodes in which they moft
" delighted when they enjoyed life and
" vigour!"   " Well, well," fays N——,
" let us fay no more about them, fince
" we are agreed, that, of all the old tapef-
" try of courts, thofe grotefque figures,
" who, without the confidence of thofe
" they ferve, continue to the laft exhibit-
" ing their antique countenances at birth-
" day balls, and in the affemblies of youth
" and beauty, are the moft ridiculous."
At that inftant the Queen paffed in her
coach with the royal children, and N——
made fome comparative remarks in his
ufual flyle; to which T—— replied,. " In
" this particular I acknowledge the hap-
" pinefs of Great Britain. I prefume not
" to make comparifons; the great character
                                    " you

" you have mentioned defies cenfure,
" and is far fuperior to my praife. But
" I muſt obferve, it appears fingular that
" you, who affect to defpife all other
" countries, and feem of opinion, that
" what is moſt valuable in nature is always
" the product of *England*, fhould bring
" your brighteſt illuſtration of that opinion
" from *Germany*."

T——, perceiving the advantage he
had gained over his antagoniſt, proceeded
vigorouſly to cenfure, what he called, the
abfurd partiality of the Engliſh in their
own favour; and obferved, that it would
be fortunate for them, if the other nations
of Europe would allow them but a few
of the numerous good qualities which they
fo laviſhly attribute to themfelves. He
feverely attacked the common people, and
denied them even the character of good-
nature, which they have been thought to
poſſefs in an eminent degree. He declared
them to be rough and infolent in

S 3   their

their manners (for the truth of this he appealed to the opinion of all their neighbours), cruel in their difpofitions (as a proof of which he inflanced fome of their favourite diverfions), and abfurd in their prejudices, which appears by their hatred and contempt of other nations; by all of whom, he afferted, they were in return moft cordially abhorred. "How, indeed, "can it be otherwife," continued he, "con-"fidering the rough, boifterous nature of "their weather?" He then expatiated on the fertility of Italy, and the mild ferenity of the climate; to which he partly attributed the fertile genius and mild character of the Italians. "No doubt," he faid, "moral caufes might contribute to the fame "effect; for more pains were taken to cul-"tivate and encourage good and quiet dif-"pofitions in the common people here than "in England. They were accuftomed to "perform their religious duties more regu-"larly; they had frequent opportunities of "hearing the moft excellent mufic in the

8 . "churches;

" churches; they were inftructed in hiftory
" by orators in the ftreet, and were made
" acquainted with the beauties of their
" beft.poets in the fame manner. All thefe
" caufes united muft neceffarily enlarge
" their minds, and make them the moft
" gentle, humane, and ingenious people in
" the world." N—— fhook his head, as if
he laid little ftrefs on the others reafoning.
For my own part, I remained filent, being
defirous that the difpute fhould go on between the two who had begun it.

Continuing our walk a little without
the town, we faw a crowd of people looking over a wall, which formed one fide of
a fquare, exprefsly built for the purpofe of
bating cattle with bull dogs. It is imagined that this renders their flefh more
tender and agreeable to the tafte ; and this
is confidered as a fufficient reafon for tor-
turing great numbers of bulls, oxen, and
cows, before they are flaughtered for the
markets; we found a multitude of fpectators enjoying this amufement. "Pray,"
fays

says Mr. N——, addressing himself to
T——, " do you imagine this humane
" practice, and the complacency which
" these refined spectators seem to take in
" beholding it, proceed from the mild-
" ness of the climate, the pains bestowed
" in teaching the people the duties of chris-
" tianity, the enlargement of their minds
" by history and poetry, or from the gen-
" tle influence of music upon their dif-
" politions?" Then turning from Mr.
T—— to me, he continued, " Not fatif-
" fied with knocking the poor animals on
" the head, those unfeeling epicures put
" them to an hour's additional torture,
" merely to gratify a caprice of their cor-
" rupted palates."

" Of all subjects," replied T——, recovering himself from the confusion into
which N——'s questions had thrown him,
" those who take upon them to be the
" panegyrists of the English nation, ought
" to avoid mentioning that species of epi-
                    " curifm

" curifm which depends on eating, left
" they be put in mind of whipping pigs
" to death, their manner of collaring
" brawn, crimping fifh, and other re-
" finements peculiar to that humane good-
" natured people."

N—— was juft going to reply, when a
a large bull, rendered outrageous by the
ftones which the populace were throwing
at him, ran fuddenly towards the gate at
the inflant the keepers were opening it
on fome other account; which threw them
into fuch confufion, that they had not time
to fhut it before the bull burft out on the
multitude. He now became an object of
terror to thofe who the moment before
had looked on him as an object of mirth.
The mighty lords of the creation, who
confider other animals as formed entirely
for *their paftime, their attire, their food,*
fled in crowds from one quadruped, and
would gladly have fallen on their knees
and worfhipped him, like fo many Egyp-
tians

tians adoring Apis, if by fo doing they
could have hoped to deprecate the juft
wrath of the incenfed animal.—They
found fafety at length, not in their own
courage or addrefs, but in the fuperior
boldnefs and agility of other animals, who
were leagued with man againft him. He
was furrounded by dogs, who attacked him
on all fides—he killed fome outright, toff-
ed and wounded many more; but perceiving his own ftrength diminifhing, and
the number of his enemies increafing
every moment, he threw himfelf into the
fea, and there found a temporary protection
from the fury of his perfecutors.—But the
dogs were infligated to follow; they at
length drove him from this laft afylum;
and the poor, torn, bleeding, exhaufted
animal was forced afhore, three or four
of the moft furious of the dogs hanging
at different parts of his head and neck.
When they were removed, he raifed his
honeft countenance, and threw an indig-
nant

nant look upon the rabble, as if to upbraid them for fuch a return for his own labours, and all the effential fervices which his whole fpecies render to mankind. Upon my foul I felt the reproach. We could not bear his looks, but fneaked away without feeling much pride on account of our near connection with thofe lords of the creation, whom we had juft beheld exerting their prerogative.

We walked along a confiderable time without fpeaking. N——— broke filence at laft: " Well," faid he, " thofe amiable " creatures whom we have quitted, are " what they call human beings;—they " are more, they are Neapolitans, men " who are moved with the concord of " fweet founds; from which I conclude " (Shakefpear may fay what he pleafes), that " fuch men are as fit for treafons, ftra- " tagems, and fpoils, as thofe who never " heard fofter melody than that of mar- " row-bones and cleavers."

" This

" This fondnefs for barbarous amufe-
" ments," faid I, " cannot be ftated ex-
" clufively to the account of Neapo-
" litans, of Englifh, or of any other par-
" ticular people. I am afraid the charge
" lies againft mankind in general; from
" whatever motive it arifes, a large pro-
" portion of the individuals in all coun-
" tries have difplayed a decided tafte for
" diverfions which may be ranged in this
" clafs."

" It ought to be remembered, how-
" ever," fays T——, " that thofe fellows
" with their dogs, who have been tor-
" menting the bull, are butchers, and the
" loweft of the vulgar of this country;
" whereas, among thofe who order fifh to
" be crimped, and pigs to be whipped
" to death, as well as among thofe
" who formerly attended Broughton's
" amphitheatre, and ftill attend cockpits,
" will be found people of the firft rank
" in England."

G   " Pray,"

" Pray," faid N——, addrefling himfelf to me, " did you ever fee a cocagna?"

I acknowledged I never had.

" Then," continued he, " I beg leave
" to give you an idea of it. It is a Neapo-
" litan entertainment, relifhed by people
" of the firft rank in this polifhed country;
" where the very vagrants in the ftreet are
" inftruĉled in hiftory, and the human
" mind is refined by poetry, foftened by
" mufic, and elevated by religion. The
" cocagna—Pray mark me—the cocagna
" is an entertainment given to the people
" four fucceeding Sundays during the car-
" nival. Oppofite to the palace, a kind of
" wooden amphitheatré is erecĉted. This
" being covered with branches of trees,
" bufhes, and various plants, real and ar-
" tificial, has the appearance of a green
" hill. On this hill are little buildings,
" ornamented with pillars of loaves of
" bread, with joints of meat, and dried
" fifh,

" fifh, varnifhed, and curioufly arranged
" by way of capitals. Among the trees
" and bufhes are fome oxen, a confiderable
" number of calves, fheep, hogs, and
" lambs, all alive, and tied to pofts. There
" are, befides, a great number of living tur-
" kies, geefe, hens, pigeons, and other
" fowls, nailed by the wings to the fcaffold-
" ing. Certain Heathen Deities appear
" alfo occafionally upon this hill, but not
" with a defign to protect it, as you fhall
" fee immediately. The guards are drawn
" up in three ranks, to keep off the po-
" pulace. The Royal Family, with all
" the nobility of the court, crowd the win-
" dows and balconies of the palace, to en-
" joy this magnificent fight. When his Ma-
" jefty waves his handkerchief, the guards
" open to the right and left ; the rabble
" pour in from all quarters, and the en-
" tertainment commences. You may eafily
" conceive what a delightful fight it muft
" be, to fee feveral thoufand hungry, half-
" naked lazzaroni rufh in like a torrent, de-
" ftroy

" ſtroy the whole fabric of loaves, fiſhes,
" and joints of meat; overturn the Hea-
" then Deities, *for the honour of Chriſ-*
" *tianity*; pluck the fowls, at the expence
" of their wings, from the poſts to which
" they were nailed; and, in the fury of their
" ſtruggling and fighting for their prey,
" often tearing the miſerable animals to
" pieces, and ſometimes ſtabbing each
" other."

" You ought, in candour, to add," interrupted Mr. T——, " that, though for-
" merly they were fixed to the poſts
" alive, yet of late the larger cattle have
" been previouſly killed."——" And pray,
" my good Sir," ſaid N——, " will you
" be ſo obliging as to inform me, what
" crime the poor lambs and fowls have
" committed, that they ſhould be torn in
" pieces alive ?" " This piece of huma-
" nity," continued he, " recalls to my
" memory a ſimilar inſtance, in a certain
" ingenious

" ingenious gentleman, who propofed, as
" the beft and moft effectual method of
" fweeping chimnies, to place a large
" goofe at the top; and then, by a ftring
" tied around her feet, to pull the animal
" gently down to the hearth. The faga-
" cious projector afferted, that the goofe,
" being extremely averfe to this method
" of entering a houfe, would ftruggle
" againft it with all her might; and, during
" this refiftance, would move her wings
" with fuch force and rapidity, as could
" not fail to fweep the chimney com-
" pletely." " Good God, Sir," cried a
lady, who was prefent when this new method was propofed, " How cruel would that
" be to the poor goofe!" " Why, Madam,"
replied the gentleman, " if you think my
" method cruel to the goofe, a couple of
" ducks will do."

LETTER LXIV.

Naples.

ON the firſt Sunday of May, we had an opportunity of ſeeing the famous Neapolitan miracle, of the liquefaction of Saint Januarius's blood, performed. This Saint, you know, is the patron of Naples; which circumſtance alone forms a ſtrong preſumption of his being a Saint of very conſiderable power and efficacy; for it is not to be imagined that the care of a city, like Naples, which is threatened every moment with deſtruction from Mount Veſuvius, would be entruſted to an under-ſtrapper. Indeed there has, on ſome occaſions, been reaſon to fear, that, great and powerful as this Saint is, the Dæmon of the mountain would have got the better of him; however, as Saint Januarius has been able to protect them hitherto, and is ſup-

VOL. II.   T   poſed

pofed to be improved in the fcience of de-
fence by long practice, the Neapolitans
think it more prudent to abide by him than
to choofe another; who, though he may
poffibly be of higher rank, and older ftanding, cannot have equal experience in this
particular kind of warfare.

Saint Januarius fuffered martyrdom about
the end of the third century. When he
was beheaded, a pious lady of this city
caught about an ounce of his blood, which
has been carefully preferved in a bottle ever
fince, without having loft a fingle grain of
its weight. This of itfelf, were it equally
demonftrable, might be confidered as a
greater miracle than the circumftance on
which the Neapolitans lay the whole ftrefs,
viz. that the blood which has congealed,
and acquired a folid form by age, is no
fooner brought near the head of the Saint,
than, as a mark of veneration, it immediately liquefies. This experiment is made
three different times every year, and is

2   confidered

bonfidered by the Neapolitans as a miracle of the firft magnitude.

As the divinity of no other religion whatever is any longer attempted to be proved by frefh miracles, but all are now trufted to their own internal evidence, and to thofe wrought at a former period, this miracle of Saint Januarius is probably the more admired on account of its being the only one, except tranfubftantiation, which remains ftill in ufe, out of the vaft abundance faid to have been performed at various periods in fupport of the Roman Catholic faith. The latter is unqueftionably the greater miracle of the two; for to change a wafer into flefh and blood, is more extraordinary than to liquefy any fubftance whatever: Yet I once imagined the liquefaction had rather the advantage in this particular; that the change is more obvious to the fenfes. But I have lately been otherwife inftructed, by an ingenious perfon, who was formerly a Jefuit. On fomebody (not

T 2   me,

me, for I never do make objections in matters of faith) having obferved, That it was
unfortunate that the great change operated
on the wafer in tranfubftantiation, was not
vifible, the perfon above alluded to pronounced the miracle to be much greater on
that account. " For pray, Sir," faid he,
addreffing himfelf to the objector, " fup-
" pofe I fhould immediately turn that fowl,
" pointing to a turkey which was at that
" moment ftalking paft; fuppofe I fhould
" immediately turn that fowl into a wo-
" man, would you not think it very ex-
" traordinary?" " Certainly," replied the
other. " Well, Sir, but after the change
" is actually made, and the fowl has to all
" intents and purpofes become a woman,
" if it ftill retained the appearance of a
" turkey, you muft acknowledge *that*
" would be more extraordinary ftill. In
" the fame manner," continued he, " in
" the celebration of mafs, the converfion
" of the wafer into the real body and blood
8   " of

" of Jefus Chrift, is a great miracle, and
" highly to be venerated; but, after this
" wonderful change has actually taken
" place, that the real body of Chrift
" fhould, even in the eyes of the fharpeft
" fighted fpectators, ftill retain its ori-
" ginal form of a wafer, is a great deal
" more amazing and ftupendous."

But, however great a fuperiority the miracle
of tranfubftantiation may have over that of
St. Januarius, in the opinion of Roman
Catholics in general, the Neapolitans imagine the latter is fufficient to convert infidels, and put heretics out of countenance.
A zealous believer of this country, having
defcribed the miracle, breaks out into the
following exclamations : " O illuftre me-
" moria ! O verità irrefragabile ! vengano
" gli Heretici, vengano, e Stupifcano,
" ed aprano gli occhi alla verità Cattolica,
" et Evangelica ; Baftarebbe quefto fangue
" di S. Gennaro fola à fare teftimonia
" della Fede. E poffibile, che a tanto, et

T 3   " fi

" fi famofo miraculo non fi converta tutta
" la Gentilità, ed Infedeltà alla verità Cat-
" tolica della Romana chiefa ?" Though I
am not fuch an enthufiaftic admirer of the
performance as this author, yet, on the
other hand, I do not think that Proteflants,
however much they may be convinced it is
a trick, have any right to call it a *clumfy
trick*, without explaining in what it confifts. This is a liberty which fome travellers of great eminence have taken. Others
have afferted, that the fubftance in the
bottle, which is exhibited for the blood of
the Saint, is fomething naturally folid, but
which melts with a fmall degree of heat.
When it is firft brought out of the cold
chapel, fay thofe gentlemen, it is in its natural folid ftate; but when brought before
the Saint by the prieft, and rubbed between
his warm hands, and breathed upon for
fome time, it melts ; and this is the whole
myftery. Though I find myfelf unable to
explain on what principle the liquefaction
depends,

depends, I am fully convinced that it muft
be fomething different from this; for I
have it from the moft fatisfactory authority,
from thofe who had opportunities of knowing, and who believe no more in the miracle than you do, that this congealed mafs
has fometimes been found in a liquid ftate
in cold weather, before it was touched by
the Prieft, or brought near the head of the
Saint ; and that, on other occafions, it has
remained folid when brought before him,
notwithftanding all the efforts of the Prieft
to melt it. When this happens, the fuperftitious, which, at a very moderate calcu-
lation, comprehends ninety-nine in a hundred of the inhabitants of this city, are
thrown into the utmoft confternation, and
are fometimes wrought up by their fears
into a ftate of mind which is highly dangerous both to their civil and ecclefiaftical
governors. It is true, that this happens but
feldom ; for, in general, the fubftance in the
phial, whatever it may be, is in a folid
form in the chapel, and becomes liquid

when brought before the Saint; but as this is not always the cafe, it affords reafon to believe, that, whatever may have been the cafe when this miracle or trick, call it which you pleafe, was firft exhibited, the principle on which it depends has fomehow or other been loft, and is not now underftood fully even by the Priefts themfelves; or elfe they are not now fo expert, as formerly, in preparing the fubftance which reprefents the Saint's blood, fo as to make it remain folid when it ought, and liquefy the inftant it is required.

The head and blood of the Saint are kept in a kind of prefs, with folding doors of filver, in the chapel of St. Januarius, belonging to the cathedral church. The real head is probably not fo frefh, and well preferved, as the blood; and on that account is not expofed to the eyes of the public, but inclofed in a large filver buft, gilt and enriched with jewels of high value. This being what appears to the people, their

idea

idea of the Saint's features and complexion are taken entirely from the buft.

The blood is kept in a fmall repofitory by itfelf.

About mid-day, the buft, inclofing the real head, was brought with great folemnity, and placed under a kind of portico, open on all fides, that the different communities, which come in proceffion, may be able to traverfe it, and that the people may have the comfort of beholding the miracle. The proceffions of that folemn day were innumerable; all the ftreets of Naples were crowded with the various orders of ecclefiaftics, dreffed in their richeft robes. The monks of each convent were muftered under their own particular banners. A fplendid crofs was carried before each proceffion; and the images, in maffy filver, of the Saints, peculiarly patronifing the convents, followed the crofs. In this order they marched from the convents to the pavilion,

pavilion, under which the head of St. Januarius was placed, and having done due
obeifance to that great projector of this
city, they marched back by a different
route, in the fame order, to their convent.
But as there are a great many convents in
Naples, and a great number of monks in
each convent, though the proceffions began foon after mid-day, the evening was
well advanced before the laft of them had
paffed. The grand proceffion of all began
when the others had finifhed. It was compofed of a numerous body of clergy, and
an immenfe multitude of people of all ranks,
headed by the archbifhop of Naples himfelf, who carried the phial containing the
blood of the Saint. The D— of H——
and I accompanied Sir W—— H—— to a
houfe directly oppofite to the portico, where
the facred head was placed. We there
found a large affembly of Neapolitan nobility. A magnificent robe of velvet, richly
embroidered, was thrown over the fhoulders
of the buft; a mitre, refulgent with jewels,
was

was placed on its head. The archbifhop,
with a folemn pace, and a look full of awe
and veneration, approached, holding forth
the facred phial which contained the precious lump of blood. He addreffed the
Saint in the humbleft manner, fervently
praying that he would gracioufly conde-
fcend to manifeft his regard to his faithful
votaries the people of Naples, by the ufual
token of ordering that lump of his facred
blood to affume its natural and original
form. In thofe prayers he was joined by
the multitude around, particularly by the
women; of whom there feemed more than
their proportion. My curiofity prompted
me to leave the balcony, and mingle with
the multitude. I got by degrees quite near
the buft. Twenty minutes had already
elapfed, fince the archbifhop had been praying with all poffible earneftnefs, and turning the phial around and around without
any effect. An old monk ftood near the
archbifhop, and was at the utmoft pains to
inftruct him how to handle, chafe, and rub
                                                                                the

the phial; he frequently took it into his own hands, but his manœuvres were as ineffectual as thofe of the archbifhop. By this time the people had become exceedingly noify; the women were quite hoarfe with praying; the monk continued his operations with increafed zeal; and the archbifhop was all over in a profufe fweat with vexation. In whatever light the failure of the miracle might appear to others, it was a very ferious matter to him; becaufe the people confider fuch an event as a proof of the Saint's difpleafure, and a certain indication that fome dreadful calamity will enfue. This was the firft opportunity he had had of officiating fince his nomination to the fee. There was no knowing what fancy might have entered into the heads of a fuperftitious populace; they might have imagined, or his enemies might have infinuated, that the failure of the miracle proceeded from St. Januarius's difapprobation of the perfon in whofe hands it was to have taken place. I never faw more evident marks of

vexation

vexation and alarm than appeared in the
countenance of the right reverend per-
fonage. This alone would have convinced
me that they cannot command the liquefaction when they pleafe. While things were
in this flate I obferved a gentleman come
haflily through the crowd, and fpeak to the
old monk, who, in a pretty loud voice, and
with an accent and a grimace very expreffive of chagrin, replied, " Cofpetto di
" bacco è dura come una pietra." At
the fame time an acquaintance whifpered
me, That it would be prudent to retire, becaufe the mob on fimilar occafions have
been ftruck with a notion, that the opera-
tion of the miracle was difturbed by the
prefence of heretics ; on which they are
apt to infult them. I directly took his
hint, and joined the company I had left.
An univerfal gloom had overfpread all their
countenances, they talked to each other in
whifpers, and feemed oppreffed with grief
and contrition. One very beautiful young
lady

lady cried and fobbed as if her heart had been ready to break. The paſſions of ſome of the rabble without doors took a different turn; inſtead of ſorrow, they were filled with rage and indignation at the Saint's obſtinacy. They put him in mind of the zeal with which he was adored by people of all ranks in Naples; of the honours which had been conferred on him; that he was reſpected here more than in any other country on earth; and ſome went ſo far as to call him, an old ungrateful yellow-faced raſcal, for his obduracy. It was now almoſt dark—and when leaſt expected, the ſignal was given that the miracle was performed.—The populace filled the air with repeated ſhouts of joy; a band of muſic began to play; Te Deum was ſung; couriers were diſpatched to the royal family, then at Portici, with the glad tidings; the young lady dried up her tears; the countenances of our company brightened in an inſtant, and they ſat down to cards without farther

ther dread of eruptions, earthquakes, or peſtilence.

I had remarked, during their ſuſpence with reſpect to the ſucceſs of the miracle, that ſome imputed the delay partly to the weather, which happened to be rainy, and colder than is uſual at this ſeaſon; and partly to the aukwardneſs of the Arch-biſhop, who, never having performed be-fore, was accuſed of not handling the phial in the ſame dexterous and efficacious man-ner that a perſon of experience would have done. While they imputed the failure to thoſe cauſes, they ſeemed equally uneaſy with the reſt of the company about the conſequences. It ſtruck me that the firſt ſentiment was perfectly inconſiſtent with the ſecond. I mentioned this to a French gentleman, who is here as travelling companion to the young Comte de G——. " If," ſaid I, " the weather, or " the unſkilfulneſs of the Archbiſhop, " has prevented the ſubſtance in the phial
" from

" from becoming liquid, this surely can-
" not be an indication that Heaven or the
" Saint is difpleafed; if, on the contrary,
" the blood continuing folid in the pre-
" fence of the Saint, proceeds from Heaven
" or the Saint being offended, then no
" kind of weather, and no kind of ex-
" pertnefs on the part of the Arch-
" bifhop, could have rendered it liquid."
——" Monfieur," faid he, " voilà ce qu'on
" appelle raifonner, ce que ces meffieurs ne
" font jamais."

The fame evening, an acquaintance
of mine, who is alfo a Roman Catholic,
and who remained clofe by the Archbifhop till all was over, affured me, that
the miracle had failed entirely; for the
old monk feeing no fymptom of the
blood liquefying, had called out that the
miracle had fucceeded; on which the fignal
had been given, the people had fhouted,
the Archbifhop had held up the bottle,
moving it with a rapid motion before the
eyes

eyes of the fpectators, and nobody chufing
to contradict what every body wifhed, he had
been allowed to cover up the phial, and carry
it back to the Chapel, with the contents, in
the fame form they had come abroad. How
far this account is exactly true, I will not
take on me to affert; I was not near
enough to fee the tranfaction myfelf, and
I have only the authority of this perfon,
having heard no other body fay they had
obferved the fame.

LETTER LXV.

THE tomb of Virgil is on the mountain of Paufilippo, a little above the grotto of that name; you afcend to it by a narrow path which runs through a vineyard; it is overgrown with ivy leaves and fhaded with branches, fhrubs, and bufhes; an ancient bay-tree, with infinite propriety, overhangs it. Many a folitary walk have I taken to this place. The earth, which contains his afhes, we expect to find clothed in the brighteft verdure. Viewed from the magic fpot, the objects which adorn the bay become doubly interefting. The Poet's verfes are here recollected with additional pleafure; the verfes of Virgil are interwoven in our minds with a thoufand interefting ideas, with the memory of our boyifh years, or the fportive

scenes

scenes of childhood, of our earlieft friends and companions, many of whom are now dead; and thofe who ftill live, and for whom we retain the firft impreffion of affection, are at fuch a diftance as renders the hopes of feeing them again very uncertain. No wonder, therefore, when in a contemplative mood, that our fteps are often directed to a fpot fo well calculated to create and cherifh fentiments congenial with the ftate of our mind. But then comes an antiquarian, who, with his odious doubts, difturbs the pleafing fource of our enjoyment; and from the fair and delightful fields of fancy, conveys us in a moment to a dark, barren, and comfortlefs defert;—he *doubts*, whether this be the real place where the afhes of Virgil were depofited; and tells us an unfatisfactory ftory about the other fide of the bay, and that he is rather inclined to believe that the Poet was buried fomewhere there, without fixing on any particular fpot.

Would

Would to heaven thofe doubters would keep their minds to themfelves, and not ruffle the tranquillity of believers!

But, after all, why fhould not this be the real tomb of Virgil? Why fhould the enthufiafts, who delight in pilgrimages to this fpot, be deprived of that pleafure? Why fhould the Poet's ghoft be allowed to wander along the dreary banks of Styx, till the antiquarians erect a cenotaph in his honour? Even they acknowledge that he was buried on this bay, and near Naples; and tradition has fixed on this fpot, which, exclufive of other prefumptions, is a much ftronger evidence in its favour than their vague conjectures againft it.

In your way to the claffic fields of Baia and Cumæ, you pafs through the grotto of Paufilippo, a fubterraneous paffage through the mountain, near a mile in length, about twenty feet in breadth, and thirty or forty in height, every where, except at the two extremities, where it is much

I   higher.

higher. People of fashion generally drive through this paſſage with torches, but .the country people and foot paſſengers find their way without much difficulty by the light which enters at the extremities, and at two holes pierced through the mountain near the middle of the grotto, which admit light from above.

Mr. Addiſon tells us, that the common people of Naples in his time believed that this paſſage through the mountain was the work of magic, and that Virgil was the magician. But this is the age of ſcepticiſm; and the common people, in imitation of people of faſhion, begin to harbour doubts concerning all their old eſtabliſhed opinions. A Neapolitan Valet-de-place aſked an Engliſh gentleman lately, Whether Signior Virgilio, of whom he had heard ſo much, had really, and bona fide, been a magician or not ? "A "magician," replied the Engliſhman; "ay, that he was, and a very great

U 3   "magician

" magician too." " And do you," refumed the Valet, " believe it was he who
" pierced this rock?" " As for this parti-
" cular rock," anfwered the Mafter, " I
" will not fwear to it from my own know-
" ledge, becaufe it was done before I was
" born ; but I am ready to make oath, that
" I have known him pierce, and even melt,
" fome very obdurate fubftances."

Two miles beyond the Grotta di Paufi-
lippe, is a circular lake, about half a mile
in diameter, called Lago d'Agnano; on
whofe margin is fituated the famous Grotta
del Cane, where fo many dogs have been
tortured and fuffocated, to fhew the effect
of a vapour which rifes about a foot above
the bottom of this little cave, and is deftructive of animal life. A dog having his head
held in this vapour, is convulfed in a few
minutes, and foon after falls to the earth
motionlefs. This experiment is repeated
for the amufement of every unfeeling perfon, who has half a crown in his pocket,
and affects a turn for natural philofophy.
                                        The

The experiment is commonly made on dogs; becaufe they, of all animals, fhow the greateft affection for man, and prefer his company to that of their own fpecies, or of any other living creature. The fellows who attend at this cave have always fome miferable dogs, with ropes about their necks, ready for this cruel purpofe. If the poor animals were unconfcious of what was to happen, it would be lefs affecting; but they ftruggle to get free, and fhow every fymptom of horror when they are dragged to this cave of torment. I fhould have been happy to have taken the effect of the vapour for granted, without a new trial; but fome of the company were of a more philofophical turn of mind than I have any pretenfions to. When the unhappy animal found all his efforts to efcape were ineffectual, he feemed to plead for mercy by the dumb eloquence of looks, and the blandifhments natural to his fpecies. While he licked the hand of his keeper, the unrelenting wretch dafhed him

U 4   a blow,

a blow, and thruſt his head into the mur-
derous vapour.

When the real utility of the knowledge
acquired by cruel experiments on animals
(a practice which has been carried to dreadful lengths of late) is fairly ſtated, and
compared with the exquiſiteneſs of *their*
ſufferings, the benefit reſulting to mankind
from thence will ſeem too dearly bought
in the eyes of a perſon of humanity. Humanity ! If language had belonged to other
animals beſides man, might not they have
choſen that word to expreſs—cruelty ? if
they had, thank God, they would have
done injuſtice to many of the human race.
I have left the poor dog too long in the
vapour ; much longer than he remained in
reality. The D— of H——, ſhocked at
the fellow's barbarity, wreſted the dog from
his hands, bore him to the open air, and
gave him life and liberty ; which he ſeemed
to enjoy with all the bounding rapture of
gladneſs and gratitude. If you ſhould ever
come this way, pray do not inſiſt on ſeeing
the

the experiment; it is not worth while; the thing is afcertained; it is beyond a doubt that this vapour convulfes and kills every breathing animal.

You come next to the favourite fields of fancy and poetical fiction. The Campi Phlegrei, where Jupiter overcame the giants; the folfaterra ftill fmoking, as if from the effects of his thunder; the Monte Nova, which was thrown fuddenly from the bowels of the earth, as if the fons of Titan had intended to renew the war; the Monte Barbaro, formerly Mons Gaurus, the favourite of Bacchus; the grotto of the Cumæan Sibyl; the noxious and 'gloomy lakes of Avernus and Acheron; and the green bowers of Elyfium.

The town of Puzzoli, and its environs, prefent fuch a number of objects, worthy of the attention of the antiquarian, the natural philofopher, and the claffic fcholar, that to defcribe all with the minutenefs they deferve, would fill volumes.

The

The Temple of Jupiter Scrapis at Puzzoli, is accounted a very interesting monument of antiquity; being quite different from the Roman and Greek temples, and built in the manner of the Afiatics, probably by the Egyptian and Afiatic merchants fettled at Puzzoli, which was the great emporium of Italy, until the Romans built Oftia and Antium.

Sylla having abdicated the Dictatorfhip, retired, and paffed the remainder of his life in this city.

The ruins of Cicero's villa, near this city, are of fuch extent, as to give a high idea of the wealth of this great orator. Had Fortune always beftowed her gifts with fo much propriety, fhe never would have been accufed of blindnefs. When the truly great are bleffed with riches, it affords pleafure to every candid mind. Neither this villa near Puzzoli, that at Tufculum, nor any of his other country-feats, were the fcenes of idlenefs or riot. They are diftinguifhed

guifhed by the names of the works he compofed there; works which have always
been the delight of the learned, and which,
ftill more than the important fervices he
rendered his country when in office, have
contributed to immortalize his name.

The bay between Puzzoli and Baia is
about a league in breadth. In crofling this
in a boat, you fee the ruins called Ponte di
Caligula, from their being thought the remains of a bridge which Caligula attempted
to build acrofs. They are by others, with
more probability, thought to be the ruins
of a mole built with arches. Having paffed
over this gulph, a new field of curiofities
prefents itfelf. . The baths and prifons of
Nero, the tomb of Agrippina, the temples
of Venus, of Diana, and of Mercury, and
the ruins of the ancient city of Cumæ; but
no vefliges now remain of many of thofe
magnificent villas which adorned this luxurious coaft, nor even of the town of Baia,
The whole of this beauteous bay, formerly
the

the feat of pleafure, and, at one period, the moft populous fpot in Italy, is now very thinly inhabited; and the contraft is ftill ftronger between the antient opulence and prefent poverty, than between the numbers of its antient and prefent inhabitants. It muft be acknowledged, that we can hardly look around us, in any part of this world, without perceiving objects which, to a contemplative mind, convey reflections on the inftability of grandeur, and the fad viciffitudes and reverfes to which human affairs are liable; but *here* thofe objects are fo numerous, and fo ftriking, that they muft make an impreffion on the moft carelefs paffenger.

LETTER LXVI.

Naples.

AS the Court are not at present at Casserta, we have not seen that place in all its splendour; we passed, however, one very agreeable day there, with Lady H—— and S— H—— F——n.

The palace at Casserta was begun in the year 1750, after a plan of Vanvitelli; the work is now carried on under the direction of his son. While the present King of Spain remained at Naples, there were generally about two thousand workmen employed; at present there are about five hundred. It will be finished in a few years, and will then, unquestionably, be one of the most spacious and magnificent palaces in Europe. It has been said, that London is too large a capital for the island of Great Britain; and it has been compared to a turgid head placed

placed on an emaciated body. The palace of Caserta also seems out of proportion with the revenues of this kingdom. It is not, properly speaking, a head too large for the body; but rather an ornament, by much too expensive and bulky for either head or body. This palace is situated about sixteen miles north from Naples, on the plain where ancient Capua stood. It was thought prudent to found a building, on which such sums of money were to be lavished, at a considerable distance from Mount Vesuvius. It were to be wished, that the contents of the cabinet at Portici were removed from the same dangerous neighbourhood. That he might not be limited in ground for the gardens, may have been his Spanish Majesty's motive for choosing that his palace should be at a distance from Naples; and that it might not be exposed to insult from an enemy's fleet, was probably the reason that determined him to place it at a distance from the sea.

3   This

This immenfe building is of a rectangular form, feven hundred and fifty feet Englifh, by five hundred and eighty; about one hundred and twelve feet high, comprehending five habitable ftories, which contain fuch a number of apartments as will accommodate the moft numerous court, without any acceffary buildings.

The rectangle is divided into four courts, each of about two hundred and fifty-two feet by one hundred and feventy. In each of the two principal fronts, are three correfponding gates, forming three openings, which pierce the whole building. The middle gate forms the entry to a magnificent portico, through which the coaches drive. In the middle of this, and in the centre of the edifice, there is a veftibule of an octogonal form; which opens into the four grand courts at four fides of the octogon; two other fides open into the portico, one to the ftaircafe; and, at the eighth fide, there is a ftatue of Hercules,

crowned

crowned by Victory, with this inscription,

VIRTUS POST FORTIA FACTA CORONAT.

The grand staircase is adorned with the richest marble; the upper vestibule to which you ascend by this noble stair, is an octogon also, and surrounded by twenty-four pillars of yellow marble, each of which is of one piece of eighteen feet high, without including the pedestal or capital. From this upper vestibule there are entries into———But I have a notion you are tired of this description, which I assure you is likewise my case. I beg, therefore, you may take it for granted, that the apartments within, particularly their Majesties, and that destined for balls and theatrical entertainments, correspond with the magnificence of the external appearance.

Among the workmen employed in finishing this palace and the gardens, there are one hundred and fifty Africans; for as the King of Naples is conftantly at war with the Barbary States, he always has a number of their failors prifoners, all of whom are immediately employed as flaves in the gallies, or at fome public work. There are at prefent at Cafferta, about the fame number of Chriftian flaves; all of thefe have been condemned to this fervitude for fome crime, fome of them for the greateft of all crimes; they are, however, better clothed and fed than the Africans. This is done, no doubt, in honour of the Chriftian religion, and to demonftrate that Chriftians, even after they have been found guilty of the blackeft crimes, are worthier men, and more deferving of lenity, than Mahometan prifoners, however innocent they may be in all *other* refpects.

The gardens belonging to this palace are equally extenfive and magnificent. A great number of fine ftatues, moft of them copies of the beft antique, are kept in a ftorehoufe till the gardens are finifhed, when they will be placed in them. The largeſt and fineſt elephant I ever ſaw is here at preſent; he is kept by African ſlaves: they ſeem to know how to manage him perfectly; he is well thriven, and goes through a number of tricks and evolutions with much docility and judgment.

In the garden, there is an artificial water and iſland. This, if one may venture to ſay ſo, ſeems a little injudicious; it brings to our memory the bay of Naples, with its iſlands, a recollection by no means favourable to this royal contrivance. In this iſland there is a kind of a caſtle, regularly ſortified, with a ditch around it, and ramparts, baſtions, ſally-ports, &c. &c. and a numerous train of artillery, ſome of them nine or ten *ouncers*. I no ſooner entered this fort, than I wiſhed that Uncle Toby and Corporal Trim had been of our party; it would have charmed the ſoul of the worthy veteran and his faithful ſervant.

I aſked

I afked the man who attended us,
What he imagined this fortification was
intended for ?—Sir H—— F—— faid,
" The cannon were certainly defigned
" againft the frogs, who were continually
" attempting to fcale the ramparts from
" the ditch."——I afked again, What
was the real defign of erecting this fort?
The man anfwered, ftretching out his
arms, and making as wide a circle with
them as he could, " Tutto, tutto per il
" follazo del Re."   " Yes," faid I, it is
" furely in the higheft degree reafon-
" able, that not only this fort, but the
" whole kingdom, fhould be appropriated
" to the amufement of his Majefty."—
" Certo," replied the man. I wifhed to
fee how far the fellow's liberality would go
—" Not only this kingdom," continued
I, " but all Europe would be highly ho-
" noured in contributing to the amufement
" of his Majefty." " Certo, certo," faid
the man.

L E T T E R LXVII.

Naples.

THE King and Queen lately paid a
visit to four of the principal nunneries in this town. Their motive was, to
gratify the curiosity of th Archduchess,
and her husband, Prince Albert of Saxony. I ought to have informed you, that
this illustrious couple left Vienna some
months after us, with an intention to make
the tour of Italy. We had the honour
of seeing them frequently while at Rome,
where they conciliated the affections of
the Italian nobles by their obliging manners, as much as they commanded respect
by their high rank. The Archduchess is
a very beautiful woman, and more distin-
guished by the propriety of her conduct,
than by either birth or beauty. As white,
by the link of contrast, is connected with

8   the

the idea of black; fo this amiable Duchefs
fometimes recals thofe to people's memories, whofe ideas of dignity are ftrongly
contrafted with hers. Confcious, from
her infancy, of the higheft rank, and
accuftomed to honours, it never enters
into her thoughts that any perfon will
fail in paying her a due refpect; while
they, eternally jealous that enough of refpect is not paid them, give themfelves
airs which would be intolerable in an
Emprefs. A fmile of benignity puts all
who approach this Princefs perfectly at
their eafe, and dignity fits as fmoothly on
her as a well-made garment; while, on
them, it briftles out like the quills of a
porcupine, or the feathers of an enraged
turkey-cock.

As nobody is permitted to enter thofe
convents, except on fuch extraordinary
occafions as this, when they are vifited
by the Sovereigns, the Britifh Minifter
feized this opportunity of procuring an
order

order for admitting the D— of H—— and me. We accordingly accompanied him, and a few others, who were in the King's fpite. I have feen various nunneries in different parts of Europe, but none that could be compared even with the meaneft of thofe four in this city, for neatnefs and conveniency. Each of them is provided with a beautiful garden; and the fituation of one is the happieft that can be imagined, commanding a profpect nearly as extenfive as that from the Carthufian convent near the caftle of St. Elmo. Thofe four nunneries are for the reception of young ladies of good families; and, into one in particular, none but fuch as are of very high rank can be admitted, either as penfioners, or to take the veil. Each of the young ladies in this fplendid convent, have both a fummer and a winter apartment, and many other accommodations unknown in other retreats of this nature. The royal vifitors were received in all of them by the

Lady

Lady Abbefs, at the head of the oldeft of
the fifterhood; they were afterwards prefented with nofegays, and ferved with
fruit, fweetmeats, and a variety of cooling
drinks, by the younger nuns. The Queen
and her amiable fifter received all very
gracioufly; converfing familiarly with the
Lady Abbeffes, and afking a few obliging
queftions of each.

In one convent the company were furprifed, on being led into a large parlour, to
find a table covered, and every appearance
of a moft plentiful cold repaft, confifting
of feveral joints of meat, hams, fowl, fifh,
and various other difhes. It feemed rather
ill-judged to have prepared a feaft of fuch
a folid nature immediately after dinner;
for thofe royal vifits were made in the afternoon. The Lady Abbefs, however,
earneftly preffed their Majefties to fit down,
with which they complied, and their example was followed by the Archduchefs and
fome of the ladies; the nuns ftood behind,

X 4

to ferve their Royal guefts. The Queen chofe a flice of cold turkey, which, on being cut up, turned out a large piece of lemon ice, of the fhape and appearance of a roafted turkey. All the other difhes were ices of various kinds, difguifed under the forms of joints of meat, fifh, and fowl, as above mentioned. The gaiety and good humour of the King, the affable and engaging behaviour of the Royal fifters, and the fatisfaction which beamed from the plump countenance of the Lady Abbefs, threw an air of cheerfulnefs on this fcene ; which was interrupted, however, by gleams of melancholy reflection, which failed not to dart acrofs the mind, at fight of fo many victims to the pride of family, to avarice, and fuperftition. Many of thofe victims were in the full bloom of health and youth, and fome of them were remarkably handfome, There is fomething in a nun's drefs which renders the beauty of a young woman more interefting than is in the power of the gayeft, richeft, and moft

laboured

laboured ornaments. This certainly does
not proceed from any thing remarkably
becoming in black and white flannel. The
Lady Abbefs and the elderly nuns made no
more impreffion in their veftal robes, than
thofe ftale, forlorn dames, whom you may
fee difplaying their family jewels and fhrivelled countenances every night at Ranelagh
or in the fide-boxes. The intereft you take
in a beautiful woman is heightened on feeing her in the drefs of a nun, by the oppofition which you imagine exifts between
the life to which her rafh vows have condemned her, and that to which her own
unbiaffed inclination would have led her.
You are moved with pity, which you know
is a-kin to love, on feeing a young blooming creature doomed to retirement and felf-
denial, who was formed by nature for fociety and enjoyment.

If we may credit the ancient poets, thofe
young women who are confined to a cloi-
fter life on any part of this coaft, are more

to be pitied than they would be under the
fame reftraint elfewhere. They tell us,
the very air in this part of Italy is repug-
nant to that kind of conftitution, and that
turn of mind, of which it would be peculiarly happy for nuns to be poffeffed. Propertius intreats his Cynthia not to remain
too long on a fhore which he feems to
think dangerous to the chafteft maiden.

Tu modo quamprimum corruptas defere Baias—
. . . .
Littora quæ fuerant caftis inimica puellis.

Martial afferts, that a woman who came
hither as chafte as Penelope, if fhe remained any time, would depart as licentious and depraved as Helen.

Penelope venit, abit Helene.

I have certainly met with ladies, after they
had refided fome time at Naples, who, in
point of character and conftitution, were
thought to have a much ftronger refemblance to Helen than to Penelope; but as
I have no great faith in the fudden opera-
tion

tion of phyfical caufes in matters of this
kind, I never doubted of thofe ladies having
carried the fame difpofition to Naples that
they brought from it. Though there are
not wanting thofe who affirm, that the influence of this feducing climate is evident
now in as ftrong a degree as it is defcribed
to have been anciently; that it pervades
people of all ranks and conditions, and that
in the convents themfelves;

Even there where frozen chaftity retires,
Love finds an altar for forbidden fires.

Others, who carry their refearches ftill
deeper, and pretend to have a diftinct
knowledge of the effect of aliment through
all its changes on the human conftitution,
think, that the amorous difpofition, imputed to Neapolitans, is only in part owing
to their voluptuous climate, but in a far
greater degree to the hot, fulphureous nature of their foil, which thofe profound na-
turalifts declare communicates its fiery qualities to the juices of vegetables; thence
they are conveyed to the animals who feed

on

on them, and particularly to man, whofe
nourifhment confifting both of animal and
vegetable food, he muft have in his veins
a double dofe of the ftimulating particles
in queftion. No wonder, therefore, fay
thofe nice inveftigators of caufe and effect,
that the inhabitants of this country are
more given to amorous indulgencies, than
thofe who are favoured with a chafter foil
and a colder climate.

For my own part, I muft acknowledge,
that I have feen nothing, fince I came to
Naples, to juftify the general imputations
above mentioned, or to fupport this very
ingenious theory. On the contrary, there
are circumftances from which the oppofers
of this fyftem draw very different conclufions; for every fyftem of philofophy, like
every Minifter of Great Britain, has an oppofition. The gentlemen in oppofition to
the voluptuous influence of this climate,
and the fiery effects of this foil, undermine
the foundation of their antagonifts' theory,

by

by afferting, that, fo far from being of a
warmer complexion than their neighbours,
the Neapolitans are of colder conflitutions,
or more philofophic in the command of
their paffions, than any people in Europe.
Do not the lower clafs of men, fay they,
ftrip themfelves before the houfes which
front the bay, and bathe in the fea without the fmalleft ceremony? Are not numbers of thofe ftout, athletic figures, during
the heat of the day, feen walking and
fporting on the fhore perfectly naked; and
with no more idea of fhame, than Adam
felt in his ftate of innocence; while the ladies from their coaches, and the fervant-
maids and young girls, who pafs along,
contemplate this fingular fpectacle with as
little apparent emotion as the ladies in
Hyde Park behold a review of the horfe-
guards?

As Sir W—— and L—y H—— are
preparing to vifit England, and the D—
feels no inclination to remain after they
are gone, we intend to return to Rome in
a few days.

L E T T E R   LXVIII.

Rome,

WE delayed vifiting Tivoli, Frefcati,
and Albano, till our return from
Naples.

The Campagna is an uninhabited plain,
furrounding the city of Rome, bounded on
one fide by the fea, and on the other by an
amphitheatre of hills, crowned with towns,
villages, and villas, which form the fineft
landfcapes that can be imagined.   The ancient Romans were wont to feek fhelter
from the fcorching heats of fummer, among
the woods and lakes of thofe hills ; and the
Cardinals and Roman Princes, at the fame
feafon, retire to their villas ; while many
of the wealthier fort of citizens take lodg-
ings in the villages, during the feafon of
gathering the vines.

On

On the road from Rome to Tivoli, about
three miles from the latter, ſtrangers are
deſired to viſit a kind of lake called Solfa-
tara, formerly Lakus Albulus, and there
ſhown certain ſubſtances, to which they give
the name of Floating Iſlands. They are nothing elſe than bunches of bullruſhes,
ſpringing from a thin ſoil, formed by duſt
and ſand blown from the adjacent ground,
and glued together by the bitumen which
ſwims on the ſurface of this lake, and the
ſulphur with which its waters are impregnated. Some of theſe iſlands are twelve or
fifteen yards in length ; the ſoil is ſuffi-
ciently ſtrong to bear five or ſix people,
who, by the means of a pole, may move
to different parts of the lake, as if they
were in a boat. This lake empties itſelf,
by a whitiſh, muddy ſtream, into the Te-
verone, the ancient Anio ; a vapour, of a
ſulphureous ſmell, ariſing from it as it
flows. The ground near this rivulet, as alſo
around the borders of the lake, reſounds,
as if it were hollow, when a horſe gallops

† over

over it. The water of this lake has the
fingular quality of covering every fubſtance
which it touches with a hard, white, ſtoney
matter. On throwing a bundle of ſmall
ſticks or ſhrubs into it, they will, in a few
days, be covered with a white cruſt; but,
what ſeems ſtill more extraordinary, this
encruſtating quality is not ſo ſtrong in the
lake itſelf, as in the canal, or little rivulet
that runs from it ; and the farther the water has flowed from the lake, till it is quite
loſt in the Anio, the ſtronger this quality
is. Thoſe ſmall, round encruſtations,
which cover the ſand and pebbles, reſem-
bling fugar-plums, are called Confetti di
Tivoli. Fiſhes are found in the Anio, both
above and below Tivoli, till it receives the
Albula ; after which, during the reſt of
its courſe to the Tiber, there are none.
The waters of this lake had a high medical
reputation anciently, but they are in no
eſteem at preſent.

Near the bottom of the eminence on
which Tivoli ſtands, are the ruins of the
vaſt

vaſt and magnificent villa built by the emperor Adrian. In this were comprehended an amphitheatre, ſeveral temples, a library, a circus, a naumachia. The emperor alſo gave to the buildings and gardens of this famous villa the names of the moſt celebrated places; as the Academia, the Lycæum, the Prytaneum of Athens, the Tempe of Theſſaly, and the Elyſian fields and infernal regions of the poets. There were alſo commodious apartments for a vaſt number of gueſls, all admirably diſtributed with baths, and every conveniency. Every quarter of the world contributed to ornament this famous villa, whoſe ſpoils have ſince formed the principal ornaments of the Campidoglio, the Vatican, and the palaces of the Roman Princes. It is ſaid to have been three miles in length, and above a mile in breadth. Some antiquarians make it much larger; but the ruins, now remaining, do not mark a ſurface of a quarter of that extent.

At no great diftance, they fhew the place to which the Eaftern Queen Zenobia was confined, after fhe was brought in triumph to Rome by the emperor Aurelian.

The town of Tivoli is now wretchedly poor; it boafts however greater antiquity than Rome itfelf, being the ancient Tibur, which, Horace informs us, was founded by a Grecian colony.

Tibur Argæo pofitum colono
Sit meæ fedes utinam feneʤæ.

Ovid gives it the fame origin, in the fourth book of the Fafti.

——Jam mœnia Tiburis udi
Stabant; Argolicæ quod pofuere manus.

This was a populous and flourifhing town in remoter antiquity; but it appears to have been thinly inhabited in the reign of Auguftus. Horace, in an Epiftle to Mæcenas, fays,

Parvum parva decent. Mihi jam non Regia Roma,
Sed vacuum Tibur placet——

Though

Though the town itfelf was not populous, the beauty of the fituation, and whole-fomenefs of the air, prompted great numbers of illuftrious Romans, both before the final deftruction of the Republic, and afterwards in Auguftus's time, to build country-houfes in the neighbourhood. Julius Cæfar had a villa here, which he was under the neceffity of felling to defray the expence of the public fhews and games he exhibited to the people during his Ædilefhip. Plutarch fays, that his liberality and magnificence, on this occafion, obfcured the glory of all who had preceded him in the office, and gained the hearts of the people to fuch a degree, that they were ready to invent new offices and new honours for him. He then laid the foundation of that power and popularity, which enabled him, in the end, to overturn the conftitution of his country. Caius Caffius had alfo a country houfe here; where Marcus Brutus and he are faid to have had frequent meetings, and to have formed the plan which terminated

the ambition of Cæfar, and again offered to
Rome that freedom which fhe had not the
virtue to accept. Here, alfo, was the villa
of Auguftus, whofe fuccefs in life arofe
at the field of Philippi from which he
fled, was confirmed by the death of the
moft virtuous citizens of Rome, and who,
without the talents, reaped the fruits of
the labours and vaft projects of Julius.
Lepidus the Triumvir, Cæcilius Metellus,
Quintilius Varus, the poets Catullus and
Propertius, and other diftinguifhed Romans, had villas in this town or its environs; and you are fhewn the fpots on which
they ftood: but nothing renders Tibur fo
interefting, as the frequent mention which
Horace makes of it in his writings. His
great patron and friend Mæcenas had a
villa here, the ruins of which are to be
feen on the fouth bank of the Anio; and
it was pretty generally fuppofed, that
the poet's own houfe and farm were very
near it, and immediately without the walls
of Tibur; but it has been of late afferted,
with

with great probability, that Horace's farm
was situated nine miles above that of Mæcenas's, at the side of a stream called Licenza,
formerly Digentia, near the hill Lucretilis,
in the country of the ancient Sabines.
Those who hold this opinion say, that
when Horace talks of Tibur, he alludes to
the villa of Mæcenas; but when he mentions Digentia, or Lucretilis, his own house
and farm are to be understood; as in the
eighteenth Epistle of the first book,

Me quoties reficit gelidus Digentia rivus,
Quem Mandela bibit, rugosus frigore pagus;
Quid sentire putas, quid credis, amice, precari?

the seventeenth Ode of the first book,

Velox amœnum sæpe Lucretilem
Mutat Lycæo Faunus;——

and in other passages. But whether the
poet's house and farm were near the town
of Tibur, or at a distance from it, his writings sufficiently show that he spent much of
his time there; and it is probable that he
composed great part of his works in that

Y 3 favourite

favourite retreat. This he himfelf in fome
meafure declares, in that fine Ode addreſſed
to Julius Antonius, fon of Mark Antony,
by Fulvia; the fame whom Auguſtus firſt
pardoned, and afterwards put privately to
death, on account of an intrigue into which
Antonius was feduced by the abandoned
Julia, daughter of Auguſtus.

—— Ego, apis Matinæ
    More modoque,
Grata carpentis thyma per laborem
Plurimum, circa nemus uvidique
Tiburis ripas, operoſa parvus
    Carmina fingo.

If you ever come to Tivoli, let it not be
with a numerous party; come alone, or
with a fingle friend, and be fure to put
your Horace in your pocket. You will
read him here with more enthufiafm than
elfewhere; you will imagine you fee the
philofophic poet · wandering among the
groves, fometimes calmly meditating his
moral precepts, and fometimes *his eye in a
fine frenzy* rolling with all the fire of po-

etic

etic enthufiafm. If Tivoli had nothing
elfe to recommend it but its being fo often
fung by the moft elegant of the poets, and
its having been the refidence of fo many
illuftrious men, thefe circumftances alone
would render it worthy the attention of
travellers; but it will alfo be interefting to
many on account of its cafcade, the Sibyl's
Temple, and the Villa Eftenfe.

The river Anio, deriving its fource from
a part of the Apennines, fifty miles above
Tivoli, glides through a plain till it comes
near that town, when it is confined for a
fhort fpace between two hills, covered with
groves. Thefe were fuppofed to have been
the refidence of the Sibyl Albunea, to whom
the temple was dedicated. The river, moving with augmented rapidity as its channel is confined, at length rufhes headlong
over a lofty precipice; the noife of its fall
refounds through the hills and groves of
Tivoli; a liquid cloud arifes from the
foaming water, which afterwards divides

Y 4

into

into numberlefs fmall cafcades, waters feveral orchards, and, having gained the plain, flows quietly for the reft of its courfe, till it lofes itfelf in the Tiber. It is not furprifing that the following lines have been fo often quoted by thofe who vifit the Sibyl's Temple, becaufe they delineate, in the moft. expreffive manner, fome of the principal features of the country around it.

Me nec tam patiens Lacedæmon,
Nec tam Lariffæ percuffit campus opimæ,
Quam domus Albuneæ refonantis,
Et præceps Anio, et Tiburni lucus, et uda
Mobilibus pomaria rivis.

The elegant and graceful form of the beautiful little temple I have fo often mentioned, indicates its having been built when the arts were in the higheft ftate of perfection at Rome. Its proportions are not more happy than its fituation, on a point of the mountain fronting the great cafcade.

Before they take their leave of Tivoli, ftrangers ufually vifit the Villa Eftenfe, belonging to the Duke of Modena. It was

. 2   built

built by Hippolitus of Efte, Cardinal of
Ferrara, and brother to the duke of that
name; but more diftinguifhed by being the
perfon to whom Ariofto addreffed his Poem
of Orlando Furiofo. The houfe itfelf is not
in the fineft ftyle of architecture. There
are many whimfical waterworks in the
gardens. Thofe who do not approve of the
tafte of their conftruction, ftill owe them
fome degree of refpect, on account of their
being the firft grand waterworks in Europe;
much more ancient than thofe of Verfailles.
The fituation is noble, the terraces lofty,
the trees large and venerable; and though
the ground is not laid out to the greateft
advantage, yet the whole has a ftriking air
of magnificence and grandeur.

LETTER LXIX.

Rome.

FRESCATI is an agreeable village, on the declivity of a hill, about twelve miles from Rome. It derives its name from the coolnefs of the air, and *frefh* verdure of the fields around. It is a bifhop's fee, and always poffeffed by one of the fix eldeft Cardinals. At prefent it belongs to the Cardinal Duke of York, who, whether in the country or at Rome, paffes the greateft part of his time in the duties and ceremonies of a religion, of whofe truth he feems to have the fulleft conviction; and who, living himfelf in great fimplicity, and not in the ufual ftyle of Cardinals, fpends a large proportion of his revenue in acts of charity and benevolence; *the world forgetting, by the world forgot,* except

except by thofe who enjoy the comforts of
life through his bounty.

Tivoli was the favourite refidence of the
ancient Romans. The moderns give the
preference to Frefcati, in whofe neighbourhood fome of the moft magnificent villas in
Italy are fituated.

The villa Aldobrandini, called alfo Belvedere, is the moft remarkable, on account
of its fine fituation, extenfive gardens, airy
terraces, its grottos, cafcades, and water-
works. Over a faloon, near the grand
cafcade, is the following infcription :

HUC EGO MIGRAVI MUSIS COMITATUS APOLLO,
HIC DELPHI, HIC HELICON, HIC MIHI DELOS ERIT.

The walls are adorned with a reprefentation of Apollo and the Mufes ; and fome
of that God's adventures are painted in
Frefco by Domenichino, particularly the
manner in which he treated Marfyas.
This, in my humble opinion, had better
been omitted ; both becaufe it is a difagreeable fubject for a picture, and becaufe it
does

does no honour to Apollo. Marſyas un-
queſtionably was an objeſt of contempt
and ridicule, on account of his preſumption ; but the puniſhment ſaid to have been
inſliſted on him exceeds all bounds, and
renders the infliſtor more deteſtable in our
eyes than the inſolent ſatyr himſelf. This
ſtory is ſo very much out of charaſter,
and ſo unlike the elegant god of poetry
and muſic, that I am inclined to ſuſ-
peſt it is not true. There is a report,
equally incredible, which has been propa-
gated by malicious people concerning his
ſiſter Diana; I do not mean her rencounter
with Aſtæon, for the Goddeſs of Chaſtity
may, without inconſiſtency, be ſuppoſed
cruel, but it is quite impoſſible to reconcile her general charaſter with the ſtories
of her noſturnal viſits to Endymion.

The villa Ludoviſi is remarkable for its
gardens and water-works. The hills on
which Freſcati is ſituated, afford great
abundance of water, a circumſtance of
which

which the owners of thofe villas have pro-
fited, all of them being ornamented with
fountains, cafcades, or water-works of
fome kind or other.

The villa Taverna, belonging to the
Prince Borghefe, is one of the fineft and
beft furnifhed of any in the neighbourhood of Rome. From this you afcend
through gardens to Monte Dracone, another palace on a more lofty fituation, belonging alfo to that Prince, and deriving
its name from the arms of his family.
The ancient city of Tufculum is fuppofed
to have ftood on the fpot, or very near it,
where Frefcati now is built; and at the
diftance of about a mile and a half, it is
generally believed, was the Tufculan villa
of Cicero, at a place now called Grotta
Ferrata. Some Greek monks of the order
of St. Bafil, flying from the perfecution
of the Saracens in the eleventh century, were
permitted to build a convent on the ruins
of Cicero's famous houfe. They ftill perform the fervice in the Greek language.

Which-

Whichever way you walk from Frefcati, you have the moft delightful fcenes
before you. I paffed two very agreeable
days, wandering through the gardens and
from villa to villa. The pleafure of our
party was not a little augmented by the
obfervations of Mr. B——, a lively old
gentleman from Scotland, a man of worth
but no antiquarian, and indeed no admirer
of any thing, ancient or modern, which
has not fome relation to his native country;
but to ballance that indifference, he feels
the warmeft regard for every thing which
has. We extended our walks as far as
the lake of Nemi, a bafon of water lying
in a very deep bottom, about four miles
in circumference, whofe furrounding hills
are covered with tall and fhady trees.
Here

Black Melancholy fits, and round her throws
A death-like filence, and a dread repofe ;
Her gloomy prefence faddens all the fcene,
Shades every flower, and darkens every green,

I never

I never faw a place more formed for contemplation and folemn ideas. In ancient times there was a temple here facred to Diana. The lake itfelf was called Speculum Dianæ, and Lacus Triviæ, and is the place mentioned in the feventh Book of the Æneid, where the Fury Alecto is defcribed blowing the trumpet of war, at whofe dreadful found the woods and mountains fhook, and mothers, trembling for their children, preffed them to their bofoms.

Contremuit nemus, et fylvæ intonuere profundæ, Audiit et triviæ longe lacus——*
Et trepidæ matres preffere ad pectora natus,

We returned by Genfano, Marino, La Riccia, and Caftel Gondolfo. All the villages and villas I have named communicate with each other by fine walks and avenues of lofty trees, whofe intermin-

* The intervening words are cold, and not much connected with the fine line which concludes the quotation.

gling

gling branches form a continued fhade for
the traveller. Caftel Gondolfo is a little
village near the lake Albano, on one extremity of which is a caftle, belonging
to his Holinefs, from which the village
takes its name; there is nothing remarkably fine in this villa, except its fituation.
Near the village of Caftel Gondolfo, is
the villa Barbarini, within the gardens of
which are the ruins of an immenfe palace, built by the Emperor Domitian.
There is a charming walk, about a mile
in length, along the fide of the lake from
Caftel Gondolfo to the town of Albano.
The lake of Albano is an oval piece of
water of about feven or eight miles circumference, whofe margin is finely adorned with groves and trees of various verdure, beautifully reflected from the tranf-
parent bofom of the lake; and which,
with the furrounding hills, and the Caftel
Gondolfo which crowns one of them, has
a fine picturefque effect.

The

The grand fcale on which the beauties
of nature appear in Switzerland and the
Alps, has been confidered by fome, as too
vaft for the pencil; but among the fweet hills
and vallies of Italy, her features are brought
nearer the eye, are fully feen and underftood, and appear in all the bloom of rural lovelinefs. Tivoli, Albano, and Frefcati, therefore, are the favourite abodes of
the landfcape-painters who travel to this
country for improvement; and in the opinion of fome, thofe delightful villages
furnifh ftudies better fuited to the powers
of their art, than even Switzerland itfelf.
Nothing can furpafs the admirable affem-
blage of hills, meadows, lakes, cafcades,
gardens, ruins, groves, and terraces,
which charm the eye, as you wander
among the fhades of Frefcati and Albano,
which appear in new beauty as they are
viewed from different points, and captivate
the beholder with endlefs variety. One
reflection obtrudes itfelf on the mind, and
difturbs the fatisfaction which fuch pleaf-

ing scenes would otherwise produce;
it arises from beholding the poverty of
infinitely the greater part of the inhabitants of those villages—Not that they seem
miserable or discontented—a few roasted
chesnuts, and some bunches of grapes,
which they may have for a penny, will
maintain them; but the easier they are
satisfied, and the less repining they are,
the more earnestly do we wish that they
were better provided for. Good heavens!
why should so much be heaped on a few,
whom profusion cannot satisfy; while a
bare competency is withheld from multitudes, whom penury cannot render discontented?

The most commanding view is from
the garden of a convent of Capucins, at
no great distance from Albano. Directly
before you is the lake, with the mountains and woods which surround it, and
the castle of Gondolfo; on one hand is
Frescati with all its villas; on the other,
the

the towns of Albano, La Riccia, and Genfano; beyond thefe you have an uninterrupted view of the Campagna, with St. Peter's church and the city of Rome in the middle; the whole profpect being bounded by the hills of Tivoli, the Apennines, and the Mediterranean.

While we contemplated all thefe objects with pleafure and admiration, an Englifh gentleman of the party faid to Mr. B——, "There is not a profpect equal "to this in all France or Germany, and not "many fuperior even in England." "That "I well believe," replied the Caledonian; "but if I had you in Scotland, I could "fhew you feveral with which this is by "no means to be compared." "Indeed! "Pray in what part of Scotland are they "to be feen?" "I prefume ·you never "was at the caftle of Edinburgh, Sir?" "Never." "Or at Stirling?" "Never." "Did you ever fee Loch Lomond, Sir?" "I never did." "I fuppofe I need not

Z 2   "afk,

" afk, whether you have ever been in
" Aberdeenfhire, or the Highlands, or—-"
" I muft confefs once for all," interrupted the
Englifhman, " that I have the misfortune
" never to have feen any part of Scot-
" land." " Then I am not furprifed,"
faid the Scot, taking a large pinch of
fnuff, " that you think this the fineft
" view you ever faw." " I prefume you
" think thofe in Scotland a great deal
" finer?" " A very great deal indeed,
" Sir; why that lake, for example, is a
" pretty thing enough ; I dare fwear, many
" an Englifh nobleman would give a
" good deal to have fuch another before
" his houfe; but Loch Lomond is thirty
" miles in length, Sir! there are above
" twenty iflands in it, Sir! that is a
" lake for you. As for their defert of a
" Campagna, as they call it, no man
" who has eyes in his head, Sir, will
" compare it to the fertile valley of Stir-
" ling, with the Forth, the moft beau-
" tiful river in Europe, twining through
" it."

" it." " Do you really in your con-
" fcience imagine," faid the Englishman,
" that the Forth is a finer river than the
" Thames?" " The Thames!" exclaimed the North Briton, " Why, my dear Sir,
" the Thames at London is a mere
" gutter, in comparifon of the Firth of
" Forth at Edinburgh." " I fuppofe
" then," faid the Englishman, recovering
himfelf, " you do not approve of the
" view from Windfor Caflle?" " I afk
" your pardon," replied the other ; " I
" approve of it very much; it is an ex-
" ceeding pretty kind of a profpect; the
" country appears from it as agreeable to
" the fight as any plain flat country,
" crowded with trees, and interfected by
" enclofures, can well do; but I own I
" am of opinion, that mere fertile fields,
" woods, rivers, and meadows, can never,
" of themfelves, perfectly fatisfy the
" eye." " You imagine, no doubt," faid
the Englishman, " that a few heath-
" covered mountains and rocks embel-

Z 3   " lifh

" lifh a country very much?" " I am
" precifely of that opinion," faid the Scot;
" and you will as foon convince me that
" a woman may be completely beautiful
" with fine eyes, good teeth, and a fair
" complexion, though fhe fhould not
" have a *nofe* on her face, as that a land-
" fcape, or country, can be completely
" beautiful without a mountain." " Well,
" but here are mountains enough," refumed the other; " look around you."
" Mountains!" cried the Caledonian,
" very pretty mountains, truly! They
" call that Caftel Gondolfo of theirs a
" caftle too, and a palace, forfooth! but
" does that make it a refidence fit for a
" Prince?" " Why, upon my word, I
" do not think it much amifs," faid the
other; " it looks full as well as the palace
" of St. James's." " The palace of St.
" James's," exclaimed the Scot, " is a
" fcandal to the nation; it is both a
" fhame and a fin, that fo great a mo-
" narch as the King of Scotland, England,

" land, and Ireland, with his Royal con-
" fort, and their large family of fmall
" children, fhould live in a fhabby old cloi-
" fter, hardly good enough for monks.
" The palace of Holyrood-houfe, indeed,
". is a refidence meet for a king." " And
" the gardens; pray what fort of gardens
" have you belonging to that palace?" faid
the Englifhman; " I have been told you do
" not excel in thofe." " But we excel
" in gardeners," replied the other, " which
" are as much preferable as the creator is
" preferable to the created." " I am fur-
" prifed, however," rejoined the South Briton, " that, in a country like yours, where
" there are fo many creators, fo very few
" fruit-gardens are created." " Why, Sir, it
" is not to be expected," faid Mr. B——,
" that any one country will excel in every
. " thing. Some enjoy a climate more favour-
" able for peaches, and vines, and nectarines;
" but, by G—, Sir, no country on earth pro-
" duces better men and women than Scot-
" land." " I dare fay none does," replied

Z 4   the

the other. " So as France excels in wine,
" England in wool and oxen, Arabia in
" horfes, and other countries in other
" animals, you imagine Scotland excels
" all others in the human fpecies." " What
" I faid, Sir, was, that the human fpecies
" in no country excel thofe in Scotland;
" and that I affert again, and will maintain,
" Sir, to my laft gafp." " I do not intend
" to deny it," faid the Englifhman; " but
" you will permit me to obferve, that, men
" being its ftaple commodity, it muft be
" owned that Scotland carries on a brifk
" trade; for I know no country that has
" a greater *exportation*; you will find
" Scotchmen in all the countries of the
" world." " So much the better for all
" the countries of the world," faid Mr.
B—; " for every body knows that the
" Scotch cultivate and improve the arts
" and fciences wherever they go." " They
" certainly improve their own fortunes
" wherever they go," rejoined the other:
" —like their gardeners, though they
" can

" can create little or nothing at home,
" they often create very good fortunes in
" other countries; and this is one reafon
" of our having the pleafure of fo much of
" their company in London." " Whe-
" ther it affords you pleafure or not,
" Sir, nothing can be more certain,"
replied the Scot in the moft ferious tone,
" than that you may *improve* very much
" by their company and example. But
" there are various reafons," continued he,
" for fo many of my countrymen fojourn-
" ing in London. That city is now, in
" fome meafure, the capital of Scotland as
" well as of England. The feat of govern-
" ment is there; the King of Scotland, as
" well as of England, refides there; the
" Scotch nobility and gentry have as good
" a right to be near the perfon of their So-
" vereign as the Englifh; and you muft
" allow, that, if fome Scotchmen make
" fortunes in England, many of our
" beft eftates are alfo fpent there. But
" you mean to fay, that the Scotch,
" in

" in general, are poor in comparison of
" the Englifh. This we do not deny, and
" cannot poffibly forget, your countrymen
" refrefh our memories with it fo often.
" We allow, therefore, that you have this
" advantage over us;—and the Perfians
" had the fame over the Macedonians at
" the battle of Arbela. But, whether
" Scotland be poor or rich, thofe Scots
" who fettle in England muft carry in-
" duftry, talents, or wealth with them,
" otherwife they will ftarve there as well
" as elfewhere; and when one country
" draws citizens of this defcription from
" another, I leave you to judge which has
" the moft reafon to complain. And let
" me tell you, Sir, upon the whole, the
" advantages which England derives from
" the Union, are manifeft and mani-
" fold." " I cannot fay," replied the
Englifhman, " that I have thought much
" on this fubject; but I fhall be obliged to
" you if you will enumerate a few of
" them." " In the firft place," refumed

the

the Scot, " Has she not greatly increased
" in wealth since that time?" " She has
" so," replied the other, smiling, " and I
" never knew the *real cause* before." " In
" the next place, Has she not acquired a
" million and a half of subjects, who other-
" wise would have been with her enemies?
" For this, *and other reasons,* they are
" equivalent to three millions.   In the
" third place, Has she not acquired secu-
" rity? without which riches are of no va-
" lue.   There is no door open *now,* Sir,
" by which the French can enter into your
" country.   They dare as soon be d——
" as attempt to invade Scotland; so if you
" can defend your own coast, there is no.
" fear of you; but without a perfect union
" with Scotland, England could not enjoy.
" the principal benefit she derives from her.
" insular situation." " Not till Scotland
" should be subdued," said the Englishman. " Subdued!" repeated the asto-
nished Scot; " let me tell you, Sir, *that*
" is a very strange hypothesis; the fruit-
" less

" lefs attempts of many centuries might
" have taught you that the thing is impof-
" fible; and, if you are converfant in hif-
" tory, you will find, that, after the de-
" cline of the Roman Empire, the courfe
" of conqueft was from *the North to the
" South.*" " You mean," faid the South
" Briton, " that Scotland would have
" conquered England." " Sir," replied
the other, " I think the Englifh as brave
" a nation as ever exifted, and therefore I
" will not fay that the Scotch are braver;
" far lefs fhall I affert, that *they*, confift-
" ing of only a fifth part of the numbers,
" could fubdue the Englifh; but I am fure,
" that rather than fubmit they would try;
" and you will admit that the trial would
" be no advantage to either country."
" Although I am fully convinced," faid
the Englifhman, " how the experiment
" would end, I fhould be forry to fee it
" made, particularly at this time." " Yet,
" Sir," rejoined the Scot, " there are
" people of your country, as I am told,
" who,

" who, even at *this time*, endeavour to ex-
" afperate the minds of the inhabitants of
" one part of Great Britain againft the na-
" tives of the other, and to create diffenfion
" between two countries, whofe mutual
" fafety depends on their good agreement ;
" two countries whom Nature herfelf, by
" feparating them from the reft of the
" world, and encircling them with her
" azure bond of union, feems to have in-
" tended for one."   " I do affure you, my
" good Sir," faid the Englifh Gentleman,
" I am not of the number of thofe who
" wifh to raife fuch diffenfion. I love the
" Scotch ; I always thought them a fen-
" fible and gallant people ; and fome of
" the moft valued friends I have on earth,
" are of your country."   " You are a man
" of honour and difcernment," faid the
Caledonian, feizing him eagerly by the
hand ; " and I proteft, without prejudice
" or partiality, that I never knew a man
" of that character who was not of your
" way of thinking."

LETTER LXX.

Florence.

WE arrived in this city the third day
after leaving Rome, though I have
delayed writing till now. I wiſhed to know
ſomething of the place, and to be a little
acquainted with the people. The laſt is not
difficult; becauſe the Florentines are naturally affable, and the hoſpitality and po-
liteneſs of the Britiſh Miniſter afford his
countrymen frequent opportunities of forming an acquaintance with the beſt company
in Florence. This gentleman has been here
about thirty years, and is greatly eſteemed
by the Florentines. It is probably owing
to this circumſtance, and to the magnificent ſtile in which ſome Engliſh Noblemen
live, who have long reſided here, that the
Engliſh, in general, are favourites with the
inhabitants of this place. L—d C——r's
conduct

conduct and difpofition confirm them in the opinion they long have had of the good-nature and integrity of the nation to which he belongs. His Lady is of an amiable character, and affords them a very favourable fpecimen of Englifh beauty.

We have had no opportunity of feeing the Grand Duchefs. She is of a domeflic turn, and lives much in the country with her children, of which fhe has a comfortable number; but the Grand Duke having come to town for two days, we had the honour of being prefented to him at the Palazzo Pitti. There is a ftriking refemblance of each other in all the branches of the Auftrian family. Wherever I had met with the Grand Duke, I fhould immediately have known that he belonged to it. He, as well his brother who refides at Milan, has, in a remarkable degree, the thick lip; which has long been a diflinguifhing feature in the Auftrian family. He is a handfome man, is rapid in his words and motions, and has more vivacity in his manner than

than either the Emperor or Archduke;
like them, he is good-hu moured, conde-
fcending and affable. After the extinction
of the Medici family, the Florentines
grumbled on account of the difadvantage
and inconveniency of having Sovereigns
who did not refide among them. They
exclaimed that their money was carried
away to a diftant country, and the moft
profitable offices at home filled by foreign-
ers. They have now got a Sovereign who
refides and fpends his revenue among them,
and has provided the State moft plentifully
in heirs; yet they ftill grumble. They
complain of the taxes—But in what country of Europe is there not the fame complaint?

Florence is, unqueftionably, a very
beautiful city. Independent of the churches
and palaces, fome of which are very magnificent, the architecture of the houfes in
general is in a good tafte, the ftreets are
remarkably clean, and paved with large
broad ftones, chifeled fo as to prevent the
horfes

horfes from fliding. This city is divided into two unequal parts by the river Arno, over which there are no lefs than four bridges in fight of each other. That called the Ponte della Trinità, is uncommonly elegant. It is built entirely of white marble, and ornamented with four beautiful ftatues, reprefenting the Four Scafone. The quays, the buildings on each fide, and the bridges, render that part of Florence through which the river runs, by far the fineft. The fame is the cafe at Paris; and It happens fortunately for thofe two cities, that thofe parts are almoft conftantly before the eye, on account of the neceffity people are continually under of paffing and repaffing thofe bridges; whereas in London, whofe river and bridges are far fuperior to any in France or Italy, people may live whole feafons, attend all the public amufements, and drive every day from one end of the town to the other, without ever feeing the Thames or the bridges, unlefs they go on purpofe. For this reafon,

when a foreigner is afked which he thinks
the fineft city, Paris or London; the moment Paris is mentioned, the Louvre, and
that ftriking part which is fituated between
the Pont Royal and Pont Neuf, prefents
itfelf to his imagination. He can recollect
no part of London equal in magnificence
to this ; and ten to one, if he decides directly, it will be in favour of Paris : but if
he takes a little more time, and compares
the two capitals, ftreet by ftreet, fquare by
fquare, and bridge with bridge, he will
probably be of a different opinion. The
number of inhabitants in Florence is calculated by fome at eighty thoufand. The
ftreets, fquares, and fronts of the palaces
are adorned with a great number of ftatues ; fome of them by the beft modern
mafters, Michael Angelo, Bandinelli, Do-
natello, Giovanni di Bologna, Benvenuto,
Cellini, and others. A tafte for the arts
muft be kept alive, independent almoft of
any other encouragement, in a city where
fo many fpecimens are continually before
the

the eyes of the inhabitants. There are towns in Europe, where ftatues, expofed night and day within the reach of the common people, would run a great rifque of being disfigured and mutilated; here they are as fafe as if they were fhut up in the Great Duke's gallery.

Florence has been equally diftinguifhed by a fpirit for commerce and for the fine arts; two things which are not always united. Some of the Florentine merchants formerly were men of vaft wealth, and lived in a moft magnificent manner. One of them, about the middle of the fifteenth century, built that noble fabric, which, from the name of its founder, is ftill called the Palazzo Pitti. The man was ruined by the prodigious expence of this building, which was immediately purchafed by the Medici family, and has continued, ever fince, to be the refidence of the Sovereigns. The gardens belonging to this palace are on the declivity of an eminence. On the fum-

A a 2   mit

mit there is a kind of fort, called Belvedere. From this, and from some of the higher walks, you have a complete view of the city of Florence, and the beauteous vale of Arno, in the middle of which it stands. The prospect is bounded on every side by an amphitheatre of fertile hills, adorned with country-houses and gardens. In no part of Italy, that I have seen, are there so many villas, belonging to private persons, as in the neighbourhood of this city; the habitations of the peasants, likewise, seem much more neat and commodious. The country all around is divided into small farms, with a neat farm-house on each. Tuscany produces a considerable quantity of corn, as well as excellent wine, and great quantities of silk. The peasants have a look of health and contentment: the natural beauty of the Italian countenance not being disgraced by dirt, or deformed by misery, the women in this country seem handsomer, and are, in reality, more blooming, than in other parts of Italy.

When

When at work, or when they bring their goods to market, their hair is confined by a filk net, which is alfo much worn at Naples; but on holidays they drefs in a very picturefque manner. They do not wear gowns, but a kind of jacket without fleeves. They have no other covering for the upper part of the arm but their fhift fleeves, which are tied with riband. Their petticoats are generally of a fcarlet colour. They wear ear-rings and necklaces. Their hair is adjufted in a becoming manner, and adorned with flowers. Above one ear they fix a little ftraw hat; and on the whole have a more gay, fmart, coquetifh air, than any country-girls I ever faw.

Churches, and palaces, and ftatues, are no doubt ornamental to a city; and the Princes are praife-worthy who have taken pains to rear and colleÃ them; but the greateft of all ornaments are cheerful, happy, living countenances. The tafte is not general; but, I thank God, I know fome

people who, to a perfect knowledge and
unaffected love of the fine arts, join a paffion for a collection of this kind, who cannot, without uneafinefs, fee one face in a
different ftyle, and whofe lives and fortunes
are employed in fmoothing the corrofions
of penury and misfortune, and *reftoring* the
original air of fatisfaction and cheerfulnefs
to the human countenance. Happy the
people whofe Sovereign is infpired with
this fpecies of virtù !

LETTER LXXI.

Florence.

I HAVE generally, since our arrival at Florence, passed two hours every forenoon in the famous gallery. Connoisseurs, and those who wish to be thought such, remain much longer. But I plainly feel this is enough for me ; and I do not think it worth while to prolong my visit after I begin to be tired, merely to be thought what I am not. Do not imagine, however, that I am blind to the beauties of this celebrated collection; by far the most valuable now in the world.

One of the most interesting parts of it, in the eyes of many, is the series of Roman Emperors, from Julius Cæsar to Gallienus, with a considerable number of their Empresses, arranged opposite to them. This series is almost complete ; but wherever the

A a 4   bust

buſt of an Emperor is wanting, the place is filled up by that of ſome other diſtinguiſhed Roman. Such an honour is beſtowed with great propriety on Seneca, Cicero, or Agrippa, the ſon-in-law of Auguſtus. But, on perceiving a head of Antinous, the favourite of Adrian, among them, a gentleman whiſpered me,—*that minion*, pointing to the head, would not have been admitted into ſuch company any where but in Florence. It ought, however, to be remembered, that the Gallery is not an Ægyptian court of judicature, where Princes are tried, after death, for crimes committed during their life. If the vices of originals had excluded their portraits, what would have become of the ſeries of Roman Emperors, and particularly of the buſt of the great Julius himſelf, who was huſband to all the wives and - - -

- - - - - - - - - - - - -

The gallery is ſacred to art, and every production which ſhe avows, has a right to a place here.

Amidſt

Amidſt thoſe noble ſpecimens of ancient
ſculpture, ſome of the works of Michael
Angelo are not thought undeſerving a place.
His Bacchus and Faunus, of which the
well-known ſtory is told, have been by
ſome preferred to the two antique figures
repreſenting the ſame.

The beautiful head of Alexander is univerſally admired by all the virtuoſi; though
they differ in opinion with regard to the
circumſtance in which the ſculptor has intended to repreſent that hero. Some imagine he is dying; Mr. Addiſon imagines
he ſighs for new worlds to conquer; others
that he faints with pain and loſs of blood
from the wounds he received at Oxydrace.
Others think the features expreſs not bodily
pain or languor, but ſorrow and remorſe,
for having murdered his faithful friend
Clitus. You ſee how very uncertain a buſineſs this of a virtuoſo is. I can hardly
believe that the artiſt intended ſimply to
repreſent him dying; there was nothing
                                    very

very creditable in the manner he brought
on his death. Nor do I think he would
choose to represent him moaning, or lan-
guishing with pain or sicknefs; there is
nothing heroic in that; nor do we sympa-
thife fo readily with the pains of the body,
as with thofe of the mind. As for the
ftory of his weeping for new worlds, he
will excite ftill lefs fympathy, if that is
the caufe of his affliction. The laft conjec-
ture, therefore, that the artift intended to
reprefent him in a violent fit of remorfe, is
the moft probable. The unfinifhed buft of
Marcus Brutus, by Michael Angelo, admirably expreffes the determined firmnefs
of character which belonged to that virtuous Roman. The artift, while he
wrought at this, feems to have had in his
mind Horace's Ode

> Juftum et tenacem propofiti virum
> Non civium ardor prava jubentium,
> Non vultus inftantis tyranni
> Mente quatit folidâ, &c.

This

This would, in my opinion, be a more suitable inscription for the bust, than the concetto of Cardinal Bembo, which is at present under it *. Michael Angelo, in all probability was pleased with the expression he had already given the features, and chose to leave it as an unfinished sketch, rather than risk weakening it by an attempt to improve it.

The virtuosi differ in opinion respecting the Arrotino, or Whetter, as much as about the head of Alexander. A young gentleman said to an antiquarian, while he contemplated the Arrotino, " I believe, " Sir, it is imagined that this statue was " intended for the slave, who, while he " was whetting his knife, overheard Ca- " tiline's conspiracy."—" That is the vul- " gar opinion," said the other; " but the " statue was, in reality, done for a pea- " sant, who discovered the plot into which

* Dum Bruti effigiem Michael de marmore fingit, In mentem sceleris venit, et abstinuit.

" the

" the two fons of Junius Brutus entered
" for the reftoration of Tarquin." " I
" afk pardon, Sir," faid the young man;
" but although one may eafily fee that
" the figure liftens with the moft exqui-
" fite expreffion of attention, yet I fhould
" think it very difficult to delineate in the
" features, whether the liftener heard a
" confpiracy, or any thing elfe which
" greatly interefted him, and abfolutely
" impoffible to mark, by any expreffion
" of countenance, what particular con-
" fpiracy he is hearing." " Your obfer-
" vation is juft, young man," faid the
antiquarian, " when applied to modern
" artifts, but entirely the reverfe when
" applied to the ancient. Now, for my
" own part, I plainly perceive in that
" man's countenance, and after you have
" ftudied thofe matters as profoundly as
" I have done you will fee the fame, that
" it is the confpiracy for the reftoration
" of Tarquin, and no other plot what-
" ever,

" ever, which he liflens to; as for Cati-
" line's confpiracy, it is not poffible he
" could know any thing about it; for,
" good God! people ought to reflect,
" that the man muft have been dead four
" hundred years before Catiline was born.".

As we are now in the famous octogonal
room, called Tribuna, I ought, if I had
any thing new to fay, to defcant a little on
the diftinguifhing excellencies of the Dancing
Faun, the Wreftlers, the Venus Urania, the
Venus Victrix; and I would moft willingly
pay the poor tribute of my praife to that
charming figure known by the name of
Venus de Medicis. Yet, in the midft of
all my admiration, I confefs I do not
think her equal to her brother Apollo in
the Vatican. In that fublime figure, to the
moft perfect features and proportions, is
joined an air which feems more than human. The Medicean Venus is unqueftionably a perfect model of female beauty;
but while Apollo appears more than a

2   man,

man, the Venus seems precisely a beautiful woman.

In the same room are many valuable curiosities, besides a collection of admirable pictures by the best masters. I do not know whether any are more excellent of their kind, but I am convinced none are more attentively considered than the two Venuses of Titian; one is said to be a portrait of his wife, the other of his mistress. The first is the finest portrait I ever saw, except the second; of this you have seen many copies: though none of them equals the beauty of the original, yet they will give a juster idea of it than any description of mine could. On the back ground, two women seem searching for something in a trunk. This episode is found much fault with; for my part, I see no great harm the two poor women do: none but those critics who search more eagerly after *deformity* than *beauty*, will take any notice of them.

Besides

Besides the Gallery and Tribuna, the hundredth part of whose treasures I have not particularised, there are other rooms, whose contents are indicated by the names they bear; as, the Cabinet of Arts, of Astronomy, of Natural History, of Medals, of Porcelain, of Antiquities, and the Saloon of the Hermaphrodite, fo called from a statue which divides the admiration of the Amateurs with that in the Borghese village at Rome. The excellence of the execution is difgraced by the vilenefs of the fubject. We are furprifed how the Greeks and Romans could take pleafure in fuch unnatural figures; in this particular their tafte feems to have been as depraved, as in general it was elegant and refined. In this room there is a collection of drawings by fome of the greatest mafters, Michael Angelo, Raphael, Andrea del Sarto, and others. There is, in particular, a fketch of the Laft Judgment by the firft-named of thefe painters, different, and, in the opinion of fome, de-

9   figned

figned with more judgment, than his famous picture on the fame fubject in Sixtus
the Fourth's chapel in the Vatican.

The large room, called the Gallery of
Portraits, is not the leaft curious in this
vaft Mufæum. It contains the portraits,
all executed by themfelves, of the moft
eminent painters who have flourifhed in
Europe during the three laft centuries.
They amount to above two hundred ; thofe
of Rubens, Vandyke, Rembrandt, and
Guido, were formerly the moft efteemed;
two have been added lately, which vie
with the fineft in this collection—thofe of
Meng's and Sir Jofhua Reynolds. The
portrait of Raphael feems to have been
done when he was young ; it is not equal
to any of the above. The Electrefs
Dowager of Saxony has made a valuable
addition to this collection, by fending
her own portrait painted by herfelf; fhe
is at full length, with the palette and
pencils in her hands. Coreggio, after
hearing

hearing the picture of St. Cecilia at Bologna cried up as a prodigy, and the *ne
plus ultra* of art, went to fee it; and confcious that there was nothing in it that required the exertion of greater powers than
he felt within himfelf, he was overheard to
fay, " Anch' io fono pittore." This illuftrious princefs was alfo confcious of her
powers when fhe painted this portrait,
which feems to pronounce to the fpectators,
Anch' io fono pittrice.

L E T T E R LXXII.

HAVING now croffed from the Adriatic to the Mediterranean, and travelled through a confiderable part of Italy, I acknowledge I have been agreeably difappointed in finding the ftate of the poorer part of the inhabitants lefs wretched than, from the accounts of fome travellers, I imagined it was; and I may with equal truth add, that although I have not feen fo much poverty as I was taught to expect, yet I have feen far more poverty than mifery. Even the extremity of indigence is accompanied with lefs wretchednefs here than in many other countries. This is partly owing to the mildnefs of the climate and fertility of the foil, and partly to the peaceable, religious, and contented difpofition of the

3   people.

people. The miseries which the poorer part of mankind suffer from cold, are, perhaps, greater than those derived from any other source whatever. But in Italy, the gentleness of the climate protects them from this calamity nine months of the year. If they can gather as much wood as to keep a moderate fire during the remaining three, and procure a coarse cloke, they have little to fear from that quarter. Those who cannot get employment, which is often the case in this country, and even those who do not choose to work, which is the case with numbers all the world over, receive a regular maintenance from some convent: with this, and what little they can pick up otherwise, in a country where provisions are plentiful and cheap, they pass through life, in their own opinion, with more satisfaction than if they had a greater number of conveniencies procured by much bodily labour. Whereas in Great Britain, Germany, and other northern

countries,

countries, the poor have no choice but to work; for if they remain idle, they are exposed to miseries more intolerable than the hardest labour can occasion to the laziest of mankind; they are invaded at once by the accumulated agonies of hunger and cold; and if they have ever had sufficient credit to contract a little debt, they are continually in danger of being thrown into a jail among pickpockets and felons. With respect to the lowest of the tradespeople and the day-labourers in this country, their wages are certainly not high; nor are they willing, by great efforts of industry, to gain all they might; but what they do gain is never wasted in intemperance, but fairly spent in their families on the real necessaries and comforts of life.

The Italians are the greatest loungers in the world, and while walking in the fields, or stretched in the shade, seem to enjoy the serenity and genial warmth of their

their climate with a degree of luxurious indulgence peculiar to themselves. Without ever running into the daring exceffes of the Englifh, or difplaying the frifky vivacity of the French, or the invincible phlegm of the Germans, the Italian populace difcover a fpecies of fedate fenfibility to every fource of enjoyment, from which, perhaps, they derive a greater degree of happinefs than any of the other. The frequent proceffions and religious ceremonies, befides amufing and comforting them, ferve to fill up their time, and prevent that ennui and thofe immoral practices which are apt to accompany poverty and idlenefs. It is neceffary, for the quiet and happinefs of every community, that the populace be employed. Some politicians imagine, that their whole time fhould be fpent in gainful induftry. Others think, that though the riches of the ftate will not be augmented, yet the general happinefs, which is a more im-

portant

'portant object, will be promoted by blend-
ing the occupations of induftry with a
confiderable proportion of fuch fuperftitious ceremonies as awaken the future
hopes, without lulling the prefent benevolence, of the multitude; but nobody
can doubt, that in countries where, from
whatever caufe, induftry does not prevail,
proceffions and other rites of the fame
nature will tend to reftrain the populace
from the vices, and of confequence prevent fome of the miferies of idlenefs.

The peafantry of this country are unqueftionably in a more comfortlefs ftate
than a benevolent mind could wifh them.
But, England and Switzerland excepted,
is not this the cafe all over Europe? In
all the countries I have feen, or had an
account of, the hufbandmen, probably
the moft virtuous, but certainly the moft
ufeful part of the community, whofe
labour and induftry maintain all the reft,
and in whom the real ftrength of the ftate
refides,

refides, are, by a moft unjuft difpenfation, generally the pooreft and moft oppreffed. But although the Italian peafantry are by no means in the affluent, independent fituation of the peafantry of Switzerland, and the tenantry of England, yet they are not fubjected to the fame oppreffions with thofe of Germany, nor are they fo poor as thofe of France.

Great part of the lands in Italy belong to convents; and I have obferved, and have been affured by thofe who have the beft opportunities of knowing, that the tenants of thefe communities are happier, and live more at their eafe, than thofe of a great part of the nobility. The revenues of convents are ufually well managed, and never allowed to be fquandered away by the folly or extravagance of any of its members; confequently the community is not driven, by craving and threatening creditors, as individuals frequently are, to fqueeze out of their vaffals

the

the means of fupplying the wafte occafioned by their own vanity and expence.
·A convent can have no incitement to fevere
and oppreffive exactions from the peafants,
except fheer avarice ; a paffion which never
rifes to fuch a height in a fociety where the
revenue is in common, as in the breaft of
an individual, who is folely to reap the
fruits of his own oppreffion.

The ftories which circulate in Proteftant
countries, concerning the fcandalous de-
bauchery of monks, and the luxurious
manner in which they live in their convents, whatever truth there may have been
in them formerly, are certainly now in a
great meafure without foundation. I remember when I was at the Grande Char-
treufe, near Grenoble, which has a confiderable diftrict of land belonging to it, I
was informed, and this information was
confirmed by what I faw, that thofe monks
were gentle and generous mafters, and that
their tenants were envied by all the peafantry

fantry around, on account of the treatment
they received, and the comparatively eafy
terms on which they held their farms.
From the enquiries I have made in France,
Germany, and Italy, I am convinced that
this is ufually the cafe with thofe peafants
who belong to convent lands; and very
often, I have been informed, befides having eafy rents, they alfo find affectionate
friends and protectors in their mafters,
who vifit them in ficknefs, comfort them in
all diftreffes, and are of fervice to their families in various fhapes.

I have been fpeaking hitherto of the peafantry belonging to convents; but I believe
I might extend the remark to the tenants
of ecclefiaftics in general, though they are
often reprefented as more proud and oppreffive mafters than any clafs of men
whatever; an afperfion which may have
gained credit the more eafily on this account,
that inftances of cruelty and oppreffion in
ecclefiaftics ftrike more, and raife a greater

9   indignation,

indignation, than the fame degree of wickednefs in other men; they raife a greater
indignation, becaufe they are more unbe-
coming of clergymen, and they ftrike
more when they do happen, becaufe they
happen feldomer. The ambition of Popes
fome centuries ago, when the Court of
Rome was in its zenith, the unlimited influence and power which particular Churchmen acquired in England and France, had
thofe effects upon their actions and characters, which ambition and power ufually
have on the characters of men; it rendered
them infolent, unfeeling, and perfecuting.
Yet, for every cruel and tyrannical Pope
that hiftory has recorded, it will be eafy to
name two or three Roman Emperors who
have furpaffed them in every fpecies of
wickednefs; and England and France have
had Prime Minifters with all the vices,
without the abilities, of Wolfey and Riche-
lieu.

Thofe who declaim againft the wickednefs of the clergy, feem to take it for
granted

granted that this body of men were the authors of the moft horrid inftances of perfecution, maffacre, and tyranny, over men's confciences, that are recorded in the annals of mankind; yet Philip II. Charles IX. and Henry VIII. were not Churchmen; and the capricious tyranny of Henry, tho. frantic fury of Charles, and the perfevering cruelty of Philip, feem to have proceeded from the perfonal characters of thefe Monarchs, or to have been excited by what they confidered as their political intereft, rather than by the fuggeftions of their Clergy.

As the fubjects of the Ecclefiaftical State are perhaps the pooreft in Italy, this has been imputed to the rapacious difpofition which fome affert is natural to Churchmen. This poverty, however, may be otherwife acounted for. Bifhop Burnet very judicioufly obferves, that the fubjects of a government, which is at once defpotic and elective, labour under peculiar difadvantages;

tages; for an hereditary Prince will naturally have confiderations for his people
which an elective one will not, " unlefs he
" has a degree of generofity not common
" among men, and leaft of all among
" Italians, who have a paffion for their
" families which is not known in other
" places *." An elective Prince, knowing that it is only during his reign that his
family can receive any benefit from it,
makes all the hafte he can to enrich them.
To this it may be added, that as Popes generally arrive at Sovereignty at an age
when avarice predominates in the human
breaft, they may be fuppofed to have a
ftronger bias than other Princes to that
fordid paffion; and even when this does
not take place, their needy relations are
continually prompting them to acts of oppreffion, and fuggefting ways and means
of fqueezing the people. Other caufes
might be affigned; but, that it does not
originate from the imputation above men-

* Vide Bifhop Burnet's Travels.

tioned,

tioned, feems evident from this, that the
peafants of particular ecclefiaftics, and of
the convents in the Pope's dominions, as
well as in other countries, are generally
lefs opprefled than thofe of the lay lords
and princes.

From what has been thrown out by
fome celebrated wits, and the common-
place invective of thofe who affect that character, one would be led to imagine that
there is fomething in the nature of the cle-
rical profeffion which has a tendency to
render men proud and oppreffive. Such
indifcriminating cenfure carries no conviction to my mind, becaufe it is contradicted
by the experience I have had in life, and
by the obfervations, fuch as they are,
which I have been able to make on human
nature. I do not mean, in imitation of the
fatirifts above mentioned, to put the
Clergy of all religions on the fame footing.
My opportunities of knowledge are too
flender to juftify *that*; my acquaintance
with

with this order of men having been in a great meaſure confined to thoſe of the Proteſtant Church, men of learning and ingenuity, of quiet, ſpeculative, and benevolent diſpoſitions ; it is uſually, indeed, this turn of mind which has inclined them to the eccleſiaſtical profeſſion. But though my acquaintance with the Roman Catholic Clergy is very limited, yet the few I do know could not be mentioned as exceptions to what I have juſt ſaid of the Proteſtant ; and, excluſive of all perſonal knowledge of the men, it is natural to think that the habitual performance of the ceremonies of the Chriſtian religion, though intermingled with ſome ſuperſtitious rites, and the preaching the doctrines of benevolence and good-will towards men, muſt have ſome influence on the lives and characters of thoſe who are thus employed. It is a common error, prevailing in Proteſtant countries, to imagine that the Roman Catholic Clergy laugh at the religion they inculcate, and regard their flocks as the dupes of an artful plan
of

of impofition. By far the greater part of
Roman Catholic priefts and monks are
themfelves moft fincere believers, and teach
the doctrines of Chriftianity, and all the
miracles of the legend, with a perfect conviction of their divinity and truth. The
few who were behind the curtain when
falfehood was firft embroidered upon truth,
and thofe who have at different periods been
the authors of all the mafks and interludes
which have enriched the grand drama of
fuperftition, have always chofen to employ
fuch men, being fenfible that the inferior
actors would perform their parts more perfectly, by acting from nature and real conviction. " Paulum intereffe cenfes," fays
Davus to Myfis, " ex animo omnia ut
" fert natura, facias an de induftria *."

The accounts we receive of their gluttony, are often as ill-founded as thofe of
their infidelity. The real character of the
majority of monks and inferior ecclefiaftics,

* Andria Terentii.

both

both in France and Italy, is that of a fimple,
fuperftitious, well-meaning race of men,
who for the moft part live in a very abfte-
mious and mortified manner, notwithftanding what we have heard of their gluttony,
their luxury, and voluptuoufnefs. Accufations are frequently thrown out by thofe
who are ill entitled to make them. I remember being in company with an acquaintance of yours, who is diftinguifhed
for the delicacy of his table and the length
of his repafts, from which he feldom retires
without a bottle of Burgundy for his own
fhare, not to mention two or three glaffes
of Champaign between the courfes. We
had dined a few miles from the town in
which we then lived, and were returning
in his chariot; it was winter, and he was
wrapped in fur to the nofe. As we drove
along, we met two friars walking through
the fnow; little threads of icicles hung
from their beards; their legs and the upper
part of their feet were bare, but their foles
were defended from the fnow by wooden
fandals.

fandals. " There goes a couple of dainty
" rogues," cried your friend as we drew
near them ; " only think of the folly of
" permitting fuch lazy, luxurious rafcals to
" live in a State, and eat up the portion of
" the poor. I will engage that thofe two
" fcoundrels, as lean and mortified as
" they look, will devour more victuals in
" a day, than would maintain two induſtri-
" ous families." He continued railing
againſt the luxury of thofe two friars, and
afterwards expatiated upon the epicurifm of
the clergy in general; who, he faid, were
all alike in every country, and of every religion. When we arrived in town, he told
me he had ordered a little nice fupper to be
got ready at his houfe by the time of our
return, and had lately got fome excellent
wine, inviting me at the fame time to go
home with him ; for, continued he, as *we
have driven* three miles in fuch weather,
we ſtand in great need of fome refreſhment.

That in all Roman Catholic countries,
and particularly in Italy, the clergy are too
VoL. II.   C c   numerous,

numerous, have too much power, too great
a proportion of the lands, and that fome
of them live in great pomp and luxury, is
undeniable. That the common people
would be in a better fituation, if manufactures and the fpirit of induftry could be introduced among them, is equally true; but,
even as things are, I cannot help thinking
that the ftate of the Italian peafantry is preferable, in many refpects, to that of the
peafants of many other countries in Europe.
They are not beaten by their ecclefiaftical
lords, as thofe of Germany are by their
mafters, on every real or imaginary offence.
They have not their children torn from
them, to be facrificed to the pomp, avarice,
or ambition of fome military defpot; nor
are they themfelves preffed into the fervice
as foldiers for life.

In England and in France the people
take an intereft in all national difputes, and
confider the caufe of their country or their
Prince as their own; they enter into the

I   fervice

fervice voluntarily, and fight with ardour
for the glory of the country or King they
love. Thofe ideas enable them to fubmit
to a thoufand hardfhips without repining,
and they feel the fenfations of happinefs in
the midft of toil, want, and danger. But
in Germany, where the paffions are anni-
hilated, and a man is modelled into a ma-
chine before he is thought a good foldier,
where his blood is fold by the Prince to the
higheft bidder, where he has no quarrel
with the enemy he murders, and no allegiance to the Monarch for whom he fights,
the being liable to be forced into fuch a fervice, is one of the moft dreadful of all calamities. Yet a regiment of fuch compelled
foldiers, dreffed in gaudy uniform, and
powdered for a review, with mufic found-
ing and colours flying, makes a far more
brilliant appearance than a clufter of peafants with their wives and children upon a
holiday. But if we could examine the
breafts of the individuals, we fhould find in
thofe of the former nothing but the terror
Cc 2   of

of punifhment, hatred of their officers,
diftruft of each other, and life itfelf fup-
ported only by the hope of defertion ; while
the bofoms of the latter are filled with all
the affections of humanity, undifturbed by
fear or remorfe.

LETTER LXXIII.

Florence.

SOCIETY feems to be on an eafy and agreeable footing in this city. Befides the converfazionis which they have here, as in other towns of Italy, a number of the nobility meet every day at a houfe called the Cafino. This fociety is pretty much on the fame footing with the clubs in London. The members are elected by ballot. They meet at no particular hour, but go at any time that is convenient. They play at billiards, cards, and other games, or continue converfing the whole evening, as they think proper. They are ferved with tea, coffee, lemonade, ices, or what other refrefhments they choofe ; and each perfon pays for what he calls for. There is one material difference between this and the Englifh clubs, that women as well as men are members.

The

The company of both fexes behave with more franknefs and familiarity to ſtrangers, as well as to each other, than is cuſtomary in public aſſemblies in other parts of Italy.

The Opera at Florence is a place where the people of quality pay and receive viſits, and converſe as freely as at the Caſino above mentioned. This occaſions a continual paſſing and repaſſing to and from the boxes, except in thoſe where there is a party of cards formed ; it is then looked on as a piece of ill manners to diſturb the players. I never was more ſurpriſed, than when it was propoſed to me to make one of a whiſt party, in a box which ſeemed to have been made for the purpoſe, with a little table in the middle. I hinted that it would be full as convenient to have the party ſomewhere elſe ; but I was told, good muſic added greatly to the pleaſure of a whiſt party ; that it increaſed the joy of good fortune, and ſoothed the affliction of bad. As I thought the people of this
country

country better acquainted than myself with the power of music, I contested the point no longer; but have generally played two or three rubbers at whist in the stage-box every opera night.

From this you may guess, that, in this city, as in some other towns in Italy, little attention is paid to the music by the company in the boxes, except at a new opera, or during some favourite air. But the dancers command a general attention: as soon as they begin, conversation ceases; even the card-players lay down their cards, and fix their eyes on the Ballette. Yet the excellence of Italian dancing seems to consist in feats of strength, and a kind of jerking agility, more than in graceful movement. There is a continual contest among the performers, who shall spring highest. You see here none of the sprightly, alluring gaiety of the French comic dancers, nor of the graceful attitudes, and smooth flowing motions of the performers in the serious

Cc 4 opera

opera at Paris. It is surprising, that a
people of such taste and sensibility as the
Italians, should prefer a parcel of athletic
jumpers to elegant dancers..

On the evenings on which there is no
opera, it is usual for the genteel company
to drive to a public walk immediately
without the city, where they remain till it
begins to grow duskish. Soon after our
arrival at Florence, in one of the avenues
of this walk we observed two men and two
ladies, followed by four servants in livery.
One of the men wore the insignia of the
garter. We were told this was the Count
Albany, and that the Lady next to him was
the Countess. We yielded the walk, and
pulled off our hats. The gentleman along
with them was the Envoy from the King of
Prussia to the Court of Turin. He whis-
pered the Count, who, returning the salu-
tation, looked very earnestly at the D— of
H——. We have seen them almost every
evening since, either at the opera or on the
public

public walk. His G— does not affect to
shun the avenue in which they happen to
be; and as often as we pass near them, the
Count fixes his eyes in a moft expreffive
manner upon the D—, as if he meant to
fay—our anceftors were better acquainted.

You know, I fuppofe, that the Count
Albany is the unfortunate Charles Stuart,
who left Rome fome time fince on the death
of his father, becaufe the Pope did not
think proper to acknowledge him by the
title which he claimed on that event. He
now lives at Florence, on a fmall revenue
allowed him by his brother. The Countefs
is a beautiful woman, much beloved by
thofe who know her, who univerfally defcribe her as lively, intelligent, and agreeable. Educated as I was in Revolution
principles, and in a part of Scotland where
the religion of the Stuart family, and the
maxims by which they governed, are more
reprobated than perhaps in any part of
Great Britain, I could not behold this unfortunate

fortunate perfon without the warmeft emotion and fympathy. What muft a man's
feelings be, who finds himfelf excluded
from the moft brilliant fituation, and nobleft
inheritance that this world affords, and reduced to an humiliating dependance on
thofe, who, in the natural courfe of events,
fhould have looked up to him for protection and fupport? What muft his feelings
be, when on a retrofpective view he be-
holds a feries of calamities attending his family, that is without example in the annals of the unfortunate; calamities, of
which thofe they experienced after their
acceffion to the throne of England, were
only a continuation? Their misfortunes
began with their royalty, adhered to them
through ages, increafed with the increafe
of their dominions, did not forfake them
when dominion was no more; and, as he
has reafon to dread, from his own experience, are not yet terminated. It will afford
no alleviation or comfort, to recollect that
part of this black lift of calamities arofe
from

from the imprudence of his anceftors; and
that many gallant men, in England, Scotland, and Ireland, have at different periods
been involved in their ruin.

Our fympathy for this unfortunate perfon is not checked by any blame which
can be thrown on himfelf. He furely had
no fhare in the errors of the firft Charles,
the profligacy of the fecond, or the impolitic and bigotted attempts of James againft
the laws and eftablifhed religion of Great
Britain and Ireland ; therefore, whilft I contemplate with approbation and gratitude
the conduct of thofe patriots who refifted
and expelled that infatuated monarch, afcertained the rights of the fubject, and fettled the conftitution of Great Britain on the
firm bafis of freedom on which it has ftood
ever fince the Revolution, and on which I
hope it will ever ftand, yet I freely acknowledge, that I never could fee the unfortunate Count Albany without fentiments
of

of compaffion, and the moft lively fympathy.

I write with the more warmth, as I have
heard of fome of our countrymen, who,
during their tours through Italy, made the
humble ftate to which he is reduced a frequent theme of ridicule, and who, as often
as they met him in public, affected to pafs
by with an air of fneering infult. The
motive to this is as bafe and abject as the
behaviour is unmanly; thofe who endeavour to make misfortune an object of ridicule, are themfelves the objects of detefta-
tion. A Britifh nobleman or gentleman
has certainly no occafion to form an
intimacy with the Count Albany; but
while he appears under that name, and
claims no other title, it is ungenerous, on
every accidental meeting, not to behave to
him with the refpect due to a man of high
rank, and the delicacy due to a man highly
unfortunate.

One

One thing is certain; that the same difpofition which makes men infolent to the
weak, renders them flaves to the powerful; and thofe who are moft apt to treat
this unfortunate perfon with an oftentatious contempt at Florence, would have
been his moft abject flatterers at St.
James's.

L·E T T E R LXXIV.

Florence.

IN a country where men are permitted to speak and write without reſtraint on the meaſures of government; where almoſt every citizen may flatter himſelf with the hopes of becoming a part of the legiſlature; where eloquence, popular talents, and political intrigues, lead to honoura, and open a broad road to wealth and power; men, after the firſt glow of youth is paſt, are more obedient to the loud voice of ambition than to the whiſpers of love. But in deſpotic ſtates, and in monarchies which verge towards deſpotiſm, where the will of the prince is law; or, which amounts nearly to the ſame thing, where the law yields to the will of the prince; where it is dangerous to ſpeak or write on general politics, and

death

death or imprifonment to cenfure the particular meafures of government; love becomes a firft, inftead of being a fecondary
objeft; for ambition is, generally fpeaking, a more powerful paffion than love;
and on this account women are the ob-
jeɗs of greater atteation and refpeɗ in
defpotic than in free countries. That
fpecies of addrefs to women which is now
called gallantry, was, if I am not miftaken, unknown to the ancient Greeks
and Romans; nothing like it appears in
any of Terence's comedies, where one
would naturally expeɗ to find it, if any
fuch thing had exifted when they were
written. It now prevails, in fome degree,
in every country of Europe, but appears
in different forms according to the different charaɗers, cuftoms, and manners,
of the various countries.

In the courts of Germany it is a formal
piece of bufinefs; etiquette governs the
arrows of Cupid, as well as the torch of
Hymen.

Hymen. Miftreffes are chofen from the number of quarters on their family coats of arms, as well as from the number of their perfonal charms; and thofe ladies who are well provided in the firft, feldom are without lovers, however deficient they may be in the fecond. But though many avenues, which in England lead to power and diftinction, are fhut up in Germany, and the whole power of government is vefted in the fovereign, yet the young nobility cannot beftow a great deal of their time in gallantry. The military profeffion, which in the time of peace is perfect idlenefs in France and England, is a very ferious, unremitting employment in Germany. Men who are continually drilling foldiers, and whofe fortunes and reputations depend on the expertnefs of the troops under their command, cannot pay a great deal of attention to the ladies.

Every French gentleman muft be a foldier; but fighting is the only part of the bufi-

nefs

nefs they go through with fpirit; they
cannot fubmit to the German precifion in
difcipline, their fouls fink under the tedi-
oufnefs of a campaign, and they languifh
for a battle from the impetuofity of their
difpofition, and impatience to have the
matter decided one way or the other.
This, with many particular exceptions, is
the general ftyle of the French nobleffe;
they all ferve an apprenticefhip to war,
but gallantry is the profeffion they follow
for life. In England, the fpirit of play
and of party draws the minds of the
young men of fortune from love or gallantry; thofe who fpend their evenings at
a gaming houfe, or in parliament, feldom
think of any kind of women but fuch as
may be had without trouble; and, of
courfe, women of character are lefs attended to than in fome other countries.
When I was laft at Paris, the Marquis de
F—— found an Englifh newfpaper on
my table; it contained a long and particular account of a debate which had

VoL. II.　　D d　　happened

happened in both houfes of parliament; he read it with great attention while I finifhed a letter, and then throwing down the paper, he faid to me, "Mais, mon ami, "pendant que vos meffieurs f'amufent à "jafer comme cela dans votre chambre "des pairs et votre parlement*, parbleu "un etranger auroit beau jeu avec leurs "femmes."

Intrigues of gallantry, comparatively fpeaking, occur feldom in England; and when they do, they generally proceed from a violent paffion, to which every confideration of fortune and reputation is facrificed, and the bufinefs concludes in a flight to the continent, or a divorce.

They manage matters otherwife in France; you hardly ever hear of flights or divorces in that country; a hundred new arrangements are made, and as many old ones broken, in a week at Paris,

* The French in general are apt to make the fame miftake with the Marquis; they often fpeak of the Houfe of Peers and the *Parliament* as two diftinct affemblies.

without

without noife or fcandal; all is conducted
quietly et felon les régles; the fair fex
are the univerfal objects of refpect and
adoration, and yet there is no fuch thing
as conftancy in the nation. Wit, beauty,
and every accomplifhment united in one
woman, could not fix the volatility of a
Frenchman; the love of variety, and the
vanity of new conquefts, would make him
abandon this phœnix for birds far lefs
rare and eftimable. The women in France,
who are full of fpirit and fenfibility, could
never endure fuch ufage, if they were
not as fickle and as fond of new conquefts
as their lovers.

In Italy, fuch levity is viewed with contempt, and conflancy is, by both fexes,
ftill claffed among the virtues.

That high veneration for the fair fex
which prevailed in the ages of chivalry, continued long after in the form of a fentimen-
tal platonic kind of gallantry. Every man
of ingenuity chofe unto himfelf a miftrefs,
and directly proclaimed her beauty and

her

her cruelty in love ditties, madrigals, and elegies, without expecting any other recompence than the reputation of a conftant lover and a good poet. By the mere force of imagination, and the eloquence of their own metaphyfical fonnets, they became perfuaded that their miftreffes were poffeffed of every accomplifhment of face and mind, and that themfelves were dying for love.

As in thofe days women were conftantly guarded by their fathers and brothers before marriage, and watched and confined by their hufbands for the reft of their lives; the refined paffions above defcribed were not expofed to the fame accidents which fo frequently befal thofe of modern lovers; they could neither fall into a decay from a more perfect knowledge of the ladies character, nor were they liable to fudden death from enjoyment. But whilft the women were adored in fong, they were miferable in reality; confinement and diftruft made them deteft their hufbands, and they endeavoured

deavoured to form connections with men
more to their taste than either jealous husbands or metaphysical lovers. To treat
a woman of character as if she were an
unprincipled wanton, is the most likely
way to make her one. In those days of
jealousy, a continual trial of skill seems to
have subsisted between husband and wife,
as if every lord, soon after marriage, had
told his lady, "Now, Madam, I know
"perfectly well what you would be at;
"but it is my business to prevent you:
"I'll guard you so well, and watch you
"so closely, that it shall never be in your
"power to gratify your inclinations."
"You are perfectly in the right, my
"lord," replied the lady, with all meek-
ness, "pray guard and watch as your
"wisdom shall direct; I, also, shall be vi-
"gilant on my part, and we shall see how
"the business will end." The business
generally did end as might have been expected; and the only consolation left the

husband

hufband was, to endeavour to affaffinate the happy lover.

But when French manners began to fpread over Europe, and to infinuate themfelves among nations the moft oppofite in character to the French, jealoufy was firft held up as the moft deteflable of all the paffions. The law had long declared againft its difmal effects, and awful denunciations had been pronounced from the pulpit againft thofe who were inflamed by its bloody fpirit; but without effect, till ridicule joined in the argument, and expofed thofe hufbands to the contempt and derifion of every fafhionable fociety, who harboured the gloomy dæmon in their bofoms.

As in England, after the Reftoration, people, to fhew their averfion to the Puritans, turned every appearance of religion into ridicule, and from the extreme of hypocrify flew at once to that of profligacy;

fligacy; fo in Italy, from the cuftom of fecluding the wife from all mankind but her hufband, it became the fafhion that fhe fhould never be feen with her hufband, and yet always have a man at her elbow.

I fhall conclude what I have to fay on this fubject in my next.

LETTER LXXV.

Florence,

BEFORE the Italian hufbands could adopt or reconcile their minds to a cuftom fo oppofite to their former prac-tice, they took fome meafures to fecure a point which they had always thought of the higheft importance. Finding the con-finement was a plan generally reprobated, and that any appearance of jealoufy fub-jeçted the hufband to ridicule, they agreed that their wives fhould go into company and attend public places, but always attended by a friend whom they could truft, and who, at the fame time, fhould not be difagreeable to the wife. This compromife could not fail of being acceptable to the women, who plainly perceived that they muft be gainers by any alteration of the former fyftem;

and

and it foon became univerfal all over Italy,
for the women to appear at public places
leaning upon the arm of a man; who,
from their frequently whifpering together,
was called her Cicifbeo. It was ftipu-
lated, at the fame time, that the lady,
while abroad under his care, fhould con-
verfe with no other man but in his prefence, and with his approbation; he was
to be her guardian, her friend, and gen-
tleman-ufher.

The cuftom at prefent is, that this ob-
fequious gentleman vifits the lady every
forenoon at the toilet, where the plan
for paffing the evening is agreed upon;
he difappears before dinner, for it is
ufual all over Italy for the hufband and
wife to dine together tête-à-tête, except
on great occafions, as when there is a
public feaft. After dinner the hufband
retires, and the Cicifbeo returns and con-
ducts the lady to the public walk, the con-
verfazioné, or the opera; he hands her
about

about wherever she goes, presents her
coffee, forts her cards, and attends with
the most pointed affiduity till the amufements of the evening are over; he accompanies her home, and delivers up his
charge to the hufband, who is then fuppofed to refume his functions.

From the nature of this connection, it
could not be an cafy matter to find a Cicifbeo who would be equally agreeable to
the hufband and wife. At the beginning
of the inftitution, the hufbands, as I have
been informed, preferred the platonic
fwains, who profeffed only the metaphy-
ficks of love, and whofe lectures, they
imagined, might refine their wives ideas,
and bring them to the fame way of thinking; in many inftances, no doubt, it
would happen, that the platonic admirer
acted with *lefs feraphic ends*; but thefe
inftances ferve only as proofs that the hufbands were miftaken in their men; for
however abfurd it may appear in the eyes
of

of some people, to imagine that the husbands believe it is only a platonic connection which subsists between their wives and the Cicisbeos; it is still more absurd to believe, as some strangers who have passed through this country seem to have done, that this whole system of Cicisbeism was from the beginning, and is now, an universal system of adultery connived at by every Italian husband. To get clear of one difficulty, those gentlemen fall into another much more inexplicable; by supposing that the men, who of all the inhabitants of Europe were the most scrupulous with regard to their wives chastity, should acquiesce in, and in a manner become subservient to, their prostitution. In support of this strange doctrine, they assert, that the husbands being the Cicisbeos of other women, cannot enjoy this privilege on any other terms; and are therefore contented to sacrifice their wives for the sake of their mistresses. That some individuals may be profligate enough to act in this manner,

ner, I make no doubt. Similar arrangements we hear inftances of in every country; but that fuch a fyftem is general, or
any thing near it, in Italy, feems to me perfectly incredible, and is contrary to the beft
information I have received fince I have been
here. It is alfo urged, that moft of the married men of quality in Italy act in the character of Cicifbeo to fome woman or other; and
thofe who are not Platonic lovers, ought to
fufpect that the fame liberties are taken
with their wives which they take with the
fpoufes of their neighbours ; and therefore
their fuffering a man to vifit their wives in
the character of a cavaliero fervente, is in
effect conniving at their own cuckoldom.
But this does not follow as an abfolute
confequence ; for men have a wonderful
faculty of deceiving themfelves on fuch occafions. So great is the infatuation of
their vanity, that the fame degree of com-
plaifance, which they confider as the effect
of a very natural and excufable weaknefs,
when indulged by any woman for themfelves,

felves, they would look on as a horrible
enormity if admitted by their wives for
another man ; fo that whatever degree of
licentioufnefs may exift in confequence of
this fyftem, I am convinced the majority
of hufbands make exceptions in their own
favour, and that their ladies find means to
fatisfy each individual that he is not involved in a calamity, which, after all, is
more general in other countries, as well as
Italy, than it ought.

Even when there is the greateft harmony
and love between the hufband and wife,
and although each would prefer the other's
company to any other, ftill, fuch is the
tyranny of fafhion, they muft feparate
every evening ; he to play the cavaliero
fervente fo another woman, and fhe to be
led about by another man. Notwithftanding this inconveniency, the couples who
are in this predicament are certainly happier than thofe whofe affections are not
centered at home. Some very loving couples
lament

lament the cruelty of this feparation, yet the world in general feem to be of opinion, that a man and his wife who dine together every day, and lie together every night, may, with a proper exertion of philofophy, be able to fupport being afunder a few hours in the evening.

The Cicifbeo, in many inftances, is a poor relation or humble friend, who, not being in circumftances to fupport an equipage, is happy to be admitted into all the focieties, and to be carried about to public diverfions, as an appendage to the lady. I have known numbers of thofe gentlemen, whofe appearance and bodily infirmities carried the cleareft refutation, with refpect to themfelves perfonally, of the fcandalous ftories of an improper connection between cavaliero ferventes and their miftreffes. I never in my life faw men more happily formed, both in body and mind, for faving the reputation of the females with whom they were on a footing

3   of

of intimacy. The humble and timid air which many of them betray in the prefence of the ladies, and the perfeverance with which they continue their fervices, notwithftanding the contemptuous ftile in which they are often treated, is equally unlike the haughtinefs natural to favoured lovers, and the indifference of men fatiated with enjoyment.

There are, it muft be confeffed, Cicifbeos of a very different ftamp, whofe figure and manners might be fuppofed more agreeable to the ladies they ferve, than to their lords. I once expreffed my furprife, that a particular perfon permitted one of this defcription to attend his wife. I was told, by way of folution of my difficulty, that the hufband was poor, and the Cicifbeo rich. It is not in Italy only where infamous compromifes of this nature take place.

I have alfo known inftances, fince I have been in this country, where the characters of the ladies were fo well eftablifhed, as not

to

to be fhaken either in the opinion of their
acquaintances or hufbands, although their
cavaliero ferventis were in every refpect
agreeable and accomplifhed.

But whether the connection between
them is fuppofed innocent or criminal, moft
Englifhmen will be aftonifhed how men
can pafs fo much of their time with women. This, however, will appear lefs
furprifing, when they recollect that the
Italian nobility dare not intermeddle in politics; can find no employment in the army
or navy; and that there are no fuch amufements in the country as hunting or drinking. In fuch a fituation, if a man of fortune has no turn for gaming, what can he
do? Even an Englifhman, in thofe defperate circumftances, might be driven to the
company and converfation of women, to
lighten the burden of time. The Italians
have perfevered fo long in this expedient,
that, however extraordinary it may feem
to thofe who have never tried it, there can

be

be no doubt that they find it to fucceed.
They tell you, that nothing fo effectually
fooths the cares, and beguiles the tedious-
nefs of life, as the company of an agreeable woman; that though the intimacy
fhould never exceed the limits of friend-
fhip, there is fomething more flattering
and agreeable in it than in male friendfhips; that they find the female heart more
fincere, lefs interefted, and warmer in its
attachments; that women in general have
more delicacy, and——. Well, well, all
this may be true, you will fay; but may
not a man enjoy all thefe advantages, to as
great perfection, by an intimacy and friend-
fhip with his own wife, as with his neigh-
bour's? " Non, Monfieur, point du tout,"
anfwered a Frenchman, to whom this queftion was once addreffed. " Et pourquoi
" donc? Parceque cela n'eft pas permis."
This you will not think a very fatisfactory
anfwer to fo natural and fo pertinent a
queftion—It is not the fafhion! This,

however, was the only anfwer I received
all over Italy.

This fyftem is unknown to the middle
and lower ranks; they pafs their time in
the exercife of their profeffions, and in the
fociety of their wives and children, as in
other countries; and in that fphere of life,
jealoufy, which formed fo ftrong a feature
of the Italian character, is ftill to be found
as ftrong as ever. He who attempts to
vifit the wife or miftrefs of any of the
trades-people without their permiffion, is
in no fmall danger of a Coltellata. I have
often heard it afferted, that Italian women
have remarkable powers of attaching their
lovers. Thofe powers, whatever they are,
do not feem to depend entirely on perfonal
charms, as many of them retain their ancient influence over their lovers after their
beauty is much in the wane, and they
themfelves are confiderably advanced in the
vale of years. I know an Italian nobleman, of great fortune, who has been
lately

lately married to a very beautiful young
woman, and yet he continues his affiduity
to his former miftrefs, now an old woman,
as punctually as ever. I know an Englifhman who is faid to be in the fame fituation,
with this difference, that his lady is ftill
more beautiful. In both thefe inftances, it
is natural to believe that the beautiful young
wives will always take care to keep their
hufbands in fuch a chafte and virtuous way
of thinking, that, whatever time they may
fpend with their ancient miftreffes, nothing
criminal will ever pafs between them.

Whatever fatisfaction the Italians find in
this kind of conftancy, and in their friendly
attachments to one woman, my friend the
Marquis de F——— told me, when I laft
faw him at Paris, that he had tried it while
he remained at Rome, and found it quite
intolerable. A certain obliging ecclefiaftic
had taken the trouble, at the earneft requeft of a lady of that city, to arrange matters between her and the Marquis, who

was put into immediate poffeffion of all the
rights that were ever fuppofed to belong to
a Cicifbeo. The woman naufeated her
hufband, which had advanced matters
mightily ; and her paffion for the Marquis
was in proportion to her abhorrence of
the other. In this ftate things had remained but a very fhort time, when the
Marquis called one afternoon to drive the
Abbé out a little into the country, but he
happened to have juft dined. The meals
of this ecclefiaftic were generally rather
oppreffive for two or three hours after they
were finifhed; he therefore declined the in-
vitation, faying, by way of apology, " Je
" fuis dans les horreurs de la digeftion."
He then enquired how the Marquis's amour
went on with the lady. " Ah, pour l'amour,
" cela eft à peu près pafsé," replied the
Marquis, " et nous fommes actuellement
" dans les horreurs de l'amitié."

LETTER LXXVI.

Florence.

THE Florentines imputed the decay of the republic to the circumflance of their Sovereign refiding in another country; and they imagined, that wealth would accumulate all over Tufcany, and flow into Florence, from various quarters, as foon as they fhould have a refiding Prince, and a Court eftablifhed. It appears, that their hopes were too fanguine, or at leaft premature. Commerce is ftill in a languid condition, in fpite of all the pains taken by the Great Duke to revive it.

The Jews are not held in that degree of odium, or fubjected to the fame humiliating diftinctions here, as in moft other cities of Europe. I am told, fome of the richeft merchants are of that religion. Another clafs of mankind, who are alfo reprobated

E e 3   in

in fome countries, are in this looked on in
the fame light with other citizens. I mean
the actors and fingers at the different
Theatres. Why Chriftians, in any country,
fhould have the fame prejudice againft
them as againft Jews, many are at a lofs to
know; it cannot, certainly, be on the fame
account. Actors and actreffes have never
been accufed of an obftinate, or fuperftitious adherence to the principles or ceremonies of any *falfe religion* whatever.

To attempt a defcription of the churches,
palaces, and other public buildings, would
lead, in my opinion, to a very unenter-
taining detail. Few cities, of its fize, in
Europe, however, afford fo fine a field of
amufement to thofe who are fond of fuch
fubjects; though the lovers of architecture
will be fhocked to find feveral of the fineft
churches without fronts, which, according
to fome, is owing to a real deficiency of
money; while others affert, they are left
in this condition, as a pretext for levying
contributions to finifh them.

The

The chapel of St. Lorenzo is, perhaps, the fineſt and moſt expenſive habitation that ever was reared for the dead; it is encruſted with precious ſtones, and adorned by the workmanſhip of the beſt modern ſculptors. Some complain that, after all, it has a gloomy appearance. There ſeems to be no impropriety in that, conſidering what the building was intended for; though, certainly, the ſame effect might have been produced at leſs expence. Mr. Addiſon remarked, that this chapel advanced ſo very ſlowly, that it is not impoſſible but the family of Medicis may be extinct before their burial-place is finiſhed. This has actually taken place : the Medici family is extinct, and the chapel remains ſtill unfiniſhed.

Of all the methods by which the vanity of the Great has diſtinguiſhed them from the reſt of mankind, this of erecting ſplendid receptacles for their bones, excites the leaſt envy. The ſight of the moſt ſuperb

edifice

edifice of this kind, never drew a repining sigh from the bosom of one poor person; nor do the unsuccessful complain, that the bodies of Fortune's favourites rot under Parian marble, while their own will, in all probability, be allowed to moulder beneath a plain turf.

I have already mentioned the number of statues which ornament the streets and squares of Florence, and how much they are respected by the common people. I am told, they amount in all to above one hundred and fifty, many of them of exquisite workmanship, and admired by those of the best taste. Such a number of statues, without any drapery, continually exposed to the public eye, with the far greater number of pictures, as well as statues, in the same state, to be seen in the palaces, have produced, in both sexes, the most perfect insensibility to nudities.

Ladies who have remained some time at Rome and Florence, particularly those who
affect

affect a tafte for virtù, acquire an intre-
pidity and a cool minutenefs, in examining
and criticifing naked figures, which is unknown to thofe who have never paffed the
Alps. There is fomething in the figure of
the God of Gardens, which is apt to alarm
the modefly of a novice; but I have heard
of female dilettantes who minded it no
more than a ftraw.

The Palazzo Pitti, where the Great
Duke refides, is on the oppofite fide of the
Arno from the Gallery. It has been enlarged fince it was purchafed from the
ruined family of Pitti. The furniture of
this palace is rich and curious, particularly
fome tables of Florentine work, which are
much admired. The moft precious ornaments, however, are the paintings. The
walls of what is called the Imperial Chamber, are painted in frefco, by various
painters; the fubjects are allegorical, and
in honour of Lorenzo of Medicis, diftinguifhed by the name of the Magnificent.
There

There is more fancy than tafte difplayed in thofe paintings. The other principal rooms are diftinguifhed by the names of Heathen Deities, as Jupiter, Apollo, Mars, Venus, and by paintings in frefco, moftly by Pietro da Cortona. In the laft mentioned, the fubjects are different from what is naturally expected from the name of the room, being reprefentations of the triumphs of Virtue over Love, or fome memorable inflance of continency. As the Medici family have been more diftinguifhed for the protection they afforded the arts, than for the virtues of continency or felf-denial, it is probable, the fubject, as well as the execution of thefe pieces, was left entirely to the painter.

I happened lately to be at this palace, with a perfon who is perfectly well acquainted with all the pictures of any merit in Florence. While he explained the peculiar excellencies of Pietro's manner, a gentleman in company, who, although he does

does not pretend to the fmalleft fkill in pictures, would rather remain ignorant for ever, than liften to the lectures of a connoiffeur, walked on, by himfelf, into the other apartments, while I endeavoured to profit by my inftructor's knowledge. When the other gentleman returned, he faid, " I " know no more of painting than my " pointer; but there is a picture in one of " the other rooms, which I would rather " have than all thofe you feem to admire " fo much; it is the portrait of a healthy, " handfome, country woman, with her " child in her arms. There is nothing in- " terefting in the fubject, to be fure, be- " caufe none of us are perfonally ac- " quainted with the woman. But I can- " not help thinking the colours very na- " tural. The young woman's countenance " is agreeable, and expreffive of fond- " nefs and the joy of a mother over a " firft-born. The child is a robuft, chub- " by-cheeked fellow; fuch as the fon of " a peafant fhould be."

We

We followed him into the room, and the picture which pleafed him fo much, was the famous Madonna della Seggiola of Raphael. Our inftructor immediately called out Viva! and pronounced him a man of genuine tafte; becaufe, without any previous knowledge or inftruction, he had fixed his admiration on the fineft picture in Florence. But this gentleman, as foon as he underftood what the picture was, difclaimed all title to praife; " becaufe," faid he, " although, when I confidered
" that picture, fimply as the reprefenta-
" tion of a blooming country wench hug-
" ging her child, I admired the art of the
" painter, and thought it one of the trueft
" copies of nature I ever faw; yet, I con-
" fefs, my admiration is much abated,
" now that you inform me his intention
" was to reprefent the Virgin Mary."
" Why fo?" replied the Cicerone; " the
" Virgin Mary was not of higher rank.
" She was but a poor woman, living in a
" little village in Galilee." " No rank
" in

" in life," said the other, " could give
" additional dignity to the perfon who
" had been told by an Angel from heaven,
" that fhe had found favour with God;
" that her Son fhould be called the Son of
" the Higheft; and who, herfelf, was con-
" fcious of all the miraculous circumftances
" attending his conception and birth. In
" the countenance of fuch a woman, be-
" fides comelinefs, and the ufual affection
" of a mother, I looked for the moft lively
" expreffion of admiration, gratitude,
" virgin modefty, and divine love. And
" when I am told, the picture is by the
" greateft painter that ever lived, I am
" difappointed in perceiving no traces of
" that kind in it." What juftice there is
in this gentleman's remarks, I leave it to
better judges than I pretend to be, to
determine.

After our diurnal vifit to the Gallery,
we often pafs the reft of the forenoon in
the gardens belonging to this palace. The
vale

vale of Arno ; the gay hills that furround it, and other natural beauties to be viewed from thence, form an agreeable variety, even to eyes which have been feafting on the moft exquifite beauties of art. The pleafure arifing from both, however, diminifhes by repetition ; but may be again excited by the admiration of a new fpectator, of whofe tafte and fenfibility you have a good opinion. I experienced this on the arrival of Mr. F——r, a gentleman of fenfe, honour, and politenefs, whofe company gave frefh relifh to our other enjoyments in this place. It is now fome time fince he left us ; and I am not at all unhappy in the thoughts of proceeding, in a day or two, to Bologna, in our road to Milan.

LETTER LXXVII.

Milan.

FOR a poft or two after leaving Florence, and about as much before
you arrive at Bologna, the road is very
agreeable; the reft of your journey between thofe two cities is over the fandy
Apennines.

We had the good fortune to find at
Bologna Sir William and Lady H——,
Mr. F——t, Mr. K——, Lord L——,
and Sir H—— F——n. Our original
intention was to have proceeded without
delay to Milan, but on fuch an agreeable
meeting it was impoffible not to remain a
few days at Bologna.

I went to the academy on the day of
diftributing the prizes for the beft fpecimens and defigns in painting, fculpture,

and

and architecture; a difcourfe in praife of the fine arts was pronounced by one of the profeffors, who took that opportunity of enumerating the fine qualities of the Cardinal Legate; none of the virtues, great or fmall, were omitted on the occafion; all were attributed in the fuperlative degree to this accomplifhed prince of the church. The learned orator acknowledged, however, that this panegyric did not properly belong to his fubject, but hoped that the audience, and particularly the Legate himfelf, who was prefent, would forgive him, in confideration that the eulogy had been wrung from him by the irrefiftible force of truth. The fame force drew forth fomething fimilar in praife of the Gonfalonier and other magiftrates who were prefent alfo; and what you may think very remarkable, the number and importance of the qualities attributed to thofe diftinguifhed perfons kept an exact proportion with their *rank*. Power in this happy city feems to have been

: 9   weighed

weighed in the fcales of juftice, and diftributed by the hand of wifdom. All the
inferior magiflrates, we were informed,
are very worthy men, endowed with many
excellent qualities; the Gonfalonier has
many more, and the Legate poffeffes every
virtue under the fun. If the Pope had
entered the room, the too lavifh profeffor
would not have been able to help him to
a fingle morfel of praife which had not
been already ferved up.

This town is at prefent quite full of
flrangers, who came to affift at the proceffion of Corpus Domini. The Duke of
Parma, feveral Cardinals, and other perfons of high diftinction, befides a prodigious crowd of citizens, attended this
great feflival. The flreets through which
the Hoft was carried under a magnificent
canopy, were adorned with tapeftry,
paintings, looking-glaffes, and all the
various kinds of finery which the inhabitants could produce. Many of the

Vol. II.   F f   painting

paintings feemed unfuitable to the occafion; they were on profane, and fome of
them on wanton fubjects; and it appeared
extraordinary to fee the figures of Venus,
Minerva, Apollo, Jupiter, and others of
that abdicated family, arranged along the
walls in honour of a triumph of the Corpus Chrifti.

On our way to Milan we flopped a
fhort time at Modena, the capital of the
duchy of that name. The whole duchy
is about fifty miles in length, and twenty-
fix in breadth; the town contains twenty
thoufand inhabitants; the ftreets are in
general large, ftraight, and ornamented
with porticoes. This city is furrounded
by a fortification, and farther fecured by
a citadel; it was anciently rendered famous by the fiege which Decimus Brutus fuftained here againft Marc Antony.

We proceeded next to Parma, a beautiful
town, confiderably larger than Modena,
and

nnd defended, like it, by a citadel and regular fortification. The ftreets are well built, broad, and regular. The town is divided unequally by the little river Parma, which lofes itfelf in the Po, ten or twelve miles from this city.

The theatre is the largeft of any in Europe ; and confequently a great deal larger than there is any occafion for. Every body has obferved, that it is fo favourable to the voice, that a whifper from the ftage is heard all over this immenfe houfe ; but nobody tells us on what circumftance in the conftruction this furprifing effect depends.

The Modenefe was the native country of Correggio, but he paffed moft of his life at Parma. Several of the churches are ornamented by the pencil of that great artift, particularly the cupola of the cathedral ; the painting of which has been fo greatly admired for the grandeur of the defign and the boldnefs of the fore-fhortenings. It is now fpoiled in fuch a manner, that its principal beauties are not eafily diftin. guifhed.

Some of the beft pictures in the Ducal Palace have been removed to Naples and elfewhere; but the famous picture of the Virgin, in which Mary Magdalen and St. Jerom are introduced, ftill remains. In this compofition, Correggio has been thought to have united, in a fupreme degree, beauties which are feldom found in the fame piece; an excellence in any one of which has been fufficient to raife other artifts to celebrity. The fame connoiffeurs affert, that this picture is equally worthy of admiration, on account of the frefhnefs of the colouring, the inexpreffible gracefulnefs of the defign, and the exquifite tendernefs of the expreffion. After I had heard all thofe fine things faid over and over again, I thought I had nothing to do but admire; and I had prepared my mind accordingly.— Would to Heaven that the refpectable body

of

of connoiffeurs were agreed in opinion, and
I fhould moft readily fubmit mine to theirs!
But while the above eulogium ftill refounded
in my ears, other connoiffeurs have afferted,
that this picture is full of affectation ; that
the fhadowing is of a dirty brown, the attitude of the Magdalen conftrained and unnatural ; that fhe may ftrive to the end of
time without ever being able to kifs the
foot of the infant Jefus in her prefent pofition; that fhe has the look of an ideot ;
and that the Virgin herfelf is but a vulgar
figure, and feems not a great deal wifer;
that the angels have a ridiculous fimper,
and moft abominable air of affectation ;
and finally, that St. Jerom has the appearance of a fturdy beggar, who intrudes his
brawny figure where it has no right to be.

Diftracted with fuch oppofite fentiments,
what can a plain man do, who has no great
reliance on his own judgment, and wifhes
to give offence to neither party ? I fhall
leave the picture as I found it, to anfwer

for itfelf, with a fingle remark in favour
of the angels.   I cannot take upon me to
fay how the real angels of heaven look; but
I certainly have feen fome *earthly* angels, of
my acquaintance, affume the fimper and
air of thofe in this picture, when they
wifhed to appear quite celeftial.

The duchies of Modena, Parma, and
Placentia, are exceedingly fertile. The foil
is naturally rich, and the climate being
moifter here than in many other parts of
Italy, produces more plentiful pafturage for
cattle, The road runs over a continued
plain, among meadows and corn fields,
divided by rows of trees, from whofe
branches the vines hang in beautiful fef-
toons. We had the pleafure of thinking,
as we drove along, that the peafants are
not deprived of the bleffings of the fmiling
fertility among which they live.   They
had in general a neat, contented, and cheerful appearance. The women are fuccefs-
fully attentive to the ornaments of drefs,
which

which is never the cafe amidft oppreffive poverty.

Notwithftanding the fertility of the country around it, the town of Placentia it-felf is but thinly inhabited, and feems to be in a ftate of decay. What firft ftrike a ftranger on entering this city, are two equeftrian ftatues, in bronze, by Giovanni di Bologna; they ftand in the principal fquare, before the Town-houfe. The beft of the two reprefents that confummate general Alexander Farnefe, Duke of Parma and Placentia, who commanded the army of Philip II. in the Netherlands. The in-fcription on the pedeftal mentions his having relieved the city of Paris, when called to the affiftance of the League into France, where his great military fkill, and cool in-trepidity, enabled him to baffle all the ardent impetuofity of the gallant Henry. He was certainly worthy of a better mafter, and of ferving in a better caufe. We can-not, without regret, behold a Prince, of

F f 4 the

the Duke of Parma's talents and character, supporting the pride of an unrelenting tyrant, and the rancour of furious fanatics.

Except the Ducal Palace, and fome pictures in the churches, which I dare fwear you will cordially forgive me for pafling over undefcribed, I believe there is not a great deal in this city worthy of attention ; at all events I can fay little about them, as we remained here only a few hours during the heat of the day, and fet out the fame evening for Milan.

LETTER LXXVIII.

Milan,

MILAN, the ancient capital of Lombardy, is the largeſt city in Italy, except Rome; but though it is thought rather to exceed Naples in ſize, it does not contain above one-half the number of inhabitants.

The cathedral ſtands in the centre of the city, and, after St. Peter's, is the moſt conſiderable building in Italy. It ought by this time to be the largeſt in the world, if what they tell us be true, that it is near four hundred years ſince it was begun, and that there has been a conſiderable number of men daily employed in completing it ever ſince; but as the injuries which time does to the ancient parts of the fabric keep them in conſtant employment, without the poſſibility of their work being ever completed,

S   pleted,

pleted, Martial's epigram, on the barber
Eutrapelus, has been applied to them with
great propriety. That poor man, it feems,
performed his operations fo very flowly,
that the beards of his patients required
fhaving again on the fide where he had begun, by the time he had finifhed the other.

EUTRAPELUS TONSOR DUM CIRCUIT ORA LUPERCI,
EXPUNGITQUE GENAS, ALTERA BARBA SUBIT.

No church in Chriftendom is fo much load-
ed, I had almoft faid disfigured, with ornaments. The number of ftatues, within-
fide and without, is prodigious ; they are
all of marble, and many of them finely
wrought. The greater part cannot be di-
ftinctly feen from below, and therefore
certainly have nothing to do above. Befides
thofe which are of a fize, and in a fituation
to be diftinguifhed from the ftreet, there
are great numbers of fmaller ftatues, like
fairies peeping from every cornice, and hid
among the grotefque ornaments, which are
here in vaft profufion. They muft have
coft much labour to the artifts who formed
them,

them, and are ſtill a ſource of toil to ſtrangers, who, in compliment to the perſon
who harangues on the beauties of this
church, which he ſays is the eighth wonder
of the world, are obliged to aſcend to the
roof to have a nearer view of them.

This vaſt fabric is not ſimply encruſted,
which is not uncommon in Italy, but in-
tirely built of ſolid white marble, and ſup-
ported by fifty columns, ſaid to be eighty-
four feet high. The four pillars under the
cupola, are twenty-eight feet in circumference. By much the fineſt ſtatue belonging to it is that of St. Bartholomew. He
appears flayed, with his ſkin flung around
his middle like a ſaſh, and in the eaſieſt
and moſt degagé manner imaginable. The
muſcles are well expreſſed; and the figure
might be placed with great propriety in the
hall of an anatomiſt; but, expoſed as it is
to the view of people of all profeſſions,
and of both ſexes, it excites more diſguſt
and horror than admiration. Like thoſe
beggars who uncover their ſores in the
ſtreet,

ftreet, the artift has deftroyed the very effect he meant to produce. This would have fufficiently evinced that the ftatue was not the work of Praxitiles, without the infcription on the pedeftal.

NON ME PRAXITILES, SED MARCUS FINXIT AORATL

The infide of the choir is ornamented by fome highly efteemed fculpture in wood. From the roof hangs a cafe of cryftal, furrounded by rays of gilt metal, and inclofing a nail, faid to be one of thofe by which our Saviour was nailed to the crofs, The treafury belonging to this church is reckoned the richeft in Italy, after that of Loretto. It is compofed of jewels, relics, and curiofities of various kinds; but what is efteemed above all the reft, is a fmall portion of Aaron's rod, which is carefully preferved there.

The Ambrofian Library is faid to be one of the moft valuable collections of books and manufcripts in Europe. It is open a certain number of hours every day; and there

there are accommodations for thofe who come to read or make extracts.

In the Mufeum, adjoining to the Library, are a confiderable number of pictures, and many natural curiofities. Among thefe they fhew a human fkeleton. This does not excite a great deal of attention, till you are informed that it confifts of the bones of a Milanefe Lady, of diftinguifhed beauty, who, by her laft will, ordained that her body fhould be diffecled, and the fkeleton placed in this Mufeum, for the contemplation of pofterity. If this Lady only meant to give a proof of the tranfient nature of external charms, and that a beautiful woman is not more defirable after death than a homely one, fhe might have allowed her body to be configned to duft in the ufual way. In fpite of all the cofmetics, and other auxiliaries which vanity employs to varnifh and fupport decaying beauty and flaccid charms, the world have been long fatisfied that death is not necef-

fary

fary to put the fair and the homely on a level; a very few years, even during life, do the bufinefs.

There is no place in Italy, perhaps I might have faid in Europe, where ftrangers are received in fuch an eafy, hofpitable manner, as at Milan. Formerly the Milanefe Nobility difplayed a degree of fplendour and magnificence, not only in their entertainments, but in their ufual ftyle of living, unknown in any other country in Europe. They are under a neceffity at prefent of living at lefs expence, but they ftill fhew the fame obliging and hofpitable difpofition. This country having, not very long fince, been poffeffed by the French, from whom it devolved to the Spaniard, and from them to the Germans, the troops of thofe nations have, at different periods, had their refidence here, and, in the courfe of thefe viciffitudes, produced a ftyle of manners, and ftamped a character on the inhabitants of this duchy, different from

from what prevails in any other part of Italy; and nice obfervers imagine they perceive in Milanefe manners the politenefs, formality, and honefty imputed to thofe three nations, blended with the ingenuity natural to Italians. Whatever uneafinefs the inhabitants of Milan may feel, from the idea of their being under German government, they feem univerfally pleafed with the perfonal character of Count Fermian, who has refided here many years as Minifter from Vienna, equally to the fatisfaction of the Emprefs Queen, the inhabitants of Milan, and the ftrangers who occafionally travel this way.

The Great Theatre having been burnt to the ground laft year, there are no dramatic entertainments, except at a fmall temporary playhoufe, which is little frequented; but the company affemble every evening in their carriages on the ramparts, and drive about, in the fame manner as at Naples, till it is pretty late. In Italy, the ladies

6 have

have no notion of quitting their carriages
at the public walks, and using their own
legs, as in England and France. On seeing the number of servants, and the splendour of the equipages which appear every
evening at the Corso on the ramparts, one
would not suspect that degree of depopula-
tion, and diminution of wealth, which we
are assured has taken place within these few
years all over the Milanese; and which,
according to my information, proceeds
from the burthensome nature of some late
taxes, and the insolent and oppressive manner in which they are gathered.

The natural productions of this fertile
country must occasion a considerable commerce, by the exportation of grain, particularly rice; cattle, cheese, and by the
various manufactures of silken and velvet
stuffs, stockings, handkerchiefs, ribands,
gold and silver laces and embroideries,
woollen and linen cloths, as well as by
some large manufactures of glass, and
earthen

earthen ware in imitation of china, which are established here. But I am told monopolies are too much protected here, and that prejudices against the profession of a merchant still exist in the minds of the only people who have money. These cannot fail to check industry, and deprefs the foul of commerce; and perhaps there is little probability that the inhabitants of Milan will overcome this unfortunate turn of mind while they remain under German dominion, and adopt German ideas. The peafants, though more at their eafe than in many other places, yet are not fo much fo as might be expected in fo very fertile a country. Why are the inhabitants of the rich plains of Lombardy, where Nature pours forth her gifts in fuch profufion, lefs opulent than thofe of the mountains of Switzerland? Becaufe Freedom, whofe influence is more benign than funshine and zephyrs, who covers the rugged rock with foil, drains the fickly fwamp, and clothes the brown heath in verdure; who dreffes

VOL. II.   G g   the

the labourer's face with fmiles, and makes
him behold his increafing family with delight and exultation ; Freedom has abandoned the fertile fields of Lombardy, and
dwells among the mountains of Switzerland.

LETTER LXXIX.

Chamberry.

WE made fo fhort a flay at Turin that I did not think of writing from thence. I fhall now give you a fketch of our progrefs fince my laft.

We left Milan at midnight, and arrived the next evening at Turin before the fhutting of the gates. All the approaches to that city are magnificent. It is fituated at the bottom of the Alps, in a fine plain watered by the Po. Moft of the ftreets are well built, uniform, clean, ftraight, and terminating on fome agreeable object. The Strada di Po, leading to the palace, the fineft and largeft in the city, is adorned with porticoes equally beautiful and convenient. The four gates are alfo highly ornamental. There can be no more agreeable walk than that around the

G g 2   ramparts.

ramparts. The fortifications are regular and in good repair, and the citadel is reckoned one of the ſtrongeſt in Europe. The royal palace and the gardens are admired by ſome. The apartments diſplay neatneſs, rather than magnificence. The rooms are ſmall, but numerous. The furniture is rich and elegant; even the floors attract attention, and muſt peculiarly ſtrike ſtrangers who come from Rome and Bologna; they are curiouſly inlaid with various kinds of wood, and kept always in a ſtate of ſhining brightneſs. The pictures, ſtatues, and antiquities in the palace are of great value; of the former there are ſome by the greateſt maſters, but thoſe of the Flemiſh ſchool predominate.

No royal family in Europe are more rigid obſervers of the laws of etiquette, than that of Sardinia; all their movements are uniform and invariable. The hour of riſing, of going to maſs, of taking the air; every thing is regulated like clock-

clock-work. Thofe illuftrious perfons
muft have a vaft fund of natural good-humour, to enable them to perfevere in fuch
a wearifome routine, and fupport their
fpirits under fuch a continued weight of
oppreffive formality.

We had the fatisfaction of feeing them
all at mafs; but as the D— of H——
grows more impatient to get to England
the nearer we approach it, he declined
being prefented at court, and we left
Turin two days after our arrival.

We ftopped a few hours, during the
heat of the day, at a fmall village, called
St. Ambrofe, two or three pofts from
Turin. I never experienced more intenfe
heat than during this day, while we were
tantalized with a view of the fnow on the
top of the Alps, which feem to overhang
this place, though, in reality, they are
fome leagues diftant. While we remained
at St. Ambrofe there was a grand proceffion. All the men, women, and chil-

dren,

dren, who were able to crawl, attended;
several old women carried crucifixes, others
pictures of the faint, or flags fixed to the
ends of long poles; they seemed to have
some difficulty in wielding them, yet the
good old women tottered along as happy
as so many young enfigns the firft time
they bend under the regimental colours.
Four men, carrying a box upon their
fhoulders, walked before the reft. I afked
what the box contained, and was informed
by a fagacious looking old man, that it
contained the bones of St. John. I enquired if all the Saint's bones were there;
he affured me, that not even a joint of his
little finger was wanting; "Becaufe," continued I, " I have feen a confiderable
" number of bones in different parts of
" Italy, which are faid to be the bones of
" St. John." He fmiled at my fimplicity,
and faid the world was full of impofition;
but nothing could be more certain, than
that thofe in the box were the true bones
of the Saint; he had remembered them
                                    ever

ever fince he was a child—and his father,
when on his death-bed, had told him, on
the *word of a dying man*, That they belonged to St. John and no other body.

At Novalezza, a village at the bottom
of Mount Cenis, our carriages were taken
to pieces, and delivered to Muleteers to be
carried to Lanebourg. I had bargained
with the Vitturino, before we left Turin;
for our paſſage over the mountain in the
chairs commonly uſed on ſuch occaſions.
The fellow had informed us there was no
poſſibility of going in any other manner;
but when we came to this place, I ſaw no
difficulty in being carried up by mules;
which we all preferred, to the great ſatisfaction of our knaviſh conductor, who thereby ſaved the expence of one half the
chairmen, for whoſe labour he was already paid.

We rode up this mountain, which has
been deſcribed in ſuch formidable terms;
with great eaſe. At the top there is a

fine

fine verdant plain of five or fix miles in
length, we halted at an Inn, called Santa
Croce, where Piedmont ends and Savoy
begins. Here we were regaled with fried
trout, catched in a large lake within fight,
from which the river Doria arifes, which
runs to Turin in conjunction with the Po.
Though we afcend no higher than this
plain, which is the fummit of Mount
Cenis, the mountains around are much
higher; in paffing the plain we felt the
air fo keen, that we were glad to have recourfe to our great-coats; which, at the
bottom of the hill, we had confidered as a
very fuperfluous part of our baggage. I
had a great deal of converfation in paffing
the mountain with a poor boy, who accompanied us from Novalezza to take back
the mules; he told me he could neither
read nor write, and had never been farther than Suza on one fide of the mountain, and Lanebourg on the other. He
fpoke four languages, Piedmontefe, which
is his native language; this is a kind of
Patois

Patois very different from Italian; the Patois of the peasants of Savoy, which is
equally different from French; he alfo
spoke Italian and French wonderfully
well; the fecond he had learnt from the
Savoyard chairmen, and the two laft from
Italian and French travellers whom he
has accompanied over Mount Cenis, where
he has paffed his life hitherto, and which
he feems to have no defire of leaving. If
you chance to be confulted by any parent
who inclines to fend their fons abroad
merely that they may be removed from
London, and acquire modern languages in
the moft œconomical manner, you now
know what place to recommend. In none
where opportunities for this branch of
education are equal, is living cheaper than
at Mount Cenis, and I know nothing in
which it has any refemblance to London,
except that it ftands on much the fame
quantity of ground. I afked this boy,
why he did not learn Englifh.—He
had all the inclination in the world.—

4   " Why

" Why don't you learn it then as well as
" French?"   " On attrape le François,
" Monfieur, bon gré, mal gré," anfwered
he, " mais Meffieurs les Anglois parlent
" peu."

When we arrived at the North fide of the
mountain we difmiffed our mules, and had
recourfe to our Alpian chairs and chairmen.
The chairs are conftructed in the fimpleft
manner, and perfectly anfwer the purpofe
for which they are intended. The chairmen are ftrong-made, nervous, little fellows. One of them was betrothed to a
girl at Lanebourg, and was to be married that evening. I could not, in con-
fcience, permit him to have any part in
carrying me, but directly appointed him
to Jack's chair. The young fellow prefented us all with ribbons, which we wore in
our hats in honour of the bride.   " Are
" you very fond of your miftrefs, friend,"
faid I? " Il faut que je l'aime beaucoup,"
anfwered he, " puifque, pauvre garçon
                              " comme

" comme me voila, je donne trente livres
" au prêtre pour nous marier." To tax
matrimony, and oblige the people who *beget
and maintain* children to pay to thofe who
maintain none, feems bad policy; and it
is furprifing that a prince who attends fo
minutely, as his Sardinian Majefty, to the
welfare of his fubjects, does not remedy fo
great an abufe.

As our carriers jogged zig-zag, according to the courfe of the road, down the
mountain, they laughed and fung all the
the way. " How comes it," faid I to the
D—, " that chairmen are generally
" merrier than thofe they carry? To hear
" thefe fellows without feeing them, one
" would imagine that *we* had the labo-
" rious part, while *they* fat at their eafe."
" True," anfwered he; " and the fame
" perfon might conclude, on hearing the
" bridegroom fing fo cheerfully, that we
" were juft going to be married and not
" he." We arrived in a fhort time at
the

the Inn at Lanebourg, nothing having
furprifed me fo much in the paſſage of
this mountain, the difficulty and danger
of which has been greatly exaggerated by
travellers, as the facility with which we
achieved it.

As foon as the fcattered members of our
carriages were joined together, we proceeded on our journey. The road is never
level, but a continued afcent and defcent
along the fide of high mountains. We
fometimes faw villages fituated at a vaſt
height above us; at other times they were
feen with difficulty in the vales, at an immenfe depth below us. The village of
Modane ſtands in a hollow, furrounded by
ſtupendous mountains. It began to grow
dark when we defcended from a great
height into this hollow; we could only
perceive the rugged fummits, and fides of
the mountains which encircle the village,
but not the village itfelf, or any part of the
plain at the bottom ; we therefore feemed
                                    defcending

defcending from the furface, by a dark abyfs leading to the centre of the globe. We arrived fafe at Modane, however, for the road is good in every refpect, fteepnefs excepted. Next morning we continued our courfe, by a miferable place called La Chambre, to Aiguebelle, a village of much the fame defcription. According to fome authors, this was the road by which Hannibal led his army into Italy. They affert, that the plain at the fummit of Mount Cenis was the place where he refted his army for four days, and from which he fhowed his foldiers the fertile plains of Italy, and encouraged them to perfevere : others affert that he led his army into Italy by Mount St. Bernard. This is a difcuffion into which I am not qualified to enter; but M—r G—l M——l, a gentleman of learning, probity, and great profeffional merit, in his way to Italy, where he now is, endeavoured to trace the route of the Carthaginian army with great attention ; and imagines he has been fuccefsful in his refearches,

searches. He has alfo afcertained the fpots
on which fome of the moft memorable battles were fought, by carefully comparing
the defcription of Polybius, and other authors, with the fields of battle, and has
detected many miftakes, which have prevailed on this curious fubject; every where
fupporting his own hypothefis by arguments which none but one who has carefully perufed the various authors, and examined the ground with a foldier's eye,
could adduce. The fame gentleman has
likewife made fome obfervations relating to
the arms of the ancient Romans, and their
tactics in general, which are equally new
and ingenious, and which, it is hoped, he
will in due time give to the public.

We arrived at the inn at Aiguebelle juft
in time to avoid an exceffive ftorm of thunder and rain, which lafted with great violence through the whole night. Thofe
who have never heard thunder in a very
mountainous country, can form no idea of

the

the loudnefs, repetition, and length of the peals we heard this night. Many of the inhabitants of thofe mountains have never feen better houfes than their own huts, or any other country than the Alps. What a rugged, boifterous piece of work muft they take this world to be!

I fancy you have by this time had enough of mountains and vallies, fo if you pleafe we fhall fkip over Montmelian to Chamberry, where we arrived the fame day on which we left Aiguebelle. To-morrow we fhall fleep at Geneva. I did not expect much fleep this night from the thoughts of it, and therefore have fat up almoft till day-break writing this letter.

LETTER LXXX.

Befançon.

THE D— of H—— went fome weeks ago to vifit an acquaintance in one of the provinces of France. As I inclined rather to pafs that time at Geneva, we agreed to meet at Paris, whither Jack and I are thus far on our way.

I muft now fairly confefs that I found myfelf fo happy with my kind friends the Genevois, that I could not fpare an hour from their company to write to you or any correfpondent, unlefs on indifpenfable bufinefs. I might alfo plead, that you yourfelf have been in fome meafure the caufe of my being feduced from my pen. In your laft letter, which I found waiting for me at the poft-houfe at Geneva, you mention a late publication in terms that gave me a curiofity to fee it; and an Englifh gentleman,

who

who had the only copy which has as yct
reached that city, was fo obliging as to
lend it me. The hours which I ufually
allot to fleep, were all I had in my power
to pafs alone; and they were very confiderably abridged by this admirable performance. The extenfive reading there
difplayed, the perfpicuity with which hiftorical facts are related, the new light in
which many of them are placed, the depth
of the reflections, and the dignity and nervous force of the language, all announce
the hand of a mafter. If the author lives
to complete his arduous undertaking, he
will do more to diffipate the hiftorical dark-
nefs which overfhadows the middle ages,
give a clearer *Hiftory of the Decline and Fall
of the Roman Empire*, and fill up, in a
more fatisfactory manner, the long interval between ancient and modern hiftory,
than all the writers who have preceded
him. This accounts for my long filence.
You fee I refume my pen the very firft opportunity, after the caufes I have affigned

VOL. II.   H h   for

for it are removed, which ought to give the more weight to my apology.

As I have frequently been at Lyons, I chose, on this occasion, to return to Paris by Franche Comté and Champagne. We accordingly set out very early yesterday morning, and were by no means in high spirits when we left Geneva, and passed along the side of the lake, through the Pais de Vaud. The beauties of that country, though they astonish at first fight, yet, like the characters of the inhabitants, they improve on intimacy. Every time I have looked at the lake of Geneva, and its delightful environs, I have discovered something new to admire. As I entered the Canton of Bern, I often turned about, and at last withdrew my eyes from those favourite objects, with an emotion similar to what you feel on taking leave of a friend, whom you have reason to think you shall never see again.

The

The firſt place we came to, on entering France from the Canton of Bern, is a poor little town on an hill; I forget its name. While the poſtillion ſtopped to put ſomething to rights about the harneſs, I ſtepped into a ſhop where they ſold wooden ſhoes; and in the courſe of my converſation with a peaſant, who had juſt purchaſed a pair for himſelf, and another for his wife, he ſaid, " les Bernois ſont bien à leur aiſe, Mon- " ſieur, pendant que nous autres Fran- " çois vivons tres durement, et cependant " les Bernois ſont des hérétiques." "Voilà," ſaid an old woman, who ſat in a corner reading her breviary ; " voilà," ſaid ſhe, taking off her ſpectacles, and laying her beads on the book, " ce que je trouve in- " compréhenſible."

This was, however, at the extremity of France, and in a province lately acquired ; for it muſt be confeſſed, that it is not common for the French to imagine that any country whatever has the advantage of

theirs

theirs in any one circumftance; and they
certainly are not fo apt to grumble as fome
of their neighbours, who have lefs reafon.
When I was laft at Geneva, a French hair-
dreffer—— Let me intreat you not to fhew
this to your friend ——, who is fo fond of
people of quality, that he thinks there is
no *life* out of their company. He would
pfhaw, and curfe my poor peafants, and
old women, and hair-dreffers, and accufe
me of being too fond of fuch low company.

As for the old women, I am much miftaken if there are not at leaft as many to
be found of both fexes in high life as in
low; for the others, I declare I have no
particular affection, but I am fond of ftrokes
of nature and character, and muft look for
them where they are to be found. I introduce the prefent hair-dreffer to your acquaintance, becaufe, if I am not miftaken,
he fpoke the fentiments of his whole nation,
high and low. You fhall judge. This
young fellow attended me every morning
                                        while

while I remained at Geneva; he had been a year or two at London; and while he dreffed my hair, his tongue generally moved as quick as his fingers. He was full of his remarks upon London, and the fine people whofe hair he pretended to have dreffed. " Do you not think," faid I, " that people may live very happily in " that country?" " Mais—pour cela oui, " Monfieur." " Do you think, then, they " are happy?" " Pour cela, non, Monfieur." " Can you guefs at the reafon why they " are not, though they have fo much reafon " to be fo?" Oui, Monfieur, elle eft toute " fimple." " Pray what is the reafon they " are not happy?" " C'eft, qu'ils ne font " pas deftinés à l'etre."

A very genteel young man, a Genevois, happened to call on me, for two minutes, while this frifeur was with me. The young gentleman had paffed fome time at Paris, and was dreffed exactly in the Parifian tafte. " He has much the air of one of

H h 3 " your

" your countrymen," faid I to the Frenchman, as foon as the other had left the
room.

" Mon Dieu! quelle différence," cried
the frifeur.", " For my part, I can fee
" none," faid I. " Monfieur," refumed he,
" foyez perfuadé qu'aucun Genevois ne fera
" jamais pris pour un François." " There
" are certainly fome *petit-maitres* to be
" found in this town," faid I. " Par-
" donnez moi," replied he, " ils ne font que
" petit-maîtres manqués."

" Did you ever fee an Englifhman," faid
I, " who might pafs for a Frenchman?"
" Jamais de la vie, Monfieur!" replied he,
with an accent of aftonifhment.

" Suppofe him," faid I, " a man of quality?" " N'importe."

" But," continued I, " fuppofe he had
" lived feveral years at Paris, that he was
" naturally very handfome, and well made,
" that he had been educated by the beft
" French

" French dancing-mafter, his clothes made
" by the beft French taylor, and his hair
" dreffed by the moft eminent frifeur in
" Paris?" "C'eft beaucoup, Monfieur, mais
" ce n'eft pas affez."

" What!" exclaimed I, " would you ftill
" know him to be an Englifhman?" " Af-
" furément, Monfieur."

" What! before he fpoke?" " Au pre-
" mier coup d'œil, Monfieur."

" The Devil you would; but how?"
" C'eft que Meffieurs les Anglois ont un
" air—une manière de fe préfenter—un—
" que fais-je moi—vous m'entendez bien,
" Monfieur—un certain air fi Gau——"

" Quel air maraud?" "Enfin un air
" qui eft charmant, fi vous voulez, Mon-
" fieur," faid he rapidly, " mais que le
" Diable m'emporte fi c'eft l'air François."

To-morrow I fhall take a view of this
town, and proceed immediately after break-
faft to Paris : mean-while I wifh you very
heartily good night.

LETTER LXXXI.

Paris.

I Made a longer ſtay at Beſançon than I intended, and am now about to inform you what detained me. The morning after the date of my laſt, as I returned to the inn from the parade, where I had been to ſee the troops, I met a ſervant of the Marquis de F——, who ran up to me the moment he knew me, and, in a breath, told me, that his maſter was at Beſancon; that he had been exceedingly ill, and thought, by the phyſicians, in great danger; but his complaint having terminated in an ague, they had now the ſtrongeſt hopes of his recovery. I defired to be conducted immediately to him.

I found the Marquis alone; pale, languid, and greatly emaciated. He expreſſed, however, equal pleaſure and ſurprife at

this

this unexpected vifit; faid, he had been in danger of making a very long journey, and added, with a fmile, that no man had ever fet out with lefs inclination, for he hated travelling alone, and this was the only journey he could ever take, without wifhing fome of his friends to accompany him. He rejoiced, therefore, that he had been recalled in time to meet me before I fhould pafs on to Paris. "But tell "me," continued he, "for I have ten "thoufand queftions to afk—but let us "take things in order; Eh bien, donnez "nous donc des nouvélles du Pape? On "nous a dit que vous aviez paffé par la ce- "remonie de la Pantoufle. Ne pourroit "on pas pendre au tragique une mifère "comme cela chez vous où le Saint Pere "paffe pour une *Babylonienne* de mauvaife "vie?" Before I could make any anfwer I chanced to turn my eyes upon a perfon whom I had not before obferved, who fat very gravely upon a chair in a corner of
the

the room, with a large periwig in full
drefs upon his head.

The Marquis, feeing my furprife at the
fight of this unknown perfon, after a very
hearty fit of laughter, begged pardon for
not having introduced me fooner to that
gentleman (who was no other than a large
monkey), and then told me, he had the
honour of being attended by a phyfician,
who had the reputation of poffeffing the
greateft fkill, and who *certainly* wore the
largeft periwigs of any doctor in the province. That one morning, while he was
writing a prefcription at his bed-fide, this
fame monkey had catched hold of his periwig by one of the knots, and inftantly
made the beft of his way out at the window
to the roof of a neighbouring houfe, from
which poft he could not be diflodged, till
the Doctor, having loft patience, had fent
home for another wig, and never after
could be prevailed on to accept of this,
which had been fo much difgraced. That,

4   *cufin,*

enfin, his valet, to whom the monkey belonged, had, ever since that adventure, obliged the culprit, by way of punishment, to sit quietly for an hour every morning, with the periwig on his head.—Et pendant ces momens de tranquilité je suis honoré de la société du vénérable personage. Then addressing himself to the monkey, "Adieu, mon ami, pour aujourdhui— "au plaisir de vous revoir;" and the servant immediately carried Monsieur le Medecin out of the room.

Afraid that the Marquis might be the worse for talking so much, I attempted to withdraw, promising to return in the evening; but this I could not get him to comply with. He assured me, that nothing did him so much harm as holding his tongue; and that the most excessive headach he had ever had in his life, was owing to his having been two hours without speaking, when he made his addresses to Madam de —— ; who could never forgive
those

thofe who broke in upon the thread of her difcourfe, and whom he *loft* after all, by uttering a few fentences before fhe could, recover her breath after a fit of fneezing: In moft people's difcourfe, added he, a fneeze paffes for a full ftop. " Mais dans " le Caquet eternel de cette femme ce " n'eft qu'un virgule."

I then enquired after my friends Dubois and Fanchon.—He told me, that his mother had fettled them at her houfe in the country, where fhe herfelf chofe, of late, to pafs at leaft one half of the year ; that Dubois was of great fervice to her, in the quality of fteward, and fhe had taken a ftrong affection for Fanchon, and that both hufband and wife were loved and efteemed by the whole neighbourhood. " I once," continued the Marquis, " propofed to Fanchon, " en badinant, to make a trip to Paris, " for fhe muft be tired of fo much folitude." " Have I not my hufband ?" faid fhe, " Your hufband is not company," rejoined I,

I, " your hufband, you know, is yourfelf.
" What do you think was her anfwer ?"
" Elle m'a répondu," continued the Marquis, " Ah, Monfieur le Marquis, plus on
" fé loigne de foi-même, plus on s'écarte
" du bonheur."

In the progrefs of our converfation, I enquired about the lady to whom he was to
have been married, when the match was fo
abruptly broken off by her father. He
told me, the old gentleman's behaviour was
explained a fhort time after our departure
from Paris, by his daughter's marriage to a
man of great fortune; but whofe tafte,
character, and turn of mind were effentially
different from thofe of the young lady.
" 1 fuppofe then," faid I, " fhe appeared
" indifferent about him from the begin-
" ning." " Pardonnez moi," replied the
Marquis, " au commencement elle joua la
" belle paffion pour fon mari, jufqu'à fcan-
" dalifer le monde, peu à peu elle devint
" plus raifonable, et fur cet article les deux

7   " epoux

" epoux jouèrent bientôt à fortune égale,
" à préfent ils s'amufent à fe chicaner de
" petites contradictions qui jettent plus
" d'amertume dans le commerce que de torts
" décidés."

. " Did you ever renew your acquaint-
" ance ?"

" Je ne pouvois faire autrement, elle a
" marqué quelques petits regrets de m'avoir
" traité fi cruellement."

" And how did you like her," faid I,
" on farther acquaintance ?"

" Je lui ai trouvé," anfwered he, " tout
" ce qu'on peut fouhaiter dans *la femme*
" *d'un autre*."

The Marquis, feeling himfelf a little
cold, and rifing from the fopha to ring for
fome wood, had a view of the ftreet. " O
" ho," cried he, looking earneftly through
the window, " regardez, regardez cet.
" homme"—"Quel homme ?" faid I. "Cet.
" homme

" homme à gros ventre," faid he ; and
while he fpoke, his teeth began to chatter.
" Ah, Diable, voilà mon chien d'accés—cet
" homme qui marche comme un Di—
" Di— Dindon, c'eft l'aumonier du. regi-
" ment." I begged he would allow himfelf to be put to bed, for by this time he
was all over fhivering with the violence of
the ague.

" Non, non, ce n'eft rien," faid he, " il
" faut abfolument que je vous conte cette
" hiftoire. Cet homme qui f'engraiffe en
" nettoy—nett—et—et—en nettoyant l'ame
" de mes foldats, faifoit les yeux doux à la
" femme d'un Ca—Ca—Caporal—Diantre
" je n'en peux plus. Adieu, mon ami, c'eft
" la plus plaifante hift—fis—pefte ! de-
" mandez mes gens."

He was put to bed directly. I found the
court below full of foldiers, who had come
to enquire after their Colonel. Before I had
reached the ftreet, the Marquis's Valet-de-
Chambre overtook me, le ris fur la bouche,

et

et les larmes aux yeux, with a meſſage from his maſter.

The ſoldiers crowded about us, with anxiety on all their countenances. I aſſured them, there was no danger; that their Colonel would be well within a very few days. This was heard with every mark of joy, and they diſperſed, to communicate the good news to their comrades.

" Ah, Monſieur," ſaid the Valet, addreſſing himſelf to me, " il eſt tant aimé de ces " braves Garçons ! et il merite ſi bien de " l'être !

Next day he looked better, and was in his uſual ſpirits; the day following, he was ſtill better; and having taken a proper quantity of the bark during the interval, he had no return of the fever. As he has promiſed to continue the uſe of the bark, in ſufficient doſes, for ſome time, and as relapſes are not frequent at this ſeaſon of the year, I am perſuaded the affair is over,

and

and that he will gradually gain ftrength till he is perfectly recovered.

He received me with lefs gaiety than ufual, the day on which I took my leave, and ufed many obliging expreffions, which, however you may fmile, I am entirely difpofed to believe were fincere ; for

Altho' the candy'd tongue lick abfurd pomp,
And crook the pregnant hinges of the knee,
Where thrift may follow fawning :
—— Why fhould the poor be Batter'd ?

Juft as I was returning, we heard the mufic of the troops marching off the parade.—" Apropos," cried he, " How do " your affairs go on with your Colonies ?" I faid, I hoped every thing would be arranged and fettled very foon.

" Ne croyez vous pas," faid he, " que " ces Meffieurs," pointing to the troops which then paffed below the window, " pourroient entrer pour quelque chofe dans " l'arrangement ?"

I faid, I did not imagine the Americans
were fuch fools as to break all connection
with their friends, and then rifk falling into
the power of their enemies.

" Il me femble," anfwered he, " que ces
" Meffieurs font affez peu de cas de votre
" amitié, et auffi, quand vous aurez prouvé
" qu'ils ont tort, il ne s'en fuivra pas que
" vous ayiez toujours eu raifon." " Allons,"
continued he, feeing that I looked a little
grave, " point d'humeur;" then feizing
my hand, " permettez moi, je vous prie,
" d'aimer les Anglois fans haïr les Amé-
" ricains."

I foon after parted with this amiable
Frenchman, whofe gaiety, wit, and agreeable manners, if I may judge from my own
experience, reprefent the character and difpofition of great numbers of his countrymen.

After a very agreeable journey by Gray,
Langres, and Troyes, we arrived at this
capital a few days ago.

LETTER LXXXII.

Paris.

ALTHOUGH it is a confiderable time
fince my arrival, yet, as you made
fo long a ftay at Paris while we were in
Germany, I could not think of refuming
my obfervations on the manners of this
gay metropolis. It has been faid, that
thofe times are the moft interefting to read
of, which were the moft difagreeable to
live in. So I find the places in which it is
moft agreeable to refide, are precifely thofe
from which we have the leaft inclination to
write. There are fo many refources at
Paris, that it always requires a great effort
to write letters, of any confiderable length,
from fuch a place. This is peculiarly my
cafe at prefent, as I have the happinefs of
paffing great part of my time with Mr.
A——— S———t, whom I found at this
hotel on my arrival. The integrity, can-

dour, and ability, of that gentleman's conduct, during a long refidence, have procured
him a great number of friends in this
capital, and have eſtabliſhed a character
which calumny attempted in vain to over-
throw. Now that I have refolution to take
up my pen, I ſhall endeavour to clear the
debt for which you dun me ſo unmerciful-
ly. I own, I am ſurprifed, that you ſhould
require my opinion on the uſes of foreign
travel, after perufing, as you muſt have
done, the Dialogues, lately publiſhed by
an eminent divine, equally diſtinguiſhed
for his learning and taſte. But as I know
what makes you peculiarly folicitous on
that fubject at prefent, I ſhall give you
my fentiments, fuch as they are, without
farther hefitation.

I cannot help thinking, that a young
man of fortune may fpend a few years to
advantage, in travelling through fome of
the principal countries of Europe, provided
the tour be well-timed, and well-con-
4   ducted;

ducted; and, without these, what part of education can be of use?

In a former letter, I gave my reasons for preferring the plan of education at the public schools of England, to any other now in use at home or abroad. After the young person has acquired the fundamental parts of learning, which are taught at schools, he will naturally be removed to some university. One of the moſt elegant and moſt ingenious writers of the present age has, in his Inquiry into the Causes of the Wealth of Nations, pointed out many deficiencies in thoſe seminaries. What that gentleman has said on this subject, may possibly have some effect in bringing about an improvement. But, with all their deficiencies, it muſt be acknowleged, that no universities have produced a greater number of men diſtinguiſhed for polite literature, and eminent for science, than thoſe of England. If a young man has, previouſly, acquired the habit of applica-

tion,

tion, and a tafte for learning, he will certainly find the means of improvement
there; and, without thefe, I know not
where he will make any progrefs in literature. But whatever plan is adopted,
whether the young man fludies at the univerfity, or at home with private teachers,
while he is ftudying with diligence and
alacrity, it would be doing him a moft
effential injury, to interrupt him by a premature expedition to the Continent, from
an idea of his acquiring the graces, elegance of manner, or any of the accomplifhments which travelling is fuppofed to give.
Literature is preferable to all other accomplifhments, and the men of rank who
poffefs it, have a fuperiority over thofe who
do not, let their graces be what they may,
which the latter feel and envy, while they
affect to defpife.

According to this plan, a youth, properly educated, will feldom begin his
foreign tour before the age of twenty; if
it

it is a year or two later, there will be no harm.

This is the age, it may be faid, when young men of fortune endeavour to get into Parliament: it is fo; but if they fhould remain out of Parliament till they are a few years older, the affairs of the nation might poffibly go on as well.

It may alfo be faid, if the tour is deferred till the age of twenty, the youth will not, after that period of life, attain the modern languages in perfection. Nor will he acquire that eafy manner, and fine addrefs, which are only caught by an early acquaintance with courts, and the affemblies of the gay and elegant. This is true to a certain degree; but the anfwer is, that by remaining at home, and applying to the purfuits of literature, he will make more valuable attainments.

I am at a lofs what to fay about thofe fame graces; it is certainly defirable to

I i 4 poffefs

poffefs them, but they muft come, as it were, fpontaneoufly, or they will not come at all. They fometimes appear as volunteers, but cannot be preffed into any fervice; and thofe who fhew the greateft anxiety about them, are the leaft likely to attain them. I fhould be cautious, therefore, of advifing a young man to ftudy them either at home or abroad with much folicitude. Students of the graces are, generally, the moft abominably affected fellows in the world. I have feen *one* of them make a whole company fqueamifh.

Though the pert familiarity of French children would not become an Englifh boy, yet it merits the earlieft and the utmoft attention to prevent or conquer that aukward timidity which fo often oppreffes the latter when he comes into company. The timidity I fpeak of, is entirely different from modefty. I have feen the moft impudent boys I ever knew, almoft convulfed with conftraint in the prefence of ftrangers, or when they were required to pronounce
a fingle

a fingle fentence of civility. But it was only on fuch occafions they were bafhful. Among their companions or inferiors, they were faucy, rude, and boifterous.

If boys of this defcription *only* were liable to bafhfulnefs, it would be a pity to remove it. But although this quality is diftinct from modefty, it is not incompatible with it. Boys of the moft modeft and moft amiable difpofition are often overwhelmed with it; from them it ought to be removed, if it can be done, without endangering that modefty which is fo great an ornament to youth, and indeed to every period of life. This, furely, may be done in England, as well as in any other country; but it is too much neglected: many confider it as a matter of no importance, or that it will wear off by time. We fee it, however, often annihilate, and always impair the effect of the greateft and moft ufeful talents. After the care of forming the heart by the principles of benevolence and
integrity,

integrity, perhaps one of the moſt important parts of education is, to habituate a boy to behave with modeſty, but without reſtraint, and to retain the full poſſeſſion of all his faculties in any company.

To attain, betimes, that eaſe and elegance of manner, which travelling is ſuppoſed to beſtow, and that the young gentleman may become perfectly maſter of the modern languages, ſome have thought of mixing the two plans; and, inſtead of allowing him to proſecute his ſtudies at home, ſending him abroad, immediately on his coming from ſchool, on the ſuppoſition that, with the aſſiſtance of a tutor and foreign profeſſors, he will proceed in the ſtudy of philoſophy, and other branches of literature, during the three or four years which are employed in the uſual tour. It will not be denied, that a young man who has made good uſe of his time at ſchool and at the univerſity, who has acquired ſuch a taſte for ſcience as to conſider

its

its purfuits as a pleafure, and not a tafk,
may, even during his travels, mix the
ftudy of men with that of books, and continue to make progrefs in the latter, when
the greater part of his time is dedicated to
the former. But that fuch a tafle will, for
the firft time, fpring up in the breaft of a
boy of fixteen or feventeen, amidft the dif-
fipation of theatres, reviews, proceffions,
balls, and affemblies, is of all things the
leaft probable.

Others, who think lightly of the importance of what is ufually called fcience to a
young man of rank and fortune, ftill contend, that a knowledge of hiftory, which
they admit may be of fome ufe *even to*
men of fortune, can certainly be acquired
during the years of travelling. But what
fort of a knowledge will it be which a boy,
in fuch a fituation, will acquire ? Not that
which Lord Bolingbroke calls philofophy,
teaching by examples, a proper conduct in
the various fituations of public and private
life,

life, but merely a fucceffion of reigns, of battles, and fieges, ftored up in the memory without reflection or application. I remember a young gentleman, whom a ftrong and retentive memory of fuch events often fet a prating very mal-à-propos ; one of his companions expreffed much furprife at his knowledge, and wondered how he had laid up fuch a ftore. " Why, truly," replied he, with franknefs, " it is all owing " to my bungling blockhead of a valet, " who takes up fuch an unconfcionable " time in dreffing my hair, that I am glad " to read to keep me from fretting; and " as there are no news-papers, or maga- " zines, to be had in this country, I have " been driven to hiftory, which anfwers " nearly as well."

But it fometimes happens, that young men who are far behind their contemporaries in every kind of literature, are wonderfully advanced in the knowledge of the town, fo as to vie with the oldeft profeffors

in

in London, and endanger their own health
by the ardour of their application. The
fooner fuch premature youths are feparated
from the conneĉtions they have formed in
the metropolis, the better; and as it will
not be eafy to perfuade them to live in
any other part of Great Britain, it will be
neceffary to fend them abroad. But, inftead of being carried to courts and capitals, the beft plan for them will be, to fix
them in fome provincial town of France or
Switzerland, where they may have a chance
of improving, not fo much by new attainments, as by unlearning or forgetting
what they have already acquired.

After a young man has employed his
time to advantage at a public fchool, and
has continued his application to various
branches of fcience till the age of twenty,
you afk, what are the advantages he is
likely to reap from a tour abroad?

He will fee mankind more at large, and
in numberlefs fituations and points of view,

in

in which they cannot appear in Great Britain, or any one country. By comparing
the various cuftoms and ufages, and hearing the received opinions of different countries, his mind will be enlarged. He will
be enabled to correct the theoretical notions
he may have formed of human nature, by
the practical knowledge of men. By contemplating their various religions, laws,
and government, *in action*, as it were, and
obferving the effects they produce on the
minds and characters of the people, he will.
be able to form a jufter eftimate of their
value than otherwife he could have done.
He will fee the natives of other countries,
not as he fees them in England, mere idle
fpectators, but bufily employed in their
various characters, as actors on their own
proper ftage. He will gradually improve
in the knowledge of *character*, not of Englifhmen only, but of men in general; he
will ceafe to be deceived either by the varnifh with which men are apt to heighten
their own actions, or the dark colours in
which

which they, too often, paint thofe of others. He will learn to diftinguifh the real from the oftenfible motive of men's words and behaviour. Finally, by being received with hofpitality, converfing familiarly, and living in the reciprocal exchange of good offices with thofe whom he confidered as enemies, or in fome unfavourable point of view, the fphere of his benevolence and good-will to his brethren of mankind will gradually enlarge. His friendfhips extending beyond the limits of his own country, will embrace characters congenial with his own in other nations. Seas, mountains, rivers, are *geographical* boundaries, but never limited the good-will or efteem of one liberal mind. As for his manner, though it will probably not be fo janty as if he had been bred in France from his earlieft youth, yet that alfo will in fome degree be improved.

However perfuaded he may be of the advantages enjoyed by the people of England,

6   land,

land, he will fee the harfhnefs and impropriety of infulting the natives of other
countries with an oftentatious enumeration
of thofe advantages; he will perceive how
odious thofe travellers make themfelves,
who laugh at the religion, ridicule the
cuftoms, and infult the police of the countries through which they pafs, and who
never fail to infinuate to the inhabitants
that they are all flaves and bigots. Such
bold Britons we have fometimes met with,
fighting their way through Europe, who,
by their continual broils and difputes,
would lead one to imagine that the angel
of the Lord had pronounced on each of
them the fame denunciation which he did
on Ifhmael the fon of Abraham, by his
handmaid Hagar. " And he will be a
" wild man, and his hand will be againft
" every man, and every man's hand
" againft him *." If the fame unfocial
difpofition fhould creep into our politics, it
might arm all the powers in Europe againft

* Vide Genefis, chap. xvi. verfe 12.

Great

Great Britain, before fhe gets clear of her unhappy conteft with America. A young man, whofe mind has been formed as it ought, before he goes abroad, when he fees many individuals preferve perfonal dignity in fpite of arbitrary government, an independent mind amidft poverty, liberal and philofophic fentiments amidft bigotry and fuperftition; muft naturally have the higheft efteem for fuch characters, and allow them more merit than thofe even of his own country, who think and act in the fame manner in lefs unfavourable circumftances.

Befides thefe advantages, a young man of fortune, by fpending a few years abroad, will gratify a natural and laudable curiofity, and pafs a certain portion of his life in an agreeable manner. He will form an acquaintance with that boafted nation, whofe fuperior tafte and politenefs are univerfally acknowledged; whofe fafhions and language are adopted by all Europe; and who,

VOL. II. K k in

in fcience, power, and commerce, are the
rivals of Great Britain. He will have opportunities of obferving the political conftitution of the German empire ; that complex
body, formed by a confederacy of princes,
ecclefiaftics, and free cities, comprehending
countries of vaft extent, inhabited by a
hardy race of men, diftinguifhed for folid
fenfe and integrity, who, without having
equalled their fprightlier neighbours in
works of tafte or imagination, have fhewn
what prodigious efforts of application the
human mind is capable of in the fevereft
and leaft amufing ftudies, and whofe armies exhibit at prefent the moft perfect
models of military difcipline. In contemplating thefe, he will naturally confider,
whether thofe armies tend moft to the
aggrandizement of the Monarch, or to defend or preferve any thing to the people
who maintain them, and the foldiers who
compofe them, equivalent to the vaft expence
of money, and the ftill greater quantity of
mifery which they occafion.

Viewing

Viewing the remains of Roman tafte and
magnificence, he will feel a thoufand emotions of the moft interefting nature, while
thofe whofe minds are not, like his, ftored
with claffical knowledge, gaze with tafte-
lefs wonder, or phlegmatic indifference;
and, exclufive of thofe monuments of antiquity, he will naturally defire to be acquainted with the prefent inhabitants of a
country, which at different periods has
produced men who, by one means or another, have diftinguifhed themfelves fo emi-
nently from their contemporaries of other
nations. At one period, having fubdued the
world by the wifdom and firmnefs of their
councils, and the difciplined vigour of their
armies, Rome became at once the feat of
empire, learning, and the arts.

After the Northern barbarians had deftroyed the overgrown fabric of Roman
power, a new empire, of a more fingular
nature, gradually arofe from its ruins, art-
fully extending its influence over the minds

of

of men, till the Princes of Europe were at length as much controlled by the bulls of the Vatican, as their anceſtors had been by the decrees of the Senate.

Commerce alſo, which rapine and ſlaughter had frightened from Europe, returned, and joined with Superſtition in drawing the riches of all the neighbouring nations to Italy. And, at a ſubſequent period, Learning, burſting through the clouds of ignorance which overſhadowed mankind, again ſhone forth in the ſame country, bringing in her train, Poetry, Painting, Sculpture, and Muſic, all of which have been cultivated with the greateſt ſucceſs; and the three laſt brought, by the inhabitants of this country, to a degree of excellence unequalled by the natives of any other country of the world. When to theſe conſiderations we add, that there is reaſon to believe that this country had arrived at a great degree of perfection in the arts before the beginning of the

Roman

Roman republic, we are almoſt tempted to believe, that local and phyſical cauſes have a conſiderable influence in rendering the mind more acute in this country of Italy, than any where elſe; and that if the infinite political diſadvantages under which it labours were removed, and the whole of this peninſula united in one State, it would again reſume its ſuperiority over other nations.

Laſtly, by viſiting other countries, a ſubject of Great Britain will acquire a greater eſteem than ever for the conſtitution of his own. Freed from vulgar prejudices, he will perceive, that the bleſſings and advantages which his countrymen enjoy, do not flow from their ſuperiority in wiſdom, courage, or virtue, over the other nations of the world, but, in ſome degree, from the peculiarity of their ſituation in an iſland; and, above all, from thoſe juſt and equitable laws which ſecure property, that mild free government

ment which abhors tyranny, protects the meaneft fubject, and leaves the mind of man to its own exertions, unreftrained by thofe arbitrary, capricious, and impolitic fhackles, which confine and weaken its nobleft endeavours in almoft every other country of the world. This animates induftry, creates fertility, and fcatters plenty over the boifterous ifland of Great Britain, with a profufion unknown in the neighbouring nations, who behold with aftonifhment fuch numbers of Britifh fubjects, of both fexes, and of all ages, roaming difcontented through the lands of defpotifm, in fearch of that happinefs, which, if fatiety and the wanton reftleffnefs of wealth would permit, they have a much better profpect of enjoying in their own country.

Cœlum non animum mutant qui trans mare
    currunt.
Strenua nos exercet inertia, navibus atque
Quadrigis petimus bene vivere. Quod petis,
    hic eft.

THE END.

TRANSLATIONS

OF THE

LATIN AND ITALIAN QUOTATIONS

IN THE

SECOND VOLUME.

Page

19. THE wretched father running to their aid,
With pious haste, but vain, they next invade.   DRYDEN.

44. How beautiful he is! O how beautiful he is!

Ibid. He is as beautiful as he is holy.

86. O God, where am I? what pleasure ravishes my soul!

90. The memory of Cassius and Brutus made a deeper impression on the minds of the spectators, on this very account, that their statues were *not* seen in the procession.

95. Many have held the empire longer; none ever relinquished it from more generous motives.

Page

99. Now by rich Circe's coaft they bend their
way.

100. Laft with her martial troops all fheathed
in brafs,
Camilla came, a queen of Volfcian race;
Nor were the web or loom the virgin's care,
But arms and courfers, and the toils of war.
She led the rapid race, and left behind
The flagging floods, and pinions of the
wind:
Lightly fhe flies along the level plain,
Nor hurts the tender grafs, nor bends the
golden grain.   PITT.

101. To Forum-Appii thence we fteer, a place
Stuff'd with rank boatmen, and with
vintners bafe.   FRANCIS.

102. The head of St. Thomas Aquinas.

104. And the fteep hills of Circe ftretch around,
Where fair Feronia boafts her ftately
grove,
And Anxur glories in her guardian Jove;
Where ftands the Pontine lake————.
      PITT.

107. Whether is it beft to go by the Numician
or Appian way to Brundufium?

108. We willingly leave Fundi, where Alifidius
Lufcus is chief magiftrate.

LATIN AND ITALIAN QUOTATIONS.

Page

108. From whom the illuſtrious race aroſe,
Who firſt poſſeſſed the Formian towers.

FRANCIS.

Ibid. My cups are neither enriched with the
juice of the Falernian grapes, nor that
of thoſe from the Formian hills.

114. ——the rich fields that Liris laves,
Where ſilent roll his deepning waves.

FRANCIS.

116. Pure ſpirits theſe; the world no purer
knows;
For none my heart with ſuch affection
glows.
How oft did we embrace! our joys how
great!
Is there a bleſſing, in the power of fate,
To be compared, in ſanity of mind,
To friends of ſuch companionable kind?

FRANCIS.

117. Formerly called another Carthage, or
another Rome; it now lies buried in
its own ruins.

124. God forbid!

125. Bleſſed Jeſus!

126. It is that which vexes me.

142. My ſon laments, that he has not killed
more than eighty birds in one day,

L l 2   whereas,

Page

whereas, I fhould think myfelf the
happieft man in the world, if I could
kill forty.

188. The knight of Aglant now has couch'd
his fpear,
Where clofely preft the men and arms ap·
pear:
Firft one, and then another, helplefs dies;
Thro' fix at once the lance impetuous flies,
And in the feventh inflicts fo deep a wound,
That prone he tumbles lifelefs to the
ground.   HOOLE.

188, 189. Thus by fome ftanding pool or
marfhy place,
We fee an archer flay the croaking race
With pointed arrow, nor the flaughter
leave,,
Till the full weapon can no more receive.
HOOLE.

197. Both Arcadians, but not equally fkilled
in finging.   -

216. What inconfiderate fellow, to terrify
people, could firft give the mournful
name of tears to that wine which, above
all others, renders the heart glad, and
excites cheerfulnefs?

LATIN AND ITALIAN QUOTATIONS.

Page

277. O illuftrious memorial! O irrefragable
truth! Come hither, ye heretics! come
hither, and be aftonifhed, and open
your eyes to catholic and evangelic
truth. The blood of St. Januarius
alone is a fufficient teftimony of the
truth. Is it poffible, that fuch a great
and famous miracle does not convert
all heretics and infidels to the truths of
the Roman Catholic church?

285. 'Sblood! it is ftill as hard as a ftone.

304. Virtue crowns him after many great
achievements.

307. All, all for the King's amufement.

Ibid. Surely.

Ibid. Surely, furely.

314. I intreat you to forfake, as foon as poffible, the corrupt coaft of Baia.

Ibid. A coaft moft unfriendly to modeft maids.

320. Confections of Tivoli.

322. May Tibur, to my lateft hours,
Afford a kind and calm retreat;
Tibur, beneath whofe lofty towers,
The Græcians fix'd their blifsful feat.

I   FRANCIS.

Page

322. The walls of the moist Tibur then stood,
which was founded by the Greeks.

Ibid. For little folks become their little fate,
And at my age, not Rome's imperial seat,

* * * * * * *

But Tibur's solitude my taste can please.

325. When retired to the cool stream of Digentia, which supplies the cold village
of Mandela with water; what, my
friend, do you imagine, are my senti-
ments and wishes?

Ibid. Pan from Arcadia's heights descends,
To visit oft my rural seat——
FRANCIS.

But as a bee, which thro' the shady groves,
Feeble of wing, with idle murmurs roves,
Sits on the bloom, and, with unceasing
toil,
From the sweet thyme extracts his flow'ry
spoil,
So I, weak bard! round Tibur's lucid
spring,
Of humble strain laborious verses sing.
FRANCIS.

328. But me not patient Lacedæmon charms,
Nor fair Larissa with such transport
warms,

Page

 As pure Albuneus' rock refounding fource,
 And rapid Anio, headlong in his courfe,
 Or Tibur, fenced by groves from folar
  beams,
 And fruitful orchards bath'd by ductile
  ftreams.   Francis.

331. Hither I, Apollo, have come, accompanied by the Mufes. This fhall henceforth be our Delphos, Delos, and Helicon.

335. The woods all thunder'd, and the mountains fhook,
 The lake of Trivia heard the note profound.

 * * * * * * *
 * * * * * * *
 * * * * * * *

 Pale at the piercing call, the mothers preft
 With fhrieks their ftarting infants to the
  breaft.   Pitt.

362. The man in confcious virtue bold,
  Who dares his fecret purpofe hold,
  Unfhaken hears the crowd's tumultuous
   cries,
  And the ftern tyrant's brow —— ——
   defies.   Francis.

TRANSLATION OF THE LATIN, &c.

Page

363. While Michael was forming this ſtatue, ſhocked with the recollection of Brutus' crime, he left his deſign unfiniſhed.

369. I alſo am a painter.

373. Do you imagine there is not little difference between acting from feeling, as nature dictates, or from art?

444. I am the workmanſhip of Marcus Agratus, not of Praxiteles.

502. If they, who through the venturous ocean range,
Not their own paſſions, but the climate, change;
Anxious thro' ſeas and land to ſearch for reſt,
Is but laborious idleneſs at beſt.

FRANCIS.

E R R A T A.

Page 126. line 18. for ſnuff boxes, or tortoiſe ſhells, and the lava, &c. read ſnuff boxes of tortoiſe ſhells, and of the lava, &c.
159. —— 21. for vote read veto
211. —— 14. for than it has been read than at any time.
384. —— 6. Before the word Accuſations read Such.
408. —— 6. for the confinement read that confinement.

www.ingramcontent.com/pod-product-compliance
Lightning Source LLC
Chambersburg PA
CBHW031726280326
41926CB00098B/510